THE ROLE OF LABOUR MOBILITY AND INFORMAL NETWORKS FOR KNOWLEDGE TRANSFER

INTERNATIONAL STUDIES IN ENTREPRENEURSHIP

Series Editors:
Zoltan J. Acs
University of Baltimore
Baltimore, Maryland USA

David B. Audretsch
Indiana University
Bloomington, Indiana USA

THE ROLE OF LABOUR MOBILITY AND INFORMAL NETWORKS FOR KNOWLEDGE TRANSFER

edited by

Dirk Fornahl
*Max Planck Institute for Research
into Economic Systems, Jena*

Christian Zellner
*Max Planck Institute for Research
into Economic Systems, Jena*

David B. Audretsch
*Max Planck Institute for Research
into Economic Systems, Jena*

Library of Congress Cataloging-in-Publication Data

A C.I.P. Catalogue record for this book is available
from the Library of Congress.

ISBN 0-387-23141-2   e-ISBN 0-387-23140-4   Printed on acid-free paper.

Printed in the United States of America.

9 8 7 6 5 4 3 2 1   SPIN 11320920

springeronline.com

Contents

vi

List of Figures

viii

List of Tables

List of Contributors

James D. Adams
Department of Economics
Rensselaer Polytechnic Institute
110 8th Street
Troy, NY 12180-2523, USA

David B. Audretsch
Max Planck Institute for Research into Economic Systems
Entrepreneurship, Growth and Public Policy Group
Kahlaische Straße 10
D-07745 Jena, Germany

Florian Arun-Taeube
Department of Economics; Chair of Economic Development and
Integration; Schumannstr: 60
D-60325 Frankfurt/ Main, Germany

Grant C. Black
School of Business and Economics
Indiana University South Bend
South Bend, IN 46634, USA

Robin Cowan
MERIT, University of Maastricht, P.O. Box 616
6200 MD Maastricht, Netherlands

Dirk Fornahl
Max Planck Institute for Research into Economic Systems
Evolutionary Economics Group
Kahlaische Straße 10
D-07745 Jena, Germany

Nicolas Jonard
CNRS, CREA, Ecole Polytechnique
1 Rue Descartes
75005 Paris, France

Max Keilbach
Max Planck Institute for Research into Economic Systems
Entrepreneurship, Growth and Public Policy Group
Kahlaische Straße 10
D-07745 Jena, Germany

Martin Kenney
Department of Human and Community Development
University of California, Davis
Davis, CA 95616, USA

Donald Patton
Department of Human and Community Development
University of California, Davis
Davis, CA 95616, USA

Michel Quéré
IDEFI-CNRS-UNSA
Université de Nice-Sophia-Anitpolis
250 rue Albert Einstein
06560 Sophia-Antipolis, Valbonne, France

Olav Sorenson
Anderson Graduate School of Management, UCLA
110 Westwood Plaza, Box 951481
Los Angeles, CA 90095-1481, USA

Albert J. Sumell
Department of Economics
Georgia State University
University Plaza
Atlanta, GA 30303, USA

Paula E. Stephan
Department of Economics
Georgia State University
University Plaza
Atlanta, GA 30303, USA

Christian Zellner
Max Planck Institute for Research into Economic Systems
Evolutionary Economics Group
Kahlaische Straße 10
D-07745 Jena, Germany

CHAPTER 1

INTRODUCTION: STRUCTURING INFORMAL MECHANISMS OF KNOWLEDGE TRANSFER

David B. Audretsch, Dirk Fornahl and Christian Zellner

Max Planck Institute for Research into Economic Systems

The role of knowledge has traditionally not played a large role in economics. Certainly the insights of the great classical economists, such as Adam Smith, focused on the allocation and distribution mechanisms of the economy, as well as the roles of capital, labor and land, while paying only nominal attention to knowledge as an economic phenomenon. Writing in the post-war era, Robert Solow followed in this classical tradition. Solow (1956) based his model of economic growth on the neoclassical production function with its key factors of production – capital and labor. Solow, of course, did acknowledge that knowledge contributed to economic growth, but in terms of his formal model, it was considered to be an unexplained residual, which "falls like manna from heaven." A generation of economists subsequently relied upon the model of the production function as a basis for explaining the determinants of economic growth.

The focus on labor and capital as the primary factors of production, and the general exclusion or trivialization of the role of knowledge, was not limited only to the sphere of macroeconomics. The most compelling theories of international trade were based on factors of capital and labor (and sometimes land). For example, the fundamental theorem for international trade, the Heckscher-Ohlin theory, later extended to the Heckscher-Samuelson-Ohlin model focused on the factors of land, labor and capital. According to the Heckscher-Ohlin theory, the proportion of productive factors determines the trade structure. If there exists an abundance of physical capital relative to labor, a country will tend towards the export of capital-intensive goods; an abundance of labor relative to physical capital leads to the export of labor-intensive goods. In fact, what became known as the Leontief Paradox, was based on the statistical evidence refuting, or at least not consistent with the Heckscher-Samuelson-Ohlin model. In particular, the Leontief Paradox pointed out that the actual patterns of U.S. trade did not correspond to the predictions of the model (Bowen, Leaner, and Sveikauskas, 1988). Rather than import labor-intensive goods and export capital-intensive goods, systematic empirical evidence found exactly the opposite for the U.S., which suggested that the comparative advantage for post-war U.S. was based on (unskilled) labor rather than on capital.

As economists struggled to resolve the Leontief Paradox, they began shifting the perspective of the model from an exclusive focus on the factors of inputs of capital and labor, to probing inclusion of various aspects of knowledge. Early extensions included human capital and skilled labor, and technology. The neo-technology theories focused on the role of R&D and the creation of new economic knowledge in shaping the comparative advantage and flows of foreign direct investment. Gruber et al. (1967) suggested that R&D expenditures reflect a temporary comparative advantage resulting from products and production techniques that have not yet been adapted by foreign competitors. Thus, industries with a relatively high R&D component are considered to be conducive to the comparative advantage of firms from the most developed nations.

The human skills hypothesis extended the Heckscher-Ohlin theory by including human capital as a third factor (Keesing, 1966 and 1967). In the presence of a relative abundance of a labor force with a high level of human capital, countries were found to export human capital-intensive goods. Similarly, the abundance of skilled labor tended to promote the export of skill-intensive goods.

The introduction of knowledge into macroeconomic growth models was formalized by Romer (1986) and Lucas (1988). Romer's (1986) critique of the Solow approach was not with the basic model of the neoclassical production function, but rather what he perceived to be omitted from that model – knowledge. Not only did Romer (1986), along with Robert E. Lucas (1988) and others argue that knowledge was an important factor of production, along with the traditional factors of labor and capital, but because it was endogenously determined as a result of externalities and spillovers, it was particularly important.

There are two assumptions implicit that drive the results of the endogenous growth models. The first is that knowledge is automatically equated with economic knowledge. In fact, as Arrow (1962) emphasized, knowledge is inherently different from the traditional factors of production, resulting in a gap between knowledge and what he termed as economic knowledge, or economically valuable knowledge. The second involves the assumed spillover of knowledge. The existence of the factor of knowledge is equated with its automatic spillover, yielding endogenous growth.

The purpose of this volume is to contest both of these assumptions and to suggest that the spillover and flow of knowledge is not at all automatic. Instead, this volume suggests that a filter exists between knowledge and its economic application. The particular focus of this volume is on several key mechanisms that serve to reduce this filter and facilitate the flow of knowledge. In particular, the volume draws on an emerging literature identifying the role of knowledge spillovers to investigate significance of labor mobility and informal networks as mechanisms facilitating the flow of knowledge.

It should be emphasized that no field in economics has dealt extensively with the microeconomics of knowledge spillovers. Thus, it is important to include the perspectives and insights of research approaches that span a broad spectrum of fields in economics. This volume brings together scholars from labor economics, regional economics, the economics of innovation and technological change, and sociology.

In Chapter 2, "The Mobility of Economic Agents as Conduits of Knowledge Spillovers", a theoretical link between the macro perspective and the microeconomic decision maker is provided by David B. Audretsch and Max Keilbach. The purpose of their chapter is to suggest that the recognition and inclusion of knowledge as an important factor has additional implications involving the mechanisms by which that knowledge spills over. While both the traditional and new growth theories have in common a macroeconomic unit of observation, in this paper the focus is on the microeconomic unit of analysis – the individual knowledge workers. Shifting the lens of analysis to the individual knowledge worker turns out to be significant. In a model where knowledge has economic value, individuals make decisions about investing in knowledge as well as appropriating the returns to those knowledge investments. As this chapter concludes, an important implication is that the mobility of knowledge workers in general, and the start-up of new firms in particular, becomes an important mechanism by which knowledge spills over.

The two important fundamental aspects identified above – informal networks and labor mobility – are closely interlinked with respect to their emergence, maintenance and re-configuration (Zellner and Fornahl 2002). By bringing together work in these two areas, this volume is an attempt to contribute to a deeper understanding of the processes and structures that facilitate yet at the same time act as constraints on knowledge flows.

The first part of this volume (Chs. 3-6) considers the role of geographic and relational proximity in shaping patterns of interaction and knowledge flows among economic agents. This approach focuses on the individual agents but accounts for the social and organisational structures these agents are embedded in. Besides belonging to a geographic region, agents are normally part of various networks. These networks are locally bound but at the same time bridge regions, hence creating cross-regional relational proximity. Patton and Kenny describe these regional and cross-regional linkages among different types of agents. In their study they use IPO data in order to explore the links between newly established semiconductor firms, firm lawyers and investment bank lawyers (treated as a proxy for the investment bank's location) as well as venture capital directors and non-VC directors. Since the spatial locations of these agents were identified, Patton and Kenny are able to analyze the pattern of network linkages and the geographical distance between the involved agents. While they discovered a strong cluster in Silicon Valley, supporting previous findings, they also found long-distance links pointing to the potential importance of cross-regional networks.

The subsequent three chapters address the question of how regional relational proximity influences start-up activities and cluster emergence; how attributes of technological knowledge are reflected in network structures (Ch. 5); and the relative importance of regional and relational proximity (Ch. 6).

Building upon the argument by Audretsch and Keilbach on the start-up of new firms as a mechanism for knowledge spillovers, Fornahl (Ch. 4) studies how regional social networks influence regional start-up activities and the location of new firms. The peculiar features of and processes in social regional networks are presented. These networks provide access to resources as well as to information, facilitating the diffusion of mental models within the population. In doing so, they influence the development of an agent through different stages leading to the entrepreneurial decision. Since the processes described have specific local features and are shaped by geographic proximity effects, it is discussed which impact regional characteristics have.

Sorenson (Ch. 5) studies the relationship between informational complexity and the degree of industry concentration, analyzing the question of when social networks play a role in structuring industrial geography. He argues that social networks become increasingly important for the transmission of knowledge as the complexity of the underlying knowledge increases. This leads to the expectation that industries based on more complex knowledge will geographically concentrate. Sorenson explores this hypothesis by investigating patent data estimating the effect of knowledge complexity on geographic dispersion of future citations. Moreover, he looks at the industry-level correlation between the distribution of knowledge complexity in the industry and the degree of geographic concentration of production, demonstrating that both these approaches lend support to his hypothesis. These findings are consistent with Patton and Kenney's results, and offer one possible explanation for clustering effects in high technology industries.

Täube (Ch. 6) draws attention to transnational networks between developing and developed countries. He focuses on the Indian software industry and analyzes the impact of transnational networks between India and Silicon Valley. He demonstrates that an important channel for knowledge and resource transfer to India is the link between overseas Indians working in Silicon Valley and organizations located in India. Such support takes place by the return of émigrés, technical assistance, venture funding or actual business outsourcing to India. The study accounts for the impact of cultural factors on knowledge transfer and on the likelihood to start a software firm, finding the software industry to be dominated by South Indian Brahmins.

The second part of this volume (Chs. 7-10) focuses on mobility patterns and the implications they have for knowledge flows, emphasizing in particular the institution of science as a key provider of knowledge for productive processes. By studying the science-industry interface from the perspective of inter-organizational labor mobility, novel insights on the relationship among institutional actors are offered. While these relationships are at the heart of the innovation systems approach, a further, closely related issue revolves around the significance of mobility for intra-institutional patterns of communication as a determinant of the intensity of scientific knowledge production.

For transferring knowledge from scientific research into productive processes, labor mobility is important in high technology sectors as it usually forms part of an entrepreneur's decision to found a firm. The phenomenon has a much broader dimension, however, to the extent that PhDs trained in scientific institutions as well as senior scientists face the option to move into large incumbent firms, and in particular into their R&D departments.

In Chapter 7 Stephan, Sumell, Black and Adams analyze the mobility of PhDs from US-universities into the top-ranked R&D departments, drawing on data from the Survey of Earned Doctorates (SED). Their empirical results show that public knowledge sources are less geographically concentrated than university R&D expenditure data would suggest and that knowledge spillovers embedded in new hires are less geographically bounded than earlier work suggests. In terms of the industries PhDs migrate to, the main destinations were shown to be telecommunications, computers, semiconductors, pharmaceuticals, electronics, transportation, and glass. Interestingly, it turns out that top R&D firms are more selective in their hiring than are "other" firms, overwhelmingly recruiting talent from programs ranked highly by the most recent National Research Council rankings.

The significance of highly trained labor for the process of innovation is rooted in the relationship between the nature of the knowledge embodied by economic agents and their destinations in the commercial sector. Zellner (Ch. 8) explores this relationship by demonstrating how a focus on individuals' mobility results in a substantially broadened perception of the socio-economic effects of basic scientific research. While the beneficial effects can accrue in a wide range of industries, the relevance of the knowledge in the private sector is discussed in some detail in the context of the German chemical industry. The chapter shows how knowledge developed and individually accumulated as part of curiosity-driven research turns out to become a vital input into commercially motivated search activities. The findings by Stephan *et al.* and Zellner indicate how a perspective on mobility patterns leads to implications for the formulation of science- and technology policy, by drawing attention to one of the most direct links between science and the productive domain.

The extent to which the commercialization of knowledsge from academic science can be stimulated through public policy measures is addressed by Quéré in Chapter 9. Adopting an Austrian economic perspective, he analyses developments in the French innovation system over the past two decades. With respect to entrepreneurship as a mechanism of knowledge transfer, Quéré argues that much "entrepreneurship" has in fact been due to scientists' opportunistic responses to changes in environmental conditions, rather than to a genuinely new individual entrepreneurial mentality. Accordingly, it is suggested that public policy should focus on encouraging entrepreneurial conducts, rather than established forms of science-industry relationships.

Cowan and Jonard (Ch. 10) use a simulation model in order to obtain insights into the processes of knowledge production and diffusion within the scientific community. In this model two ways of knowledge diffusion exist: the job market and networking. It is shown that both these processes are relevant for knowledge accumulation but that distinct mechanisms and dynamics take place. They point out that there is an optimum amount of networking and that a too highly skewed distribution of networking activity hinders knowledge production. Furthermore, network linkages lead to more specialization because the agents can profit from the adjacent knowledge other agents hold that can lead to a positive feedback.

Taken together, these individual chapters provide considerable insights into the process by which knowledge spills over from the source producing it to the agents and firms actually involved in commercializing new ideas. A number of compelling themes emerge from the chapters. First, the flow and spillover of knowledge requires the interaction of multiple analytical units of analysis, spanning the cognitive process of individual economic agents, to the organizational structure of firms, and finally to the platform for knowledge flows provided by geographic space. While endowments of knowledge factors, such as research and development and human capital are a necessary condition to generate knowledge spillovers, this book makes it clear that they are also not a sufficient condition. Rather, the mobility of knowledge agents, that form the basis of regional clusters, plays a central role in the spillover of knowledge, and ultimately, economic growth.

ACKNOWLEDGEMENTS

This book is the result of the workshop "The Role of Labour Mobility and Informal Networks for Knowledge Transfer", held at the Max Planck Institute for Research into Economic Systems, Jena (Germany) in December 2002. We are indebted to the Max Planck Society for providing us with the opportunity to organize the workshop and bring together this group of scientists, to discuss ideas and produce this book. Furthermore, the editors would like to thank all the authors for contributing their papers and taking part in the refereeing process.

REFERENCES

Arrow, K. (1962). Economic Welfare and the Allocation of Resources for Invention, in R. Nelson (Ed.), *The Rate and Direction of Inventive Activity*, Princeton: Princeton University Press.

Bowen, H.P., E.E. Leamer, and L. Sveikauskas, (1987). Multicountry, Multifactor Rests of the Factor Abundance Theory, *American Economic Review*, 78, 791-809.

Gruber, W.H., D. Mehta and R. Vernon, (1967). The R&D Factor in International Trade and Investment of the Untied States, *Journal of Political Economy* 75, 20-37.

Keesing, D. B., (1966). Labor Skills and Comparative Advantage, *American Economic Review*, 56, 249-258.

Keesing, D.B., (1967). The Impact of Research and Development on United States Trade, *Journal of Political Economy* 75, 38-48.

Krugman, P., (1991). *Geography and Trade*, Cambridge: MIT Press.

Lucas, R.E. Jr. (1993). Making a Miracle, *Econometrica*, 61, 251-272.

Romer, P. M., (1986). Increasing Returns and Long-Run Growth, *Journal of Political Economy, 94(5)*, 1002-37.

Solow, R. , (1956). A Contribution to The Theory of Economic Growth, *Quarterly Journal of Economics*, 70, 65-94.

Zellner, C. and D. Fornahl, (2002). Scientific Knowledge and Implications for its Diffusion, *Journal of Knowledge Management, 6 (2)*, 190-198.

CHAPTER 2

THE MOBILITY OF ECONOMIC AGENTS AS CONDUITS OF KNOWLEDGE SPILLOVERS

David B. Audretsch and Max Keilbach

Max Planck Institute for Research into Economic Systems, Jena

1. INTRODUCTION

This volume brings two relatively new concepts together – the mobility of economic agents and knowledge spillovers. Not only is research on each of these phenomenon limited, but understanding about the intersection of these two concepts is virtually non-existent. While most of this Volume focuses on filling this void and making an explicit link between agent mobility and knowledge spillovers, it is also important to understand why such a link is important in the first place. This chapter provides a context explaining not only why the mobility of economic agents serves as a conduit of knowledge spillovers, but even more importantly, why this function matters for economics. In particular, it matters for economic growth. Economic growth has been a dominant concern in economics, dating back at least to the classical economists. In the post-war models of economic growth, neither knowledge nor knowledge spillovers had any relevance for economic growth.

When Robert Solow (1956) proposed a model of economic growth, the production function emerged as the basis for explaining the determinants of economic growth. According to the neoclassical model of the production function, two key factors of production – capital and labor – provided the inputs for output and growth.

The role of science and knowledge is not particularly obvious in the neoclassical model of the production function. The implications from this model were that (1) the impact of science and ideas was essentially embodied in capital, and (2) the mobility of scientists, engineers and other knowledge workers should have no significance other than labor mobility in general. That is, labor mobility was generally viewed as important because it is a mechanism for equilibrating wages in the labor market.

Romer's (1986) critique of the Solow approach was not with the basic model of the neoclassical production function, but rather what he perceived to be omitted from that model – knowledge. Not only did Romer (1986), along with Lucas (1988) and others argue that knowledge was an important factor of production, along with the traditional factors of labor and capital, but because it was endogenously determined as a result of externalities and spillovers, it was particularly important.

The purpose of this paper is to suggest that the recognition and inclusion of knowledge as an important factor has additional implications involving the mechanisms by which that knowledge spills over. While both the traditional and new growtheories have in common a macroeconomic unit of observation, in this paper the focus is on the microeconomic unit of analysis – the individual knowledge workers. Shifting the lens of analysis to the individual knowledge worker turns out to be significant. In a model where knowledge has economic value, individuals make decisions about investing in knowledge as well as appropriating the returns to those knowledge investments. As this paper suggests, an important implication is that the mobility of knowledge workers in general, and the startup of new firms in particular, becomes an important mechanism by which knowledge spills over.

2. THE KNOWLEDGE PRODUCTION FUNCTION

Contrary to the approach where the unit of analysis on innovation and technological change for most theories of innovation is the firm (Cohen and Levin, 1989; Griliches, 1979, in this paper we will instead focus on the individual. In the traditional theories, the firms are exogenous and their performance in generating technological change is endogenous (Cohen and Levin, 1989).

For example, in the most prevalent model found in the literature of technological change, the model of the knowledge production function, formalized by Zvi Griliches (1979), firms exist exogenously and then engage in the pursuit of new economic knowledge as an input into the process of generating innovative activity.

The most important input in the model of the knowledge production function is new economic knowledge. As Cohen and Klepper point out, the greatest source generating new economic knowledge is generally considered to be R&D (Cohen and Klepper, 1991 and 1992). Other inputs in the knowledge production function have included measures of human capital, skilled labor, and educational levels (Griliches, 1979 and 1992). Thus, the model of the knowledge production function from the literature on innovation and technological change can be represented as

$$I_i = \alpha RD_i^{\beta} HK_i^{\gamma} \varepsilon_i \tag{1}$$

where I stands for the degree of innovative activity, RD represents R&D inputs, and HK represents human capital inputs. The unit of observation for estimating the model of the knowledge production function, reflected by the subscript i, has been at the level of countries, industries and enterprises (Griliches, 1984)

Empirical estimation of the model of the knowledge production function, represented by Equation (1), was found to hold most strongly at broader levels of aggregation (Griliches, 1979, 1992). Empirical evidence (Griliches, 1992) clearly supported the existence of the knowledge production function at the unit of observation of countries. This is intuitively understandable, because the most innovative countries are those with the greatest investments to R&D. little innovative output is associated with less developed countries, which are characterized by a paucity of production of new economic knowledge.

Similarly, the model of the knowledge production function was found to exist at the level of the industry (Griliches, 1979). The most innovative industries also tend to be characterized by considerable investments in R&D and new economic knowledge. Not only are industries such as computers, pharmaceuticals and instruments high in R&D inputs that generate new economic knowledge, but also in terms of innovative outputs. By contrast, industries with little R&D, such as wood products, textiles and paper, also tend to produce only a negligible amount of innovative output. Thus, the knowledge production model linking knowledge generating inputs to outputs certainly holds at the more aggregated levels of economic activity.

Where the relationship became problematic was at the disaggregated microeconomic level of the enterprise, establishment, or even line of business. While Audretsch (1995) found that the simple correlation between R&D inputs and innovative output was 0.84 for four-digit standard industrial classification (SIC) manufacturing industries in the United States, it was only about half, 0.40 among the largest U.S. corporations.

The model of the knowledge production function becomes even less compelling in view of the recent wave of studies revealing that small enterprises serve as the engine of innovative activity in certain industries. For example, Audretsch (1995) found that while large enterprises (defined as having at least 500 employees) generated a greater number of new product innovations than did small firms (defined as having fewer than 500 employees), once the measures were standardized by levels of employment, the innovative intensity of small enterprises was found to exceed that of large firms. The innovation rates, or the number of innovations per thousand employees, have the advantage in that they measure large- and small-firm innovative activity relative to the presence of large and small firms in any given industry. That is, in making a direct comparison between large- and small-firm innovative activities, the absolute number of innovations contributed by large firms and small enterprises is somewhat misleading, since these measures are not standardized by the relative presence of large and small firms in each industry. When a direct comparison is made between the innovative activity of large and small firms, the innovation rates are presumably a more reliable measure of innovative intensity because they are weighted by the relative presence of small and large enterprises in any given industry. Thus, while large firms in manufacturing introduced 2,445 innovations, and small firms contributed slightly fewer, 1,954, small-firm employment was only half as great as large-firm employment, yielding an average small-firm innovation rate in manufacturing of 0.309, compared to a large-firm innovation rate of 0.202 (Audretsch, 1995).

These results are startling, because the bulk of industrial R&D is undertaken in the largest corporations; and small enterprises account only for a minor share of R&D inputs, raising the question of where such firms obtained access to R&D inputs. Either the model of the knowledge production did not hold, at least at the level of the enterprise (for a broad spectrum across the firm-size distribution), or else the appropriate unit of observation had to be reconsidered. In searching for a solution, scholars chose the second interpretation, leading them to move towards spatial units of observation as an important unit of analysis for the model of the knowledge production function.

3. KNOWLEDGE SPILLOVERS

As it became apparent that the unit of analysis of the enterprise was not completely adequate for estimating the model of the knowledge production function, scholars began to look for externalities. In refocusing the model of the knowledge production to a spatial unit of observation, scholars confronted two challenges. The first one was theoretical. What was the theoretical basis for knowledge to spill over yet, at the same time, be spatially bounded within some geographic unit of observation? The second challenge involved measurement. How could knowledge spillovers be measured and identified? More than a few scholars heeded Krugman's warning (1991, p. 53) that empirical measurement of knowledge spillovers would prove to be impossible because "knowledge flows are invisible, they leave no paper trail by which they may be measured and tracked."

In confronting the first challenge, which involved developing a theoretical basis for geographically bounded knowledge spillovers, scholars turned towards the incipient literature on the new economic geography. In explaining the asymmetric distribution of economic activity across geographic space, Krugman (1991) and Romer (1986) relied on models based on increasing returns to scale in production. By increasing returns, however, Krugman and Romer did not necessarily mean at the level of observation most familiar in the industrial organization literature – the plant, or at least the firm – but rather at the level of a spatially distinguishable unit, say a region or area. In fact, it was assumed that externalities across firms and even industries that yield convexities in production. In particular, Krugman (1991) focused on convexities arising from spillovers from (1) a pooled labour market; (2) pecuniary externalities enabling the provision of nontraded inputs to an industry in a greater variety and at lower cost; and (3) information or technological spillovers.

That knowledge spills over was barely disputed. Arrow (1962) had identified the externalities associated with knowledge, in particular the non-exclusivity and non-rivalrous use. However, the geographic range of such knowledge spillovers has been greatly contested. In disputing the importance of knowledge externalities in explaining the geographic concentration of economic activity, Krugman (1991) and others did not question the existence or importance of such knowledge spillovers. In fact, they argue that such knowledge externalities are so important and forceful that there is no compelling reason for a geographic boundary to limit the spatial extent of the spillover. According to this line of thinking, the concern is not that knowledge does not spill over but that it should stop spilling over just because it hits a geographic border, such as a city limit, state line, or national boundary.

Rather, in applying the model of the knowledge production function to spatial units of observation, not only were theories of knowledge externalities needed but also theories about why those knowledge externalities should be spatially bounded. Thus, it took the development of localization theories explaining not only that knowledge spills over but also why those spillovers decay as they move across geographic space.

Such theories of localization (Jacobs, 1969) suggest that *information*, such as the price of gold on the New York Stock Exchange, or the value of the Yen in London, can be easily codified and has a singular meaning and interpretation. By contrast, *knowledge* or what is sometimes referred to as *tacit knowledge,* is vague, difficult to codify and often only serendipitously recognized. Information is codified and can be formalized, written down, but tacit knowledge is non-codifiable and cannot, by definition, be formalized and written down. Geographic proximity matters in transmitting knowledge, because as Kenneth Arrow (1962) pointed out some three decades ago, such tacit knowledge is inherently non-rival in nature, and knowledge developed for any particular application can easily spill over and have economic value in very different applications. As Glaeser, Kallal, Scheinkman and Shleifer (1992, p. 1126) have observed, "intellectual breakthroughs must cross hallways and streets more easily than oceans and continents."

Feldman (1994) developed the theory that firms cluster to mitigate the uncertainty of innovation, proximity enhances the ability of firms to exchange ideas, discuss solutions to problems, and be cognizant of other important information, hence reducing uncertainty for firms that work in new fields. In addition, Feldman (1994) further suggests that firms producing innovations tend to locate in areas where there are necessary resources and that resources accumulate due to a region's past success with innovations.

An implication of the distinction between information and tacit knowledge is the marginal cost of transmitting information across geographic space has been rendered invariant by the telecommunications revolution, while the marginal cost of transmitting knowledge, and especially tacit knowledge, rises with distance.

Studies identifying the extent of knowledge spillovers are based on the model of the knowledge production function applied at spatial units of observation. In what is generally to be considered to be the first important study refocusing the knowledge production function, Jaffe (1989) modified the traditional approach to estimate a model specified for both spatial and product dimensions:

$$I_{si} = \alpha IRD^{\beta_1} UR_{si}^{\beta_2} (UR_{si} GC_{si}^{\beta_3}) \; \varepsilon_{si} \qquad (2)$$

where I is innovative output, IRD is private corporate expenditures on R&D, UR is the research expenditures undertaken at universities, and GC measures the geographic coincidence of university and corporate research. The unit of observation for estimation was at the spatial level, s, a state, and industry level, i. Estimation of equation (2) essentially shifted the knowledge production function from the unit of observation of a firm to that of a geographic unit. Jaffee (1989) found empirical evidence that $\beta_1 \geq 0$, $\beta_2 \geq 0$, $\beta_3 \geq 0$ supports the notion of knowledge spills over for third-party use from university research laboratories as well as industry R&D laboratories. Acs, Audretsch and Feldman (1992) and Feldman (1994) confirmed that the knowledge production function represented by equation (2) held at a spatial unit of observation using a direct measure of innovative activity, new product introductions in the market. This was subsequently confirmed by Anselin, Acs and Varga (1997 and 2000).

Implicitly contained within the knowledge production function model is the assumption that innovative activity should take place in those regions, s, where the direct knowledge-generating inputs are the greatest, and where knowledge spillovers are the most prevalent. Jaffee (1989) dealt with the measurement problem raised by Krugman (1991) by linking the patent activity within technologies located within states to knowledge inputs located within the same spatial unit.

Thus, the empirical evidence suggests that location and proximity clearly matter in exploiting knowledge spillovers. Not only have Jaffe, Trajtenberg and Henderson (1993) found that patent citations tend to occur more frequently within the state in which they were patented than outside of that state, but Audretsch and Feldman (1996) found that the propensity of innovative activity to cluster geographically tends to be greater in industries where new economic knowledge plays a more important role. This effect was found to hold even after holding the degree of production at that location constant. Audretsch and Feldman (1996), follow Krugman's (1991) example, and calculate Gini coefficients for the geographic concentration of innovative activity to test this relationship. The results indicate that a key determinant of the extent to which the location of production is geographically concentrated is the relative importance of new economic knowledge in the industry. Even after controlling for the geographic concentration of production, the results suggest a greater propensity for innovative activity to cluster spatially in industries in which industry R&D, university research and skilled labor are important inputs. In this work, skilled labor is included as a mechanism by which knowledge spillovers may be realized as workers move between jobs in an industry taking their accumulated skills and know-how with them.

Zucker, Darby and Armstrong (1994) show that in biotechnology, which is an industry based almost exclusively on new knowledge, the firms tend to cluster together in just a handful of locations. This finding is supported by Audretsch and Stephan (1996) who examine the geographic relationships of scientists working with biotechnology firms. The importance of geographic proximity is clearly shaped by the role played by the scientist. The scientist is more likely to be located in the same region as the firm when the relationship involves the transfer of new economic knowledge. However, when the scientist is providing a service to the company that does not involve knowledge transfer, local proximity becomes much less important.

There is also reason to believe that knowledge spillovers are not homogeneous across firms. In estimating Equation (1) for large and small enterprises separately, Acs, Audretsch and Feldman (1994) provide some insight into the puzzle posed by the recent wave of studies identifying vigorous innovative activity emanating from small firms in certain industries. How are these small, and frequently new, firms able to generate innovative output while undertaking generally negligible amounts of investment into knowledge generating inputs, such as R&D? The answer appears to be through exploiting knowledge created by expenditures on research in universities and on R&D in large corporations. Their findings suggest that the innovative output of all firms rises along with an increase in the amount of R&D inputs, both in private corporations as well as in university laboratories. However, R&D expenditures made by private companies play a particularly important role in providing knowledge inputs to the innovative activity of large firms, while expenditures on research made by universities serve as an especially key input for generating innovative activity in small enterprises. Apparently large firms are more adept at exploiting knowledge created in their own laboratories, while their smaller counterparts have a comparative advantage at exploiting spillovers from university laboratories.

4. MOBILITY OF ECONOMIC AGENTS AS A SPILLOVER MECHANISM

The literature identifying mechanisms actually transmitting knowledge spillovers is sparse and remains underdeveloped. However, one important area where such transmission mechanisms have been identified involves entrepreneurship. Entrepreneurship involves the startup and growth of new enterprises. This mechanism for knowledge spillovers may not be the most dominant or even the most important. However, it is important to recognize that it may represent at least one mode by which spillovers of knowledge are transmitted.

Why should the mobility of economic agents serve as a mechanism for the spill over of knowledge from the source of origin? At least two major channels or mechanisms for knowledge spillovers have been identified in the literature. Both of these spillover mechanisms revolve around the issue of appropriability of new knowledge. Cohen and Levinthal (1989) suggest that firms develop the capacity to adapt new technology and ideas developed in other firms and are therefore able to appropriate some of the returns accruing to investments in new knowledge made externally. This view of spillovers is consistent with the traditional model of the knowledge production function, where the firm exists exogenously and then undertakes (knowledge) investments to generate innovative output.

By contrast, Audretsch (1995) proposes shifting the unit of observation away from exogenously assumed firms to individuals, such as scientists, engineers or other knowledge workers – agents with endowments of new economic knowledge. When the lens is shifted away from the firm to the individual as the relevant unit of observation, the appropriability issue remains, but the question becomes, *How can economic agents with a given endowment of new knowledge best appropriate the returns from that knowledge?* If the scientist or engineer can pursue the new idea within the organizational structure of the firm developing the knowledge and appropriate roughly the expected value of that knowledge, he has no reason to leave the firm. On the other hand, if he places a greater value on his ideas than do the decision-making bureaucracy of the incumbent firm, he may choose to start a new firm to appropriate the value of his knowledge. Small enterprises can compensate for their lack of R&D is through spillovers and spin-offs. Typically an employee from an established large corporation, often a scientist or engineer working in a research laboratory, will have an idea for an invention and ultimately for an innovation. Accompanying this potential innovation is an expected net return from the new product. The inventor would expect to be compensated for his/her potential innovation accordingly. If the company has a different, presumably lower, valuation of the potential innovation, it may decide either not to pursue its development, or that it merits a lower level of compensation than that expected by the employee.

In either case, the employee will weigh the alternative of starting his/her own firm. If the gap in the expected return accruing from the potential innovation between the inventor and the corporate decision maker is sufficiently large, and if the cost of starting a new firm is sufficiently low, the employee may decide to leave the large corporation and establish a new enterprise. Since the knowledge was generated in the established corporation, the new start-up is considered to be a spin-off from the existing firm. Such start-ups typically do not have direct access to a large R&D laboratory. Rather, these small firms succeed in exploiting the knowledge and experience accrued from the R&D laboratories with their previous employers.

The research laboratories of universities provide a source of innovation-generating knowledge that is available to private enterprises for commercial exploitation. Jaffe (1989) and Acs, Audretsch, and Feldman (1992), Audretsch and Feldman (1996) and Feldman and Audretsch (1999), for example, found that the knowledge created in university laboratories "spills over" to contribute to the generation of commercial innovations by private enterprises. Acs, Audretsch, and Feldman (1994) found persuasive evidence that spillovers from university research contribute more to the innovative activity of small firms than to the innovative activity of large corporations.

In the metaphor provided by Albert O. Hirschman (1970), if voice proves to be ineffective within incumbent organizations, and loyalty is sufficiently weak, a knowledge worker may resort to exit the firm or university where the knowledge was created in order to form a new company. In this spillover channel the knowledge production function is actually reversed. The knowledge is exogenous and embodied in a worker. The firm is created endogenously in the worker's effort to appropriate the value of his knowledge through innovative activity.

One group of studies has focused on how location has influenced the entrepreneurial decision, or the decision to start a new firm. Within the economics literature, the prevalent theoretical framework has been the general model of income choice. The model of entrepreneurial choice dates back at least to Knight (1921), but was more recently extended and updated by Lucas (1978), Kihlstrom and Laffont (1979), Holmes and Schmidtz (1990) and Jovanovic (1994). In its most basic rendition, individuals are confronted with a choice of earning their income either from wages earned through employment in an incumbent enterprise or else from profits accrued by starting a new firm. The essence of the entrepreneurial choice model is made by comparing the wage an individual expects to earn through employment, W^*, with the profits that are expected to accrue from a new-firm startup, P^*. Thus, the probability of starting a new firm, $Pr(s)$, can be represented as

$$Pr(s) = f(P^*-W^*) \qquad\qquad (3)$$

The model of entrepreneurial choice has been extended by Kihlstrom and Laffont (1979) to incorporate aversion to risk, and by Lucas (1978) and Jovanovic (1994) to explain why firms of varying size exist, and has served as the basis for empirical studies of the decision to start a new firm.

Audretsch and Stephan (1999) examined how the decision made by scientists to start a new biotechnology company is shaped by the experience trajectory of the scientist. They apply the framework of Stephan and Levin (1991) and Levin and Stephan (1991), which focuses on the incentive and reward structure facing scientists. This leads to the prediction that scientists from a trajectory involving employment in the private sector, typically a large pharmaceutical company, will have an incentive to start a company at a younger point in her career than her counterpart coming from an academic trajectory. In fact, the empirical evidence provides clear evidence that scientists from the academic trajectory start companies at a systematically older age than do their counterparts from pharmaceutical company trajectories.

Klepper (2002) finds evidence that companies started by the mobility involved in spin-offs from high performance automobile companies exhibited a higher level of performance than did companies started from entrepreneurs with experience in either low performance automobile companies or no experience at all in the automobile industry. He interprets his findings as suggesting that the learning process is superior in a high performance company, and that the spillover of knowledge is transmitted by the spin-off and startup of a new company.

Similarly, Audretsch and Lehman (2002) find compelling evidence that the trajectory and previous experience of board members also influences the performance of new firms. Based on a sample of high-technology and knowledge-intensive German startup companies, they find empirical evidence suggesting that the human capital of the board members has a positive impact on firm performance.

Geographic location should influence the entrepreneurial decision by altering the expected return from entrepreneurial activity, P*. The theory of knowledge spillovers suggests that P* will tend to be greater in agglomerations and spatial clusters, since access to tacit knowledge is greater. Geography and spatial location also influences entrepreneurship. The important role that geographic clusters and networks play as a determinant of entrepreneurial activity was identified in Europe and only recently has been discovered within the North American context (Porter, 1990 and 2000; Saxenien, 1994).

For example, in studying the entrepreneurial networks located in California's Silicon Valley, Saxenian (1990, pp. 96-97) describes the entrepreneurship capital of Silicon Valley, "It is not simply the concentration of skilled labor, suppliers and information that distinguish the region. A variety of regional institutions – including Stanford University, several trade associations and local business organizations, and a myriad of specialized consulting, market research, public relations and venture capital firms – provide technical, financial, and networking services which the region's enterprises often cannot afford individually. These networks defy sectoral barriers: individuals move easily from semiconductor to disk drive firms or from computer to network makers. They move from established firms to startups (or vice versa) and even to market research or consulting firms, and from consulting firms back into startups. And they continue to meet at trade shows, industry conferences, and the scores of seminars, talks, and social activities organized by local business organizations and trade associations. In these forums, relationships are easily formed and maintained, technical and market information is exchanged, business contacts are established, and new enterprises are conceived. This decentralized and fluid environment also promotes the diffusion of intangible technological capabilities and understandings."

By contrast, there is a longer and richer tradition of research linking entrepreneurship to spatial clusters and networks in Europe. However, most of these studies have been in social science fields other than economics. For example, Becattini (1990) and Brusco (1990) identified the key role that spatial clusters and networks play in promoting SMEs in Italy. While such networks and clusters were generally overlooked or ignored in North America, with publication of Saxenien's book, *Regional Advantage*, which documented how spatial networks generated entrepreneurial activity in Silicon Valley and Route 128 around Boston, it became clear and accepted that spatial agglomerations were also important in the North American context.

An important distinction between the European literature and studies and the emerging literature in North America was the emphasis on high technology and knowledge spillovers in the North American context. By contrast, the European tradition focused much more on the role of networks and clusters in fostering the viability of SMEs in traditional industries, such as textiles, apparel and metalworking. For example, seminal studies by Becattini (1990) and Brusco (1990) argue that small and new firms enjoy a high degree of stability when supported by networks in Italy. A rich literature has provided a compelling body of case studies, spanning the textile industries of northern Italy to the metal working firms of Baden Wuerttemberg, documenting the long-term viability and stability of small and new firms embedded in the so-called industrial districts of Europe. Examples of such industrial districts include Prato, Biella, Carpi and Castelgoffredo, which specialize in textile (coolants in Castelgoffredo); Vigevano, Montebellune and Montegranaro where shoes are manufactured (ski boots in Montebellune); Pesaro and Nogara which manufacture wooden furniture; Sassuolo where ceramic tiles are produced.

Brusco (1990) emphasizes the cooperation among network firms within an industrial district. Such cooperation presumably reduces any size-inherent disadvantages and improves the viability of small firms operating within the network. Grabher (1993) similarly argues that the social structure underlying industrial networks contributes to the viability of small firms that would otherwise be vulnerable if they were operating in an isolated context.

Feldman (2001) and Feldman and Francis (2001) examine the impact of agglomeration on entrepreneurship. In particular, they focus on the formation of clusters through entrepreneurship. Based on entrepreneurship and interviews with entrepreneurs to explore the development of an Internet and biotechnology cluster around Washington, D.C., Feldman (2001) and Feldman and Francis (2001) provide compelling evidence that clusters form not because resources are initially located in a particular region, but rather through the work of entrepreneurs. Early entrepreneurs locate their businesses in a region and adapt to the particularities of the location. As their businesses begin to thrive, resources such as money, networks, experts, and services arise in, and are attracted to, the region. With this infrastructure in place, more entrepreneurial ventures locate and thrive in the region, which ultimately may create a thriving cluster where none previously existed.

Sorenson and Stuart (2001) show that location matters in obtaining venture capital. By analyzing the determinants of venture capital investment in the United States between 1986 and 1998, they find that the likelihood of a venture capitalist investing in a given target declines with increasing geographical distance between the venture capitalist and the company.

Gompers and Lerner (1999) have shown how geography affects the location of venture capital. In particular, they show that the geographic distribution of venture capital is highly spatially skewed. Gompers and Lerner (1999) provide evidence showing California, New York, and New England as the major location of venture capital funds.

If the mobility of economic agents serves as a mechanism for knowledge spillovers, it should not only be reflected by the model of entrepreneurial choice, or the decision to start a new firm. Rather, measures reflecting the mobility of economic agents should also be positively linked to the growth performance of regions. The view of entrepreneurship that is based on its role as an agent of change in a knowledge-based economy implies that a positive economic performance should be linked to entrepreneurial activity. This hypothesis has raised two challenges to researchers: (1) What is meant by economic performance and how can it be measured and operationalized? and (2) Over which units of analysis should such a positive relationship between entrepreneurship and economic performance be manifested? In fact, these two issues are not independent from each other. The answer to the second question, the appropriate unit of analysis, has influenced the first question, the performance criteria and measure.

The most prevalent measures of performance has been employment growth. The most common and almost exclusive measure of performance is growth, typically measured in terms of employment growth. These studies have tried to link various measures of entrepreneurial activity, most typically startup rates, to economic growth. Other measures sometimes used include the relative share of SMEs, and self-employment rates.

For example, Audretsch and Fritsch (2002) analyzed a database identifying new business startups and exits from the social insurance statistics in Germany to examine whether a greater degree of turbulence leads to greater economic growth, as suggested by Schumpeter in his 1911 treatise. These social insurance statistics are collected for individuals. Each record in the database identifies the establishment at which an individual is employed. The startup of a new firm is recorded when a new establishment identification appears in the database, which generally indicates the birth of a new enterprise. While there is some evidence for the United States linking a greater degree of turbulence at the regional level to higher rates of growth for regions, Audretsch and Fritsch (2002) find that the opposite was true for Germany during the 1980s. In both the manufacturing and the service sectors, a high rate of turbulence in a region tends to lead to a lower and not a higher rate of growth. They attribute this negative relationship to the fact that the underlying components – the startup and death rates – are both negatively related to subsequent economic growth. Those areas with higher startup rates tend to experience lower growth rates in subsequent years. Most strikingly, the same is also true for the death rates.

Audretsch and Fritsch (2002) conjectured that one possible explanation for the disparity in results between the United States and Germany may lie in the role that innovative activity, and therefore the ability of new firms to ultimately displace the incumbent enterprises, plays in new-firm startups. It may be that innovative activity did not play the same role for the German *Mittelstand* as it does for SMEs in the United States. To the degree that this was true, it may be hold that regional growth emanates from SMEs only when they serve as agents of change through innovative activity.

The empirical evidence suggested that the German model for growth provided a sharp contrast to that for the United States. While Reynolds et al (1995) had found that the degree of entrepreneurship was positively related to growth in the United States, a series of studies by Audretsch and Fritsch (2002) could not identify such a relationship for Germany. However, the results by Audretsch and Fritsch were based on data from the 1980s.

Divergent findings from the 1980s about the relationship between the degree of entrepreneurial activity and economic growth in the United States and Germany posed something of a puzzle. On the one hand, these different results suggested that the relationship between entrepreneurship and growth was fraught with ambiguities. No confirmation could be found for a general pattern across developed countries. On the other hand, it provided evidence for the existence of distinct and different national systems. The empirical evidence clearly suggested that there was more than one way to achieve growth, at least across different countries. Convergence in growth rates seemed to be attainable by maintaining differences in underlying institutions and structures.

However, in a more recent study, Audretsch and Fritsch (2002) find that different results emerge for the 1990s. Those regions with a higher startup rate exhibit higher growth rates. This would suggest that, in fact, Germany is changing over time, where the engine of growth is shifting towards entrepreneurship as a source of growth. The results of their 2002 paper suggest a somewhat different interpretation. Based on the compelling empirical evidence that the source of growth in Germany has shifted away from the established incumbent firms during the 1980s to entrepreneurial firms in the 1990s, it would appear that a process of convergence is taking place between Germany and the United States, where entrepreneurship provides the engine of growth in both countries. Despite remaining institutional differences, the relationship between entrepreneurship and growth is apparently converging in both countries.

Audretsch and Keilbach (2002) and link the mobility of workers in general, and knowledge workers in particular, as it is manifested by the startup of new firms, to the output of German regions in the context of a production function model. Their results indicate that a higher degree of worker mobility and especially knowledge worker mobility that leads to a new-firm startup has a significant and positive impact on output and productivity growth.

5. CONCLUSIONS

Romer (1986), Lucas (1978 and 1992) and Grossman and Helpman (1992) established that knowledge spillovers are an important mechanism underlying endogenous growth. However, they shed little light on the actual mechanisms by which knowledge is transmitted across firms and individuals. The answer to this question is important, because a policy implication commonly drawn from the new economic growth theory is that, as a result of convexities in knowledge and the resultant increasing returns, knowledge factors, such as R&D should be publicly supported. While this may be valid, it is also important to recognize that the mechanisms for spillover transmission may also play a key role and may also serve as a focus for public policy enhancing economic growth and development. This paper proposes the mobility of economic agents from one economic context to a different economic context as one such channel transmitting spillovers.

There are at least two important implications arising from the view that the mobility of economic agents transmits the spillover of knowledge. The first is that the basic assumptions of the knowledge production view of the firm may, in fact, not hold, at least in knowledge-based industries. The knowledge production view assumes the firm exists exogenously and then invests in knowledge to endogenously generate innovative activity. This paper suggests a very different interpretation. Economic agents have an endowment of knowledge that can be considered to be exogenous at any moment of time. In order to appropriate the value of their knowledge they may remain in their current situation at an incumbent firm, or they may choose to leave that firm and go to a different enterprise, or even to start a new firm. In this case, the knowledge is exogenous and the new firm is endogenously created in an attempt to appropriate the value of knowledge. The mobility of economic agents with a knowledge endowment may not involve direct immediate commercialization, but rather movement to situations where the accumulation of knowledge capital is greater than in the status quo situation. Thus, the mobility of economic agents across different contexts and their creation of trajectories becomes an important mechanism for the process by which knowledge spills over from one context and organization to another.

The second implication may be that the propensity for economic agents to engage in mobility may not be constant across industries, regions and countries but is presumably shaped by contextual factors. These contextual factors, which Audretsch and Keilbach (2002) term as constituting entrepreneurship capital, may in fact, constitute a key missing factor in explaining variations in growth across geographic space. Those regions with a rich endowment of entrepreneurship capital would be expected to experience a relatively high degree of mobility among economic agents, which would consequently result in higher levels of economic performance. What exactly constitutes such entrepreneurship capital and how it impacts growth needs to be identified and analyzed in what promises to be a rich and rewarding line of scholarly research.

REFERENCES

Acs, Z. J., D. B. Audretsch and Feldman M. P. (1992). Real Effects of Academic Research. *American Economic Review, 82(1)*, 363-367.
Acs, Z. J., D. B. Audretsch and Feldman, M. P. (1994). R&D Spillovers and Recipient Firm Size. *Review of Economics and Statistics, 100(2)*, 336-367.
Anselin, L, A. Varga and Z. J. Acs, (1997). Local Geographic Spillovers between University Research and High Technology Innovations. *Journal of Urban Economics, 42*, 422-448.
Arrow, K. (1962). Economic Welfare and the Allocation of Resources for Invention. In: Nelson, R. (Ed.). *The Rate and Direction of Inventive Activity*. Princeton, Princeton University Press.
Audretsch, D. (1995). *Innovation and Industry Evolution*. Cambridge, MIT Press.
Audretsch, D. and Feldman, M. (1996). R&D Spillovers and the Geography of Innovation and Production. *American Economic Review, 86(4)*, 253-273.
Audretsch, D. and Stephan, P. (1996). Company-Scientist Locational Links: The Case of Biotechnology. *American Economic Review, 86(4)*, 641-652.
Audretsch, D. B. and Lehman, E. (2002). Does the New Economy Need New Governance? Ownership, Knowledge and Performance. Centre for Economic Policy Research (CEPR), Discussion Paper 3626.
Audretsch, D. B. and Keilbach, M. (2002). Entrepreneurship Capital and Economic Performance. Centre for Economic Policy, Research Discussion Paper.
Audretsch, D. B. and Fritsch, M. (2002). Growth Regimes over Time and Space. *Regional Studies, 36(2)*, 113-124.
Becattini, G., (1990). The Marshallian Industrial District as a Socio-Economic Notion. In: Becattini, G., Pyke, F. and Sengenberger W. (1990). *Industrial Districts and Inter-Firm Co-operation in Italy*. Geneva, International Labor Studies, 37-51.
Brusco, S., (1990). The Idea of the Industrial District: Its Genesis. In Becattini, G., Pyke, F. and Sengenberger, W. (1990), *Industrial Districts and Inter-Firm Co-operation in Italy*. Geneva, International Labor Studies, 10-19.
Cohen, W. and Levinthal, D. (1989). Innovation and Learning: The Two Faces of R&D. *Economic Journal, 99(3)*, 569-596.
Cohen, W. M. and Levin, R.C. (1989). Empirical Studies of Innovation and Market Structure. In Schmalensee, R. and Willig, R. (Eds.). *Handbook of Industrial Organization, Volume II*. Amsterdam, NorthHolland, 1059-1107.
Cohen, W. M. and Klepper, S. (1991). Firm Size versus Diversity in the Achievement of Technological Advance. In: Acs, Z. and Audretsch, D. (Eds.). *Innovation and Technological Change: An International Comparison*. Ann Arbor, University of Michigan Press, 183-203.
Cohen, W. M. and Klepper, S. (1992). The Tradeoff between Firm Size and Diversity in the Pursuit of Technological Progress. *Small Business Economics, 4(1)*, 1-14.
Feldman, M.P. (1994). Knowledge Complementarity and Innovation. *Small Business Economics, 6(3)*, 363-372.
Feldman, M., P. and Audretsch, D.B. (1999). Innovation in cities: science-based diversity, specialization and localized competition. *European Economic Review, 43*, 409-429.
Feldman, M. P. and Francis, J. (2001). The Entrepreneurial Spark: Individual Agents and the Formation of Innovative Clusters. In: Curzio, A. and Fortis, M. (Eds.) (2002). *Complexity and Industrial Clusters: Dynamics and Models in Theory and Practice*. Heidelberg, Physica-Verlag, 195-212.
Feldman, M. P. (2001). The Entrepreneurial Event Revisited: Firm Formation in a Regional Context. *Industrial and Corporate Change*, 861-891.
Gompers, P. and J. Lerner, (1999). *The Venture Capital Cycle*. Cambridge, MIT Press.
Grabher, G. (ed.) (1993). *The Embedded Firm: On the Socioeconomics of Industrial Networks*. London: Routledge.

Griliches, Z (1979). Issues in Assessing the Contribution of R&D to Productivity Growth. *Bell Journal of Economics, 10*, 92-116.

Griliches, Z. (1992). The Search for R&D Spill-Overs. *Scandinavian Journal of Economics, 94*, 29-47.

Grossman, G.M. and Helpman, E. (1991). *Innovation and Growth in the Global Economy.* Cambridge, MIT Press.

Hirschman, A. O. (1970). *Exit, Voice, and Loyalty.* Cambridge, Harvard University Press.

Holmes, T. J. and Schmitz, J.A., Jr. (1990). A Theory of Entrepreneurship and its Application to the Study of Business Transfers. *Journal of Political Economy, 98(4)*, 265-294.

Jaffe, A., Trajtenberg, M. and Henderson, R. (1993). Geographic Localization of Knowledge Spillovers as Evidenced by Patent Citations. *Quarterly Journal of Economics, 63*, 577-598.

Jaffe, A. B., (1989). Real Effects of Academic Research. *American Economic Review, 79(5)*, 957-970.

Jovanovic, B. (1994). Entrepreneurial Choice: When People Differ in their Management and Labor Skills. *Small Business Economics, 6(3)*, 185-192.

Kihlstrom, R.E. and Laffont, J.J. (1979). A General Equilibrium Entrepreneurial Theory of Firm Formation Based on Risk Aversion. *Journal of Political Economy, 87(4)*, 719-748.

Klepper, S. (2002). The Evolution of the U.S. Automobile Industry and Detroit as its Capital. Paper presented at the International Workshop in The Post-Entry Performance of Firms: Technology, Growth and Survival, University of Bologna, 22-23 November.

Knight, F.H. (1921). *Risk, Uncertainty and Profit.* New York, Houghton Mifflin.

Krugman, P. (1991). *Geography and Trade.* Cambridge, MIT Press.

Levin, S. G. and Stephan, P.E. (1991). Research Productivity over the Life-Cycle: Evidence for Academic Scientists. *American Economic Review, 81*, 114-32.

Lucas, R. (1988). On the Mechanics of Economic Development. *Journal of Monetary Economics, 22*, 3-39.

Lucas, R.E. Jr. (1993). Making a Miracle. *Econometrica, 61*, 251-272.

Porter, M. (1990). *The Comparative Advantage of Nations.* New York, Free Press.

Powell, W., Koput, K. W. and Smith-Doerr, L. (1996). Interorganizational Collaboration and the Locus of Innovation: Networks of Learning in Biotechnology. *Administrative Science Quarterly, 42 (1)*, 116-145.

Reynolds, P. D., Miller, B. and Maki, W.R. (1995). Explaining Regional Variation in Business Births and Deaths: U.S. 1976-1988. *Small Business Economics, 7*, 389-407.

Romer, P. M. (1986). Increasing Returns and Long-Run Growth. *Journal of Political Economy, 94(5)*, 1002-37.

Saxenian, A. (1990). Regional Networks and the Resurgence of Silicon Valley. *California Management Review, 33*, 89-111.

Saxenian, A., (2001). The Role of Immigrant Entrepreneurs in New Venture Creation. In: Schoonhoven, C. and Romanelli, E. (Eds.). *The Entrepreneurship Dynamic.* Palo Alto, Stanford University Press, 40-67.

Saxenien, A. (1994). *Regional Advantage.* Cambridge, Harvard University Press.

Solow, R. (1956). A Contribution to The Theory of Economic Growth. *Quarterly Journal of Economics, 70*, 65-94.

Sorenson, O. and Stuart, T. (2001). Syndication Networks and the Spatial Distribution of Venture Capital Investments. *American Journal of Sociology, 106 (6)*, 1546-1588.

Sorenson, O. and Audia, P.G. (2000). The Social Structure of Entrepreneurial Activity: Geographic Concentration of Footwear Production in the United States, 1940-1989. *American Journal of Sociology, 106, (2)*, 424-462.

Stephan, P.E. (1996). The Economics of Science. *Journal of Economic Literature,* 34(3), 1199-1235.

Stephan, P. and Eberhart, S. (1998). The Changing Rewards to Science. *Small Business Economics, 10*, 141-51.

Stephan, P.E. and Levin, S.G. (1991). *Striking the Mother Lode in Science: The Importance of age, Place and Time.* Oxford, Oxford University Press.

Stephan, P.E. (2002). *Using Human Resource Data to Track Innovation: Summary of a Workshop.* Washington, D.C., National Science Foundation.

Thorton, P.H. and Flynne, K.H. (2003). Entrepreneurship, Networks and Geographies. In Acs, Z. and Audretsch, d. (Eds.), *The International Handbook of Entrepreneurship.* Dordrecht, Kluwer Academic Publishers.

Zucker, L., Darby, M. and Brewer, M. (1994). Intellectual Capital and the Birth of U.S. Biotechnology Enterprises. NBER Working Paper 4653.

Zucker, L., Darby, M. and Torrero, M. (1997). Labor Mobility from Academic to Commerce. NBER Working Paper No. 6050.

PART I

Geographic and Relational Proximity

CHAPTER 3

THE SPATIAL DISTRIBUTION OF ENTREPRENEURIAL SUPPORT NETWORKS: EVIDENCE FROM SEMICONDUCTOR INITIAL PUBLIC OFFERINGS FROM 1996 THROUGH 2000

Donald Patton and Martin Kenney

University of California, Davis

1. INTRODUCTION

Theory and recent research demonstrates that entrepreneurship is a spatially and socially embedded activity.[1] In certain regions, dense support networks of institutions dedicated to assisting entrepreneurial start-ups have been established and a wide variety of authors have given credit to these networks for supporting regional entrepreneurship (Kenney and von Burg 1999; Saxenian 1994; Bahrami and Evans 2000). As Marshall (1890) recognized many, but not all, industries exhibit a strong clustering effect (see also, e.g., Storper and Walker 1988; Porter 1990; 1998). Research on these networks has been hampered by a lack of empirical data that contains spatial variables and identifies the relationship between various actors (i.e., venture capitalists, law firms and investment bankers) and the start-up firm. Thus research has been qualitative and anecdotal or when quantitative limited to certain industries usually biotechnology.

Because these institutions are dedicated to the formation of new firms their presence within a region serves to lower the entry costs of new firms into the region. The role of start-ups in the transmission of knowledge within a cluster has been widely noted as they are one of the key ways in which Marshall's "mysteries of the trade" are diffused within a cluster such as the Silicon Valley (Brown and Duguid 2000). Therefore the economic actors that comprise an entrepreneurial support network within a region serve, in their promotion of start-ups, as an important conduit of knowledge spillovers.

This study is an examination of the spatial location of a firm's entrepreneurial support network, which we define as the network of actors that a start-up firm relies upon for financial, legal, and managerial support and expertise. In particular, this study is an examination of some of these actors with respect to start-up semiconductor firms that have reached a stage in their development where they have decided to go public with an initial public offering (IPO) of their stock. Although this is but one path a successful start-up may choose, the others being remaining as a private firm or being acquired or merging with another company, it is the one path that allows outside observers access to the inner workings of the new firm. This access is made available through the documents a firm going public must submit to the U.S. Securities and Exchange Commission, and it is these documents that provide the basis of this study.

2. ECONOMIC CLUSTERS, ENTRENEURIAL SUPPORT NETWORKS, AND THE FORMATION OF NEW FIRMS

The tendency of different types of economic activity to concentrate geographically is a widely observed phenomenon over time and across countries. These concentrations of activity are most frequently referred to as clusters or industrial districts, and the relationship between innovation, entrepreneurship, and geography of these clusters has attracted the attention of academics from a variety of disciplines in the last decade. The importance of industrial clustering for firm growth and innovation has been widely noted beginning with Alfred Marshall (1890), extending through Michael Piore and Charles Sabel (1984) to contemporary geographers (Malecki 1980; Scott 1993; Storper 1995).

Krugman (1991), in a restatement of Alfred Marshall's observations from 1890, concludes that there are three distinct reasons for localization. First, clusters allow for a large market of workers with highly specialized skills. For many firms such skilled labor can only be found within a cluster. Second, a cluster supports a wide range of specialized local suppliers of inputs and services. Again, some specialized inputs are only readily available in clusters. Technological spillovers, the tendency for knowledge to spill over from firms and individuals within a cluster, yet be geographically bounded by the cluster, is given as a final reason for industrial localization.

The literature investigating clusters has found that both traded and untraded interdependency benefits are responsible for the success of these regional economic agglomerations (Storper 1995; Porter 1990). Michael Porter (1998), in conclusions not very different from those of Paul Krugman above or economic geographers such as Walker (1985; 1988), identified three broad ways in which clusters affect competition. First, the externalities present in a cluster operate to increase the productivity of all member firms. Second, the cluster accelerates the innovative capacity of its firms. Third, the concentration of specialized skills and knowledge within the cluster reduces the barriers to entry and facilitates new firm formation. Baptista and Swann (1998) found evidence to suggest that all of these factors are at work and that innovation, firm entry and growth are all stronger in clusters. In qualitative work directed at particular industrial clusters, Kenney and von Burg (1999) have argued that these benefits are responsible for the success of innovative regions such as Silicon Valley and Route 128. Saxenian (1994) argues that the interactive nature of the Silicon Valley environment is the reason that Silicon Valley was more successful than Route 128.

Silicon Valley hosts a set of interdependent institutions that observers have termed an "ecosystem", a "social structure of innovation", or an "incubator region" (Bahrami and Evans 2000; Florida and Kenney 1990; Schoonhoven and Eisenhardt 1989). Silicon Valley can be considered as two intertwined but analytically separable economies. The first set of organizations consist of established firms, corporate research laboratories, and universities that are the constituents of the existing economy that are in one form or another not unusual for any industrial cluster. Silicon Valley, however, has another set of organizations that combine to create an "economy" predicated on facilitating entrepreneurs in the creation of new firms. Kenney and von Burg (2000) argue that this other economy is the *differentia specifica* of high-technology regions such as Silicon Valley, and is the trait that sets them apart from most other regions of industrial clustering.

The organizations of the first economy, either because of their charter to do research as in the case of universities and R&D laboratories, or as a by-product of their normal activities as in the case of firms, create inventions that may be capable of being capitalized in an independent firm. This ability to extrude an invention from an existing firm is facilitated by the rapid pace in high-tech industry, which often creates technological discontinuities and accompanying economic opportunities. In the electronics industry there have been recurring discontinuities, and very often the existing firms are unwilling or unable to exploit them, or simply miss them because they are preoccupied with their current businesses and customers (Christensen 1997).

The organizations of the second economy comprise the institutional infrastructure that has evolved to enable the creation and growth of new firms (Bahrami and Evans 1989; Florida and Kenney 1988; Schoonhoven and Eisenhardt 1989; Todtling 1994). Just as computers and microprocessors are the actual products of the firms found in the first economy, new firms can be seen as the products of the institutional infrastructure of the second economy dedicated to the creation of new firms. The components of this infrastructure are organizations whose primary or sole purpose is related to servicing start-ups. The capital gains derived from these start-ups fuel the entire process, whether these organizations receive fees for services rendered or receive equity in the enterprise. We refer to the particular constituents within this infrastructure that a start-up wishing to go public must turn to as the firm's entrepreneurial support network.

The history of the development of the semiconductor industry in Silicon Valley illustrates not only the remarkable technological importance of this industry to Silicon Valley and the power of Moore's Law,[2] but also the role of members of a firm's support network, particularly venture capitalists. Silicon Valley's capture of the semiconductor industry was the result of a series of small events that would make an enormous difference, starting in 1955 when William Shockley, coinventor of the transistor at Bell Laboratories, decided to establish a firm to exploit his invention.

Shockley hired eight brilliant young scientists and engineers and brought them with him to Palo Alto. Shockley proved to be an ineffective manager, and the eight resigned in 1957 to form their own start-up. Not knowing how to find capital in the San Francisco Bay Area, they went through a U.S. East Coast investment bank to get funding from an East Coast firm, Fairchild Camera and Instrument Company, owned by Sherman Fairchild. The firm founded by these eight engineers was named Fairchild Semiconductor. Fairchild quickly became a technological leader in the transistor industry and spearheaded the transition to the integrated circuit.

With the Sputnik-related military buildup throughout the 1960s and the adoption of transistors and integrated circuits by the manufacturers of consumer electronics and computers, sales boomed and profits were exorbitant (Hanson, 1982). As a by-product of the exuberant growth of the semiconductor industry in the 1960s, many firm founders and early employees became very wealthy (Tilton, 1971). Their success, and willingness to invest in new ventures, put in motion a path-dependent logic, in terms of an example and an incentive for others to follow. Earlier successes justified future ventures. The dimensions of this spin-off process were immense; a genealogy of semiconductor start-ups through 1986 indicated that 124 start-ups could trace their roots to Fairchild.

Fairchild and its spin-offs were important in the history of Silicon Valley venture capital. In addition to Arthur Rock, who arranged the Fairchild investment in 1958, organized the funding for Intel, and provided funding to many other start-ups such as Apple, other important venture capitalists that began their career at Fairchild are Donald Valentine and Pierre Lamond of Sequoia Partners, and Eugene Kleiner of Kleiner Perkins. Most important, the success of Fairchild's spin-offs (such as Intel, Advanced Micro Devices, National Semiconductor, LSI Logic, and their spin-offs) created enormous capital gains for their founders, key employees, and investors in venture capital funds. Some gains were reinvested in venture capital funds and independent start-ups. The final important contribution of Fairchild and its early start-ups was the number of managers and engineers that had become independently wealthy and were able to invest in or join start-ups without risking their financial future.

3. THE CONSTITUENT ACTORS OF AN ENTREPRENEURIAL SUPPORT NETWORK

One of the principal advantages of choosing to locate a new firm in a cluster is to access the knowledge spillovers that are to be found there. But as Powell et. al. (2002) argue, the existence of an infrastructure within a cluster that fosters knowledge transfer and the provision of capital is an important element in the firm's decision as well. This infrastructure, or support network, is comprised of universities, law firms, research institutes, venture capitalists and other professionals. This entrepreneurial support network maintains channels of communication among market participants that not only support the public good nature of technological knowledge, these channels also reduce the transaction costs of comprehending and utilizing such information (Antonelli, 2000).

In capitalist economies, quite naturally, access to capital is a requirement. In this study, two financial intermediaries, the venture capitalists and investment bankers, are included. The role of spatial and network proximity for financial intermediaries has attracted significant attention recently. Agnes (2002) in a study of the interest rate swaps industry found that "different financial services have differing informational contents, with implications for the local embeddedness of financial services firms." This is confirmed by the finding that formal institutional networks are actually embedded in informal relationships through which transactions and information flows (Clark and O'Connor 1997; Pryke and Lee 1995; Thrift and Leyshon 1994). In other words, as Uzzi (1999) illustrates formal relationships such as the lender-borrower relationship are embedded in a social context, and this social embeddedness, what Garud and Jain (1996) in their study of technological change refer to as "just-embedded," actually reduces the cost of loans and reduces risk. Abolafia (1997) finds that the necessity of social and physical proximity differs by the nature of the financial product. So, for highly standardized products such as listed equities and government bonds, traders need not be proximate, whereas for other more idiosyncratic financial instruments proximity is of greater importance.

There is an ample literature suggesting that venture capital investing is a locally embedded practice, because of the importance of their monitoring and informal assistance functions that go beyond simply providing capital (Florida and Kenney 1988; Sorenson and Stuart 2001; Gilson and Black, 1998). Indeed, Greenwald and Stiglitz (1992) have observed that the venture capital industry shares many aspects with early financial market communities.

Because venture capital firms operate in a tightly knit community and have detailed information of the projects they fund and the industries in which their entrepreneurs operate, there is a strong reliance upon trust and reputation in the relationship between venture capitalists and the firms they fund. The critical venture capitalists in a start-up are what are termed the "lead" venture capitalists who are the board members and those most responsible for monitoring and assisting the firm (Gompers and Lerner 1999), and it is these venture capitalists that one would expect to be local.

Investment banks are another part of a firm's entrepreneurial support network. Their expertise and connections with venture capitalists and entrepreneurs are core assets, from which other specialties have arisen. Here we would hypothesize that repeated transactions take place between individual venture capitalists and investment bankers, and that they will be located in close physical proximity to each other despite the fact that many of the investment banks such as Goldman Sachs and Morgan Stanley are located on the East Coast, though historically there were a number of smaller boutique investment banks on the West Coast including Hambrecht and Quist, Robertson Stephens (during the 1990s they were acquired by larger banks). However, very often the newly acquired investment-banking arm was not relocated, so an attribution of the source of the investment banking service to the headquarters would be incorrect.

The legal profession is, quite naturally, local in practice even though most large legal firms have numerous branch offices. High-technology lawyers for small start-ups often have a multifaceted role that extends far beyond merely providing the legal services such as incorporation documents etc. They often advise entrepreneurs and provide introductions to venture capital firms and other business services (Suchman 2000). Of course, for firms in more remote locations such legal advice may not be available leading one to hypothesize that the start-up would either have a relatively unsophisticated local lawyer or be forced to retain counsel from a distant high-technology cluster.

4. PROXIMITY, TACIT INFORMATION, AND ENTREPRENEURIAL NETWORKS

David Audretsch (2000) has observed that an irony of globalization is that as technological advances in communication have drastically reduced the cost of transmitting information over distance, the perceived importance of geographically bound clusters of economic activity as engines of innovation and global competitiveness has grown. The ability to send information almost costlessly anywhere in the world would tend to lead to the death of distance (Brown and Duguid, 2002), yet distance in the exchange of knowledge among economic actors is of great importance for a large number of such relationships. The importance of distance, then, derives from the attributes of the knowledge being transmitted. Knowledge, or information, that can be easily standardized and codified can be sent, and understood, over distance at very low cost. Knowledge that is difficult to articulate and is tacit in nature is more open to interpretation and uncertainty and therefore relies upon face-to-face interaction to be transmitted effectively (Feldman, 2000).

A large number of empirical studies demonstrate that knowledge spillovers are geographically mediated, which is to say that innovation is found in clusters. As early as Malecki (1980) it was observed that there was regional variation in R&D and from this he argued that there were significant differences between the ability of regions to innovate. Feldman (1994), using data collected by the Small Business Administration, found that innovations in particular industries were highly concentrated in states such as California and Massachusetts for electronics and New Jersey and New York for medical instruments. Audretsch and Feldman (1996) found that even after the geographical concentration of production is accounted for, innovations are found to cluster in industries where industry R&D, skilled labor, and university research are important inputs.

This phenomenon of clustering of innovation as measured by patents was first observed by Jaffe et. al. (1993) who found that patents will cite other patents originating in the same location more frequently than patents outside the location controlling for the existing geography of related research activity. Almeida and Kogut (1997) obtained similar results in studying patents in the semiconductor industry, indicating that patent citations are localized.[3]

In their studies of geographical proximity and the transmission of tacit scientific information, Zucker, Darby, and Brewer (1998), and Audretsch and Stephan (1996) examined the proximity of biotechnology firms to scientists conducting research in the field of biotechnology. Zucker et. al. found that the presence of star researchers in biotechnology in a region, as identified by a publishing record in genetic sequencing, was strongly and positively related to the number of biotechnology start-ups in a region. Audretsch and Stephan dealt with this same issue though a database linking start-ups with their specific scientific advisors. They found that scientists who were founders or were chair of a firm's Scientific Advisory Board were much more likely to be locally linked to the firm than other affiliated scientists, indicating that those scientists intimately involved in the transfer of knowledge must do so through proximate, face-to-face contact.

While proximity of actors is critical to the transmission of tacit or sticky knowledge among them, proximity is also important in the interactions among members of entrepreneurial networks as well.

Gompers and Lerner (1999), in a study of venture capital oversight of firms, examined the geographical proximity of 271 biotechnology firms between 1978 and 1989 and the venture capitalists that funded them. It was found that the proximity of the venture capitalist to the firm was highly significant in explaining their service on the board of directors even after the venture capitalist firm's ownership and age were accounted for. Because effective oversight of a firm by a venture capitalist requires frequent visits and close involvement in the firm's affairs, the costs of oversight are highly dependent on the distance between the venture capitalist and the firm.

Powell et. al. (2002) found a strong pattern of spatial co-location of biotechnology firms and venture capital. Those venture capital firms that did invest outside their region tended to be older and larger. In their comprehensive study of venture capital investment across all industries from 1986 to 1998, Sorenson and Stuart (2001) observed that venture capitalists were more likely to invest in geographically distant firms when they had prior investing experience with other members of the investment syndicate. In general venture capital firms that have established numerous relationships with other VC firms tend to invest more across geographic distance than do those firms that have not established such relationships.

Our study extends these earlier efforts by focusing on the entire entrepreneurial network not just a single component such as venture capital. In this way, we provide a more comprehensive understanding of high-technology entrepreneurship than has earlier research.

5. DATA AND METHODOLOGY

Every firm wishing to go public must file a prospectus with the U.S. Securities and Exchange Commission (SEC) prior to its initial offering of stock. This initial public offering (IPO) is a defining event in the history of any firm. The IPO performs two important functions: First, it provides the firm with capital so that it can continue its expansion. Second, after the IPO, the stakes of both management and investors (subject to certain lock-up delays) becomes liquid. In return, however, the firm must conform to the reporting and transparency requirements imposed by the SEC under the Securities Act of 1933. One of the primary objectives of the Securities Act of 1933 is to require companies making a public offering of their securities to publicly disclose relevant business and financial information about their company so that potential investors can make an informed investment decision regarding the offering. To achieve this end the 1933 Act requires companies going public to file disclosure documents with the Securities and Exchange Commission, the most important of which are the general form S-1 registration statement and the 424B prospectus. These documents, in effect, provide us with a detailed snapshot of the firm at the time it goes public, and it is these documents, which provide the basis of the data used in this study.

5.1 The Data

The semiconductor firms selected for this study were obtained from the Venture Economics database listing IPOs over the time period of June 1996 through the year 2000. These firms were identified by their Standard Industry Code (SIC) and were restricted to those filing an S-1 registration statement.[4] A population of 44 firms was selected by this criterion.

Although the IPO prospectus of a firm contains a great deal of information about the company going public regarding its finances, management, ownership, business strategy and the like, we have initially restricted our attention to the geographical location of the actors associated with the IPO.

On the lead page of every S-1 registration statement the names and addresses of the lawyers and their law firms involved in the IPO are given. In almost every instance the lawyers of two law firms are provided; one law firm representing the issuer, or firm going public, and one law firm representing the underwriters, or lead investment banker, of the IPO.[5] The addresses of these law firms allow us to map the precise location of two actors in the IPO process; firm lawyers and investment bank (IB) lawyers.

The location of the firm's lawyer has a straightforward meaning. The location of the investment bank's, or lead underwriter's, lawyer is less so. Originally we had hoped to obtain the name of the lead investment banker, but when this was found to be infeasible we considered identifying the lead banker's location by selecting the investment bank's branch office having the closest proximity to the firm going public. This approach, though, has two difficulties. First, it is unclear how accurately one can identify all of the branch offices of an IB at some point in history and second, even if such a listing were accurate selecting the most proximate office may be an arbitrary selection. Therefore we rely upon the location of the investment banks' law firm as a proxy for the lead IB location. The lead IB is identified in the prospectus as the underwriter having agreed to purchase from the firm, or issuer, the largest number of shares of stock for the IPO.

The SEC requires that each firm include a discussion of its management in its prospectus. This section on management includes a table that provides the name, age, and title of the executive officers and directors of the firm or other key employees. In addition, a one-paragraph biography of each individual in the table is provided which indicates the individual's current and previous employment status and affiliation. On the basis of this information we constructed a list of independent directors in the sense that they were not employed by the firm at the time of the IPO.

This group of independent directors was in turn broken into two mutually exclusive sets; those board members that were affiliated with a venture capital (VC) firm, and the remaining board members that were not so affiliated. Determining whether a board member was affiliated with a venture capitalist firm was based on their biography. The address and location of all directors was found through extensive searching over the internet. The addresses of these directors allow us to map the precise location of two additional actors in the IPO process; non-VC directors and VC directors.

5.2 Geographical Distribution of Actors

The distribution of the actors geographically is shown below in Table 3.1. The most obvious feature of Table 3.1 is the dominance of California in firms that have gone public and the other actors in the startup process.

Table 3.1. Distribution of IPO Actors

State	Firms	Firm Lawyers	IB Lawyers	Non-VC Directors	VC Directors	Total
Arizona				1		1
N. California	27	30	31	52	40	180
S. California	5	3	4	9	3	24
Colorado	1		2	1		4
Connecticut				1	2	3
Delaware	1			1		2
Florida				2		2
Illinois					1	1
Massachusetts	2	2	4	4	10	22
Maryland					1	1
Michigan		1		3		4
North Carolina				1		1
New Hampshire					1	1
New Jersey	2			2		4
Nevada				2		2
New York	1	4	3	5	5	18
Oklahoma				1		1
Oregon	2	2		4		8
Pennsylvania	1			3		4
Texas	2	2		2	9	15
Virginia				2		2
Washington					1	1
National Total	44	44	44	96	73	301
Foreign	0	0	0	12	9	21
Not located	0	0	0	5	1	6
Total	44	44	44	113	83	328

Massachusetts, New York, and Texas are of secondary importance while Oregon is of some importance as well. The dominance of California comes of course from the Silicon Valley, but Southern California as a region is of importance on its own. Restricting attention to just national data by excluding foreign actors and those that could not be located, the relative importance of these states can be seen in Figures 1 and 2.

Figure 3.1 shows the contribution of six regions; Silicon Valley (including the San Francisco Bay area), Southern California (LA and San Diego), Massachusetts, New York, Oregon, and Texas, to the ranks of the different actors. Figure 3.2 illustrates this same data by showing the contribution of the different actors to each of six regions plus all other.

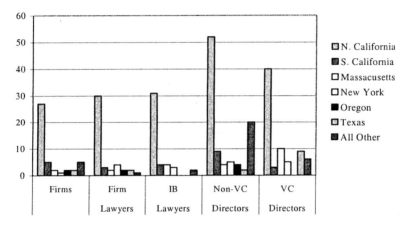

Figure 3.1. Contribution of six regions to the ranks of the different actors

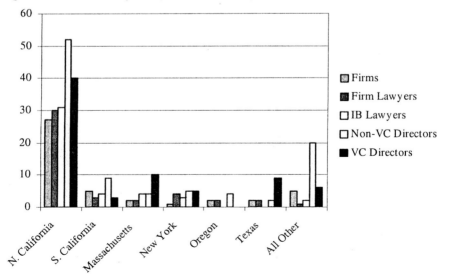

Figure 3.2. Contribution of the different actors to each of six regions

These figures show that while the Silicon Valley dominates in these IPOs, southern California, Massachusetts and New York have all the actors required for facilitating IPOs. The importance of Boston for venture capital firms and the importance of corporate banking in New York City stand out, as does the presence of venture capitalists in Dallas and Austin Texas.

5.3 Proximity of Actors

The proximity of these actors to the firm going public in addition to their distribution over regions is of interest. The histograms in Figure 3.3 and 3.4 for law firms and Figure 3.5 and 3.6 for directors show their proximity to a firm in straight line miles for those actors we have precisely located.[6]

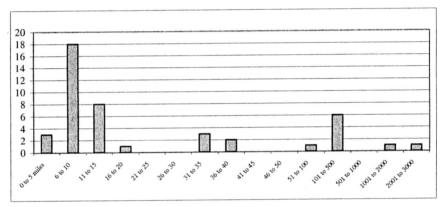

Figure 3.3. Firm Lawyers

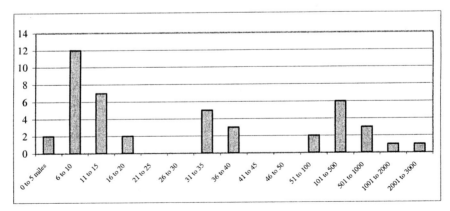

Figure 3.4. IB Lawyers

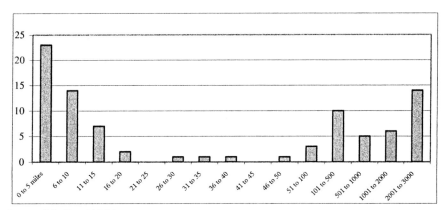

Figure 3.5. Non-VC Directors

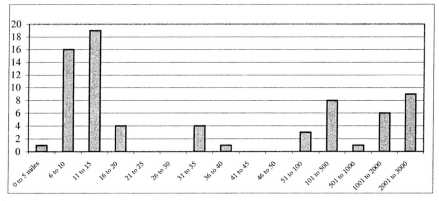

Figure 3.6. VC Directors

In comparing the proximity of law firms it is interesting to see how similar are the proximity distributions of firm and investment bank lawyers. In addition the number of law firms having an exact proximity of 25 miles or less is 30 out of 44 for firm lawyers, and 23 out of 44 for IB lawyers. It is striking how close most firm lawyers are to the firms they represent.

In comparing directors proximity differs somewhat with non-VC directors having a tendency to be either very close or on the other side of the country. This bicoastal pattern also emerges for VC directors. The exact proximity of these directors does not differ much though with 52.3% of all non-VC directors being within 25 miles of the firm compared to 55.6% for VC directors.

The significance of the proximity of these actors can be seen more clearly by including all of the actors that can be located by state or country. We define an actor as being inside a firm's region if it is within 50 miles of the firm, and outside the region otherwise.[7] Table 3.2 shows this breakdown by category of actor.

Table 3.2. Proximity of IPO Actors to Firms

	Firm Lawyers	IB Lawyers	Lawyer Total	Non-VC Directors	VC Directors	Director Total	Lawyers and Directors Together
Inside region	35	31	66	55	45	100	166
	79.55%	70.45%	75.0%	50.93%	54.88%	52.63%	59.71%
Outside region	9	13	22	53	37	90	112
	20.45%	29.55%	25.0%	49.07%	45.12%	47.37%	40.29%
Total	44	44	88	108	82	188	278
χ^2			0.97			0.29	12.51
Mean distance	128.43	201.00		572.27	494.04		
Median distance	11	19		16.5	15.5		

The results found in Table 3.2 are consistent with the above discussion of proximity. A Chi-square test indicates that a firm lawyer is not significantly more likely to be located inside a firm's region than is an IB lawyer, nor is there a statistically significant difference between the proximity of non-VC and VC directors. However, taken as a group it is true at the .005 level of significance that lawyers are more likely to be within the region of a company than are directors.

Because lawyers are so intimately involved in the negotiations surrounding the IPO and act as intermediaries among the actors it is not surprising that they should require close proximity to the firm during the IPO process. We would have hypothesized, though, that VC directors would in general have greater proximity than non-VC directors in agreement with the results of Gompers and Lerner (1999) on venture capital oversight. Since Silicon Valley dominates this industry segment this result could be driven to some degree by the geographical distribution of these two types of directors and the firms they serve in the Valley.

5.4 Networks and Regional Relations among Actors

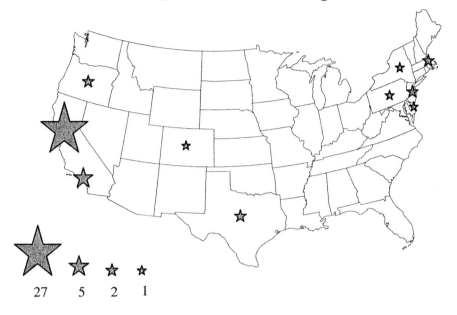

Figure 3.7. National Distribution of Semiconductor IPOs

The density of semiconductor IPOs across the U.S. indicates that semiconductor activity is concentrated in California and along the Northeast corridor with pockets of activity in Texas, Oregon and Colorado. We found that maps showing the distribution of all of the actors obscured much that can be known from this data. The density of activity in various centers such as Boston, New York City, and particularly the Silicon Valley, could not be clearly shown on a map of this sort. Moreover, the networks that exist within and among these regions are not shown. However, the networks that exist among these actors and the firms they serve in the IPO process can be shown through regional diagrams illustrating the relationships between each firm and members of its support network.

The firms and actors in this study are found primarily in the Silicon Valley and five other regions. All of the dyad relationships between a firm and a member of its support network can be placed within this regional framework. The regional figure shown below, Firm Lawyer→ Firm Dyads, should be interpreted as follows. The 27 firms in northern California all have law firms within northern California, two law firms in northern California represent firms in southern California, and one northern California law firm represents a firm in New Jersey. Three out of five southern California firms have lawyers within southern California. One New York law firm represents a New York firm, while the other three represent firms in Delaware, New Jersey, and Pennsylvania. Both Oregon firms are represented by lawyers within the state, as are both Texas firms. Finally, the semiconductor firm going public in Colorado is represented by a Michigan law firm. The arrow in these figures always points towards the firm.

This figure, together with the one illustrating regional relationships between firms and investment bank (IB) lawyers, shows just how localized the relationships between a firm and the legal counselors involved in its IPO can be. Every single firm within the major regions shown here chose a lawyer from its region with the exception of two southern California firms that relied on law firms from the Silicon Valley.

The reduced importance of proximity of newly public firms and the directors that serve on their board of directors is shown in the second set of regional dyad figures. A bicoastal distribution of directors, particularly of lead venture capitalists, is evident.

Taken as a whole these figures also tell us something about the regions themselves in the IPO process. West coast firms are quite dependent on the law firms of northern California for legal counsel. Similarly New York, although being home to only one semiconductor IPO, is the center of legal representation along the Northeast corridor. Massachusetts emerges as the center of venture capital for the eastern United States while the Silicon Valley provides venture capital to the entire country.

Silicon Valley, of course, dominates among all of these actors indicating that its preeminence in semiconductor manufacturing and new firm formation is matched by its being the core of entrepreneurial activity as well. None of this is surprising and is exactly what one would expect given the advantages of location within clusters for both new firms and members of the entrepreneurial networks examined here.

However, the degree of geographical clustering among some actors within the Silicon Valley was somewhat surprising. Figure 3.12 provides visual confirmation of the density of the networks that exist in the Silicon Valley. All 27 of the semiconductor firms that went public in northern California can be found within a 7.5 mile radius off Highway 237. A more extraordinary clustering of actors can be found within a one half-mile radius of Page Mill Road in Palo Alto where 19 out of 44 firm lawyers and 15 out of 44 investment bank lawyers can be found.[8] In addition, 24 out of 82 total venture capitalist directors can be found in a one-mile radius off Sand Hill Road in Menlo Park.

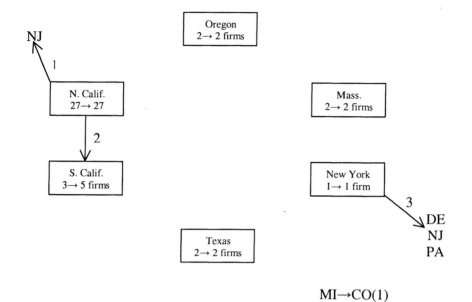

Figure 3.8. Firm Lawyer → Firm Dyads

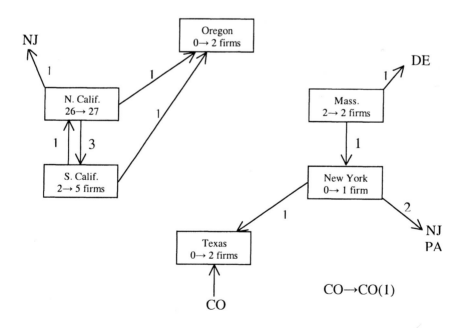

Figure 3.9. IB Lawyer → Firm Dyads

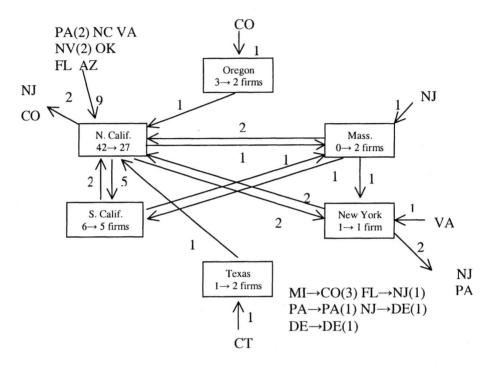

Figure 3.10. Non-VC Director → Firm Dyads

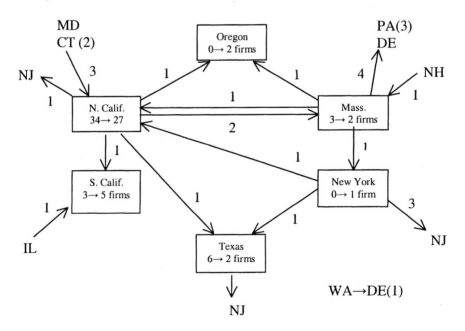

Figure 3.11. VC Director → Firm Dyads

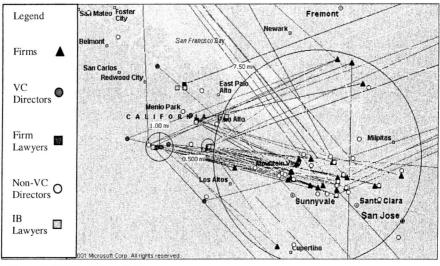

Figure 3.12. The Silicon Valley

While VC directors and non-VC directors have the same proximity to firms in this population, their distribution within the Silicon Valley is quite distinct. VC directors are concentrated around Sand Hill Road and are found almost exclusively in Palo Alto, Menlo Park and parts north. Non-VC directors, on the other hand, are distributed throughout the region but are found in abundance in Sunnyvale, Santa Clara, and San Jose. The general pattern then is for many non-VC directors to reside throughout Santa Clara County where the firms are located, while VC directors are much more concentrated in the location of San Mateo County.

6. CONCLUSION

The investigations of the spatial location of the multiple constituents of the start-up environment has been limited. All of the studies have focused upon the venture capital-firm dyad, however even these studies have suffered from a lack of ability to identify the key venture capitalists. This study is the first step in an effort to overcome these shortcomings. This descriptive study confirms many of the results from the existing dyad-based literature, however it also advances the literature by providing a more comprehensive view of the institutions that support entrepreneurship in the semiconductor industry.

The attraction of the Silicon Valley to start-up semiconductor firms for all of the reasons cited in the literature on clustering was clearly in evidence as over 60% of all semiconductor firms going public from 1996 through 2000 nationwide choose to locate within a 7.5-mile radius in the Valley. The degree of clustering within the Silicon Valley also extended to the actors involved in the start-up process. Almost 40% of all legal counselors in the IPO process were found within a half-mile radius in Palo Alto, and almost 70% of all law firms representing both firms and investment bankers were located in the Silicon Valley. Such proximity would be expected if as Suchman (2000) claims, lawyers perform a not only the function of providing advice on the formal aspects of legally creating a firm, but also act as intermediaries among the actors in the process as well.

Although venture capitalist directors in the Silicon Valley were heavily concentrated around Sand Hill Road, the dominance of Silicon Valley in providing venture capital to the semiconductor industry was not complete, as venture capitalists in Boston, Texas, and, to some extent, New York City also provided financial support. The importance of outside venture capital to Silicon Valley firms provides support to the observations made by Powell et. al. (2002) and Sorenson and Stuart (2001) regarding the role of local venture capitalists, but also the recognition that venture capitalists outside the region also invested. Even though this was a small sample, it extends upon Sorenson and Stuart's results by just focussing on the key venture capitalists in the firm (these are the venture capitalists most responsible for the firm). In this small sample, we were surprised to find that, in some cases, one of the key ventures located outside the region.

There are limitations to a study of this type. In our case the population is limited to only those start-ups that have been sufficiently successful to undertake an initial public offering. In addition the population is quite small at 44 firms, and is a rather eclectic group as it includes semiconductor equipment and solar cell manufacturers. Nevertheless it provides a foundation for future work. Our future work will compare spatial location and network patterns among the constituents of entrepreneurial support networks over several industry groups. Since the importance of tacit information exchange among actors in the IPO process almost certainly varies across industries, it seems likely that the role of geographical location and proximity among these actors would vary across industries as well (Audretsch 2000). Second, the collection of financial data after the IPO offering is quite simple, thus we will be able to examine whether various characteristics affect a firm's economic performance. This will provide an outcome measure for each firm as a function of its financial makeup and relationships with the market actors of the start-up process. With this we will be able to test one part of Schoonhoven and Eisenhardt's (1989) claim that the higher growth rates of semiconductor start-ups from 1978 to 1986 in the Silicon Valley were attributable to the Valley being an incubator consisting of institutions that nurtured and sped the growth of these start-ups. Expanding such an investigation to other industries would allow us to identify the extent to which such incubators exist in other locations and industries.

NOTES

[1]   On social embeddedness, see Granovetter (1985). On the embeddedness of economic activity in a regional context, see Storper and Salais (1997).

[2]   Gordon Moore, one of the founders of Fairchild and later Intel, observed that the number of transistors on an integrated circuit doubled approximately every eighteen months even as the cost of the integrated circuit remained the same.

[3]   In an examination of labor mobility patterns among semiconductor engineers, Angel (1991) found that these engineers moved around the U.S. However, if they moved to Silicon Valley their mobility continued, but now their mobility was confined to the Silicon Valley.

[4]   This eliminates firms considered by the SEC to be small businesses that file an SB-2 registration statement rather than an S-1. Although these small firms would be of interest, the most reliably complete list of IPOs at this time is comprised of larger, S-1 firms.

[5]   In the case of a spin-off both the new firm and the parent firm have legal representation.

[6]   All firm lawyers and IB lawyers could be precisely located. Therefore their straight line distance from the company going public could be determined. 88 out of 96 non-VC directors, and 72 out of 73 VC directors could be precisely located nationally. The remaining directors could be generally located within a state in Table 3.1.

[7]   In Table 3.2 every actor that can be located is included, including foreign actors, who will obviously be outside the region of the firm.

[8]   It would be more correct to say firm lawyer or investment bank lawyer deals or events. Wilson Sonsini, a single law firm, was involved in 13 IPO deals as a legal representative of a firm in this population, and so this is

REFERENCES

Abolafia, M. (1997). *Making markets: Opportunism and restraint on Wall Street.* Cambridge, Mass.: Harvard University Press.

Agnes, P. (2002). The 'end of geography' in financial services: Local embeddedness and territorialization in the interest rate swaps industry. *Economic Geography,* 76, 347-366.

Almeida, P. and Kogut, B. (1997). The exploration of technological diversity and the geographical localization of innovation. *Small Business Economics,* 9, 21-31.

Angel, D. (1991). High-technology agglomeration and the labor market: The case of silicon valley. *Environment and Planning A,* 23, 1501-1516.

Antonelli, C. (2000). Collective knowledge communication and innovation: The evidence oftechnological districts. *Regional Studies,* 34 (6).

Audretsch, D. (2000). Corporate form and spatial form. In: G. L. Clark, Feldman M.P. and Gertler, M.S.(Eds.). *The Oxford handbook of economic geography.* New York: Oxford University Press.

Audretsch, D. B. and Feldman, M.P. (1996). R&D spillovers and the geography of innovation and production. *American Economic Review,* 86 (3), 630-640.

Audretsch, D. B. and Stephan, P.E. (1996). Company-scientist locational links: The case of biotechnology. *American Economic Review,* 86 (3), 641-652.

Bahrami, H. and Evans, S. (2000). Flexible recycling and high-technology entrepreneurship. In: M. Kenney (Ed.). *Understanding silicon valley.* Stanford, CA: Stanford University Press, 165-189.

Bahrami, H. and Evans, S. (1995). Flexible re-cycling and high-technology entrepreneurship. *California Management Review,* 37 (3), 62-89.

Baptista, R. and Swann, P. (1998). Do firms in clusters innovate more?" *Research Policy,* 27, 525-540.

Brown, J.S. and Duguid, P. (2002). *The social life of information.* Boston: Harvard Business School Press.

Brown, J.S. and Duguid, P. (2000). Mysteries of the region: Knowledge dynamics in silicon valley. In: W.F.Miller, Lee, C., Hancock, M.G. and Rowen, H.S. (Eds.). *The silicon valley edge: A habitat for innovation and entrepreneurship.* Stanford, CA: Stanford University Press, 16-45.

Christensen, C. (1997). *The innovator's dilemma: When new technologies cause great Firms to fail.* Boston: Harvard Business School Press.

Clark, G. L. and O'Connor, K. (1997). The informational content of financial products and the spatial structure of the global finance industry. In: K. R. Cox (Ed.). *Spaces of globalization reasserting the power of the local.* New York: Guilford press.

Feldman, M. P. (2000). Location and innovation: The new economic geography of innovation, spillovers and agglomeration. In: G. L. Clark, Feldman M.P. and Gertler, M.S.(Eds.). *The Oxford handbook of economic geography.* New York: Oxford University Press.

Feldman, M. (1994). *The geography of innovation.* Boston: Kluwer Academic Publishers.

Florida, R. and Kenney, M. (1990). *The breakthrough illusion: Corporate america's failure to move from innovation to mass production.* New York: Basic Books.

Florida, R. and Kenney, M. (1988). Venture capital, high technology and regional development. *Regional Studies,* 22, 33-48.

Garud, R. and Jain, S. (1996). Technology embeddedness. In J. Baum and Dutton, J. (Eds.) *Advances in strategic management.* Connecticut: JAI Press, 389-408.

Gilson, R. J. and Black, B.S. (1998). Venture capital and the structure of capital markets. *Journal of Financial Economics,* 47, 243-277.

Gompers, P. A. and Lerner, J. (1999). *The venture capital cycle.* Cambridge, Mass.: MIT Press.

Granovetter, M. Economic action and social structure: The problem of embeddedness. *American Journal of Sociology,* 91, 481-510.

Greenwald, B. and Stiglitz, J.F. (1992). Information, finance and markets: The architecture of allocative mechanisms. *Industrial and Corporate Change*, 1, 37-63.

Hanson, D. (1982). *The new alchemists: Silicon valley and the microelectronics revolution.* Boston: Little, Brown and Company.

Jaffe, A.B., Trajtenberg, M. and Henderson, R. (1993). Geographic localization of knowledge spillovers as evidenced by patent citations. *Quarterly Journal of Economics*, 108, 577-598.

Kenney, M. and von Burg, U. (2000). Institutions and economies: Creating silicon valley." In: M. Kenney (Ed.). *Understanding silicon valley.* Stanford, CA: Stanford University Press, 165-189.

Kenney, M. and von Burg, U. (1999). Technology and path dependence: The divergence between silicon valley and route 128. *Industrial and Corporate Change*, 8 (1), 67-103.

Krugman, P. (1991). *Geography and trade.* Cambridge, MA: The MIT Press.

Malecki, E. (1980). Dimensions of r&d location in the United States. *Research Policy*, 9, 2-22.

Marshall, A. (1890). *Principles of economics.* London: Macmillan & Company.

Piore, M. and Sabel, C. (1984). *The second industrial divide.* New York: Basic Books.

Porter, M. (1998). Clusters and the new economics of competition. *Harvard Business Review* (November-December), 77-90.

Porter, M. (1990). *The competitive advantage of nations.* New York: Free Press.

Powell, W. W., Koput, K.W., Bowie, J.I. and Smith-Doerr, L. (2002). The spatial clustering of science and capital: Accounting for biotech firm-venture capital relationships. *Regional Studies*, 36 (3), 291-305.

Pryke, M. and Lee, R. (1995). Place your bets: Towards an understanding of globalization, socio-financial engineering and competition within a financial centre. *Urban Studies*, 32, 329-344.

Saxenian, A. (1994). *Regional advantage.* Cambridge, MA.: Harvard University Press.

Schoonhoven, C.B. and Eisenhardt, K. (1989). The impact of incubator region on the creation and survival of new semiconductor ventures in the U.S. 1978-1986. *Report to the economic development administration*, U.S. department of commerce (August).

Scott, A. J. (1993). *Technopolis: High-technology industry and regional development in southern California.* Berkeley: University of California Press.

Sorenson, O. and Stuart, T.E. (2001). Syndication networks and the spatial distribution of venture capital investments. *American Sociological Review*, 106 (6), 1546-1588.

Storper, M. (1995). The resurgence of regional economies, ten years later: The region as a nexus of untraded interdependencies. *European Urban and Regional Studies*, 2 (3), 191-221.

Storper, M. and Salais, R. (1997). *Worlds of production: Frameworks of action in the economy.* Cambridge: Harvard University Press.

Storper, M. and Walker, R. (1989). *The capitalist imperative: Territory, technology, and industrial growth.* London: Basil Blackwell.

Suchman, M. C. (2000). Dealmakers and counselors: Law firms as intermediaries in the development of silicon valley. In: M. Kenney (Ed.). *Understanding silicon valley.* Stanford, CA: Stanford University Press, 71-97.

Thrift, N. and Leyshon, A. (1994). A phantom state? The detraditionalization of money, the international financial system and international financial centres. *Political Geography*, 13, 299-327.

Tilton, J. (1971). *The international diffusion of technology: The case of semiconductors.* Washington, D.C.: Brookings Institution.

Todtling, F. (1994). Regional networks of high-technology firms - The case of the greater Boston region. *Technovation*, 14 (5), 323-343.

Uzzi, B. (1999). Embeddedness in the making of financial capital: How social relations and networks benefit firms seeking financing. *American Sociological Review*, 64 (4), 481-505.

Walker, R. (1988). The geographical organization of production-systems. Environment and Planning D. *Society and Space*, 6, 377-408.

Walker, R. (1985). Technological determination and determinism: Industrial growth and location. In: M. Castells (Ed.). *High technology, space and society.* Beverly Hills, CA: Sage Publications, 226-264.

Zucker, L. G., Darby, M. R. and Brewer, M. B. (1998). Intellectual human capital and the birth of U.S. biotechnology enterprises. American Economic Review, 88 (1), 290-306.

CHAPTER 4

THE IMPACT OF REGIONAL SOCIAL NETWORKS ON THE ENTREPRENEURIAL DEVELOPMENT PROCESS

Dirk Fornahl

Max Planck Institute for Research into Economic Systems, Jena

1. INTRODUCTION

In recent years entrepreneurial and especially start-up activities have gained an increasing share of attention in economic research. There is a practical and political interest in understanding entrepreneurial activities in general and the regional factors that influence their distribution in particular. This is due to the fact that these activities have an influence on regional and national variables like competitiveness, innovativeness and the rate of unemployment (see for example, Bednarzik 2000, Audretsch & Thurik 2000). Furthermore, it was noticed by empirical studies that the regional distribution of entrepreneurial activities is uneven (Reynolds et al. 1995, Bade & Nerlinger 2000) and that start-ups play an important role in the formation and development of localized industrial clusters (Saxenian 1994, Rosegrant & Lampe 1992, Fornahl & Menzel 2002). In addition, the theoretical explanations of these entrepreneurial processes are still rudimentary so that there exists a motivation to analyze and to explain entrepreneurial behavior and divergent regional development theoretically to gain new insights into the processes.

The aim of this paper is to analyze how regional social networks influence the start of a new firm. The results give some hints about how regional disparities in entrepreneurial activities do emerge. Several studies pointed to the crucial role of social networks for the start-up of new firms (Birley 1985, Foss 1993). These social networks enable the exchange of information as well as of tangible and intangible resources. Moreover, the creation of a new business is fostered by the advice and assistance offered in the entrepreneurial development by the social environment (Birley 1985). Sorenson and colleagues extended this research on social networks by taking into account the regional perspective. They showed that some clusters emerge and local industrial structure reproduce themselves because entrepreneurs locate in certain geographic areas because of the role (regional) social networks play in the process of founding new companies (Sorenson 2003, Stuart and Sorenson 2003, Sørenson and Sorenson 2003, Sorenson and Audia 2000, Sorenson and Stuart 2001). Furthermore there exist several empirical studies that analyze the impact of networks on start-up activities inside specific regions (see for example: Saxenian 2000, Castilla et al. 2000 on Silicon Valley). This paper addresses the question of why entrepreneurs of one specific industry have a tendency to agglomerate in one or a few specific locations.

Research on the impact of social networks in general and regional one in particular provided very interesting results shedding light on the two important questions of who becomes a successful entrepreneur and how regional disparities in the founding behavior can be explained. In order to get a deeper understanding of the processes, this paper takes up the results of these studies and adds some elements that seem to be important to explain the regional entrepreneurial behavior. This paper is complementary to the described approaches because it shifts attention to the effects these networks have during the whole developmental process to become an entrepreneur and start a firm. The approaches are extended in two respects: firstly, in addition to the effects regional social networks have on information and resource flows, which are often discussed in the literature, this paper takes into account the impact that positive examples and role models have on the mental model of the agent and on his behavior. Secondly, the development process to become an entrepreneur is analyzed in detail. Besides opportunity perception and the necessity of resources for starting a firm, especially the willingness of an agent to start a firm is considered.

It is not the purpose of this paper to provide a complete in-depth analysis of the links between social networks and start-ups, but rather to develop a conceptual framework that might inform theoretical and empirical advance. For this purpose several aspects linked to the effects of social networks on start-ups are discussed and hypotheses are generated which can be tested empirically.

The paper proceeds as follows. Section 2 presents a short stylized stage model of the starting-up process of a new firm. Section 3 examines some basic structural and developmental features of social networks. Section 4 deals with the specific role of proximities and locality for the establishment and maintenance of social networks. In section 5 the question is addressed of how regional social networks influence the processes going on in the different stages of the start-up process and the development through the stages. The basic theoretical insights that result from the previous sections are used. The implications are discussed and the resulting hypotheses for future work are presented in section 6. The last section concludes and gives an outlook.

2. AN IDEALIZED STAGE MODEL OF THE START-UP PROCESS

In the following section a framework to analyze the development of an agent to become an entrepreneur is built. Since the interaction of the entrepreneur with his social environment is of specific interest for this development process, this is described first.

2.1 Entrepreneurship in a Social Environment

Agents' behavior strongly depends on the information they receive from their environment and the mental models[1] the agents hold. Since an individual agent only possesses limited information-gathering capacities, he does not have (technical) access to all the information necessary and his willingness to gather new information is limited because, for example, the involved costs and the time required are too high. Mental models focus the scarce attention and help, the agent to discriminate and 'decide' which information to pay attention to. But in addition to this effect on perception, mental models also influence the memorizing of information, its evaluation and in the end the agent's behavior (Anderson 2000). When the mental model of an agent changes, this can have far-reaching impacts on his behavior. Such a change can result from new experiences the agent makes as well as from interaction, observation or communication processes (Bandura 1986, Chapter 2) inside a group or network. This learning is strongly influenced by the frequency and intensity of interaction, communication and observation between agents. The higher the frequency, the more likely it is that the agents will exchange mental models because of social learning processes. Hence, the social environment influences the behavior of entrepreneurs by shaping the information the agent receives and the mental model the agent holds

This approach has parallels with already existing theories on entrepreneurship: A socio-psychological perspective takes into consideration how the social environment influences the agents to become entrepreneurs (e.g. Simonton 1975). The closer social environment like families, social milieus or reference groups is especially important here. The Austrian Economic Perspective assumes an uneven distribution of information and knowledge among economic agents. This prior knowledge, information and beliefs influence the likelihood that an agent can discover and exploit opportunities (Shane 2000, van Praag 1996). Cognitive theories about entrepreneurial behavior use an individualistic perspective but also take into consideration the external (cultural and social) environment. Decisions are affected by the perception and interpretation of the environment. Entrepreneurial 'intention is a function of the interaction of a person's 'thinking' with the individual's past history, current personality, and social and economic development' (Busenitz & Lau 1996, p. 26).

In all these theories the development of important individual characteristics (to become an entrepreneur) is assumed to be the result of learning, adoption processes and information exchange in a social environment. Entrepreneurs are not born as entrepreneurs but develop to become one. The starting up of a new firm is a complicated process in which several stages have to be passed until in the end an entrepreneur with a (successful) firm emerges (Figure 1).

Figure 4.1. Stage model of entrepreneurs

2.2 An Entrepreneurial Stage Model

Based on the considerations in the previous section, here a stylized stage model starting with an 'economic agent' and ending with the early development of the firm after the actual start-up is presented. In such an approach not only the actual starting of the firm and the first phase of its operation is analyzed, but especially the development up to the founding decision is the core of the analysis.

The regional population of 'economic agents' and potential entrepreneurs is heterogeneous. The agents differ, for example, with regard to their knowledge and capabilities, personality characteristics, social and technical skills, involvement in social structures or information access. The social environment the agents are part of and in which they grew up shapes these differences.[2] Economic agents and potential entrepreneurs differ in one respect: potential entrepreneurs are actively searching for business opportunities to found a firm while economic agents do not. Besides this difference they are similar. An economic agent does not have the concrete intention to start a firm but is just pursuing his job or other activities. Nevertheless, he is able to discover such opportunities. In comparison, a potential founder has realized that the idea of starting a firm or entrepreneurial activities, in general, is a good alternative and starts to actively search for opportunities investing time and (financial) resources. Note that this does not imply that all potential entrepreneurs necessarily have a higher likelihood of discovering opportunities and starting a firm or that they have a higher probability of continued success with their firm once they have started up. But, on average, the likelihood of discovering an opportunity is higher in this group since they focus cognitive attention and material resources on search activities. Not all individuals independent of whether they are actively searching or not are equally likely to recognize a given entrepreneurial opportunity (Shane 2000). In any case, the discovery of opportunities strongly depends on the agent's prior knowledge of and information about, for example, technologies, markets or customer wishes, their information channels and information-processing abilities, as well as on the mental model, which might focus the search on specific areas.

Once an opportunity is discovered and a first idea emerges, a business conception has to be developed and evaluated with respect to its potential market success ('market test'). Furthermore, the task is to transform a general (technical) business idea into an economically successful firm strategy by developing a marketable product or service. In addition, the actual founding decision depends on the perception and evaluation of opportunities, alternatives and own abilities ('ability test'), as well as on the willingness to start a business. This, in turn, is influenced by personal factors and characteristics, the access to relevant information, as well as by the mental model the agent possesses. According to Witt (1999), a self-sorting takes place in which the agent decides whether to take the risk of becoming an entrepreneur or not. This sorting is a result of multilateral subjective opportunity costs that include pecuniary considerations (like expected profits and opportunity costs) as well as non-pecuniary ones.

Van Praag (1996) has a similar approach when stating that the start-up of a firm depends on the interaction between opportunity and willingness. Opportunity is '(...) defined as the possibility to become an entrepreneur if one wants to' (p. 39) and willingness is a result of a comparison of becoming an entrepreneur and working as an employee. This interaction is fundamental to the start-up decision and 'only' restricted by a lack of financial capital, human capital or unfavorable environmental circumstances.

The ability as well as the market test and thus the founding decision are strongly influenced by psychological factors, e.g. over-optimism of entrepreneurs leads them to form unrealistic expectations about their ventures, competence and expected competition especially in new industries (Camerer and Lovallo 1999, Cooper et al. 1988, Sorenson and Audia 2000). In interplay with easily available resources, which might lower the selection threshold for entry, an over-shooting results in the number of firms results, which in turn can lead to higher failure rates (Barnett, Swanson and Sorenson 2003).

The stage at which the actual founding takes place consists of the planning and the direct founding process including some legal steps and questions like where to start, how to get the financing and which employees to hire and so on. It is by no means certain that the involved agents already know exactly how their business conception should look like. If the evaluation of the general conception has a positive result, it is possible that the firm is founded first and after that an active search process takes place to decide exactly what to do and how to do it. This last stage also includes all the operative and strategic decisions that are based on the business conception and which are important for the survival of the firm. At this stage, the entrepreneur tries to exploit the perceived opportunities and at the same time actively searches for new ones, which are again tested for realization. The quality of the decisions made here influences the success of the firm.

There are several important processes going on inside each stage and the step from one stage to the other is important in explaining the development of the entrepreneur until the firm has really started up and is operating. In reality, it is hard to separate these different stages from one another, but it serves as an analytical tool for distinguishing between the different effects presented in the next sections. The order of willingness and opportunity is of specific interest because this order might influence the future success of the firm, since it might be the case that agents willing to found a firm discover opportunities too easily. Although mainly one direction is presented here, it is also possible that an agent just stays at one stage without developing further or switches back to an earlier stage, for example an agent who tried to run a firm, went bankrupt and does not want to start a firm ever again. Thus, the presented model and the development of agents from one stage to another is by no means a linear and deterministic process.

To summarize the argumentation: the starting-up process can be, at least theoretically, structured in different stages that include the elements willingness, opportunity, ability test, market test and based on this the final decision to start the firm. Of specific importance are the processes that influence these elements in such a way that the firm is really started in the end. These considerations will be taken up again in section 5.

3. SOCIAL NETWORKS: ESTABLISHMENT AND EFFECTS

From the last sections it can be concluded that the social environment of the agents influence the development to become an entrepreneur. Therefore, the social environment is an interesting object of investigation. In the following sections the establishment, maintenance and effects of social networks as an important part of the social environment of agents are analyzed.

The social environments in which agents interact are not identically structured and social relations do not occur at random. The interaction between agents and exchanges among them are embedded in a social context, mainly represented and structured by social networks (Burt 1987, Marsden and Friedkin 1993, Granovetter 1985). In this paper social networks are defined generally as being composed of different individual agents (the nodes in the network) connected by (personal) social relationships among these agents as well as of the mechanisms that govern the interactions (Castilla et al. 2000). Social networks link a large variety of agents, for example, family members, friends, work groups / colleagues, employers, research and business partners, firms and industry or supporting organizations (including for example clubs or round-tables) and services (including banks or venture capital firms) (for some of these networks see for example Birley 1985). Thus, the social networks also differ a lot depending on the kinds of agents in the network. The networks can consist of direct social ties linking two members of the network directly and indirect ties that link two agents via the direct ties of these agents to the same other agents (Shane and Cable 2002). The interactions and relations between the agents that are part of the network are relatively long lasting and voluntary (Granovetter 1985).

3.1 Establishment and Maintenance of Social Networks

The establishment of networks in most cases follows the same process: An agent at least once has to meet another agent in a face-to-face interaction to found a direct social tie among them. Normally such an encounter does not take place only once, but intense personal interactions, contacts and face-to-face communication, are the key for the establishment of these networks to form sustainable connections between the agents. The same holds for the maintenance of networks: without frequent contacts the likelihood of deterioration increases. Since a social network leads to higher frequency of interaction with other members of the network, stronger links are built between the network members and the network is stabilizing and rebuilding itself in a self-reinforcing manner.

In general, social network can be distinguished in two groups: 1) Some networks are established on purpose because the members of the network want to pursue a specific goal or want to profit from positive network effects. 2) The social network is not purposefully established to serve specific needs or to follow economic reasoning but originates for various reasons. Especially the latter networks are mainly based on an overlap in the past personal, work or academic history of the agents. They may originate from family ties, a certain neighborhood or spontaneous contacts, they may have been established as a by-product of e.g. formal co-operations, during school, university or former jobs. Thus, social networks can be goal-oriented and purposefully designed and constructed. But in most cases social networks are based on unintended interactions or the other mentioned reasons (Strambach 1995).

In the formation of networks social and cultural factors also play a role: Networks tend to form among agents sharing one or more characteristics. This might be due to the reason that agents have common focal points or similar foci of cognitive attention (Sugden 1995) because they have the same cultural background that makes it easier for them to get in contact, communicate, establish and maintain social ties. Sorenson, Rivkin and Fleming (2002) (referring to Blau 1977 and to Lazarsfeld and Merton (1954)) point to the relevance of the social background of agents that influences the likelihood that agents meet each other and the willingness to form social ties. People prefer to interact with and form ties to others who share similar characteristics (McPherson, Smith-Lovin and Cook 2001).

3.2 Effects of Social Networks on Economic Activities

In the following the effects of social networks on economic activities are presented. First, general effects of networks are described briefly and after that the focus is on three processes social networks facilitate and which are relevant for firm founders and firms in general, namely the exchange of information, the access to tangible and intangible resources and the diffusion of mental models. The latter processes in particular depend strongly on the kind of network, e.g. on the kind of network members. For example, information on technologies is only valuable and can be passed on, if other people of the network have the same technological background that may be the case in networks of former workmates or networks originating in academic education.

It can be argued that it is much easier for agents who are part of a network to observe specific modes of behavior and to notice other network members. Besides the mere observability, the frequency of (face-to-face) interaction, communication and observation between agents who are part of the same network is high. Networks can favor coincidental contacts because an agent can meet other members with whom he is only weakly tied and develop strong ties to them. In addition, while interacting the agents are likely to develop common norms, shared values, expectations, identities and world views which in turn can lead to social obligations and sanctions, mutual trust and understanding. The interaction between various partners and information exchanges between network members foster the development of reputation and reciprocity (Granovetter 1985). This influences the speed, quantity, quality and reliability of exchanges (Maskell and Malmberg 1999). Furthermore, the pecuniary and non-pecuniary costs of information gathering are reduced (Coleman 1988). Furthermore, these processes govern the interactions and stabilize the network.

Social networks open up channels for (non-public) information transfer (Hägerstrand 1953). The type of information diffusing in the network is very heterogeneous ranging from formal technical, market or organizational information to gossip. These transfers play a major role for getting a large variety of information, e.g. on vacant jobs, on markets, technologies, the abilities of agents, on the past behavior of actual or potential business partners and on other relevant topics for firms or individual agents. Furthermore, information such as know-how, know-where and know-who is exchanged. By using not only the strong and direct ties but also the weak and indirect ones, network members can obtain more information than they could obtain alone (Burt 1997). Some of this information is exclusive for members of the networks only disseminates very slowly to the outside of the network (Sorenson, Rivkin and Fleming 2002). Even if not all these transfers have an economic impact, it can be assumed that active as well as passive information gathering through these network connections influence economic activities to a certain degree.

These processes of information exchange and social obligation (and similar processes described above) lead to the possibility to cope better with risks, uncertainty and ambiguity in social interactions. This is of specific importance for entrepreneurs that often have to make decision under uncertainty. It is, for example, possible to get more accurate and more reliable information about business partners like their competences and their tendency to behave opportunistically (Shane and Cable 2002, Burt 1992).

Most firms, and especially firm founders, are operating in a dynamic environment where they have to react to changes and have to find suitable, reliable and cheap tangible and intangible resources. These resources include (tacit) knowledge, employees, financial capital as well as capital goods like machinery or laboratory equipment. As was pointed out in the previous paragraph the mere information about these resources by the use of social networks is already an important input for economic activities and decisions. Additionally, the direct access to and the accumulation of these resources by using social networks is an important element contributing to the success of the firm. Social networks are, for example, one important way to get access to knowledge (Zellner and Fornahl 2002), labor (Granovetter 1973, Saxenian 1994, Castilla et al. 2000) and financial capital (Shane and Cable 2002). Thus, for an efficient and beneficial knowledge exchange the existence of a magnitude of informal direct and indirect ties between agents working in different firms or organizations but in at least related industries or technological fields, are helpful (Liebeskind et al. 1995).

Social-cognitive learning processes linked to positive models – other agents that serve as behavioral examples for the own behavior – are an important factor for the development of mental models. For these learning activities, processes like interaction, communication or observation as well as factors like the comparability of an agent with the model are important. These factors are strongly influenced by social networks in which information on possible role models and their attributes diffuses intentionally or unintentionally and in which a shared social background develops. As a consequence, new mental models can be introduced and diffused in a network which has consequences for the perception of information, business opportunities, the own evaluation and in the end for the behavior of the agents. For a detailed analysis of how mental models are influenced by social networks and which impact this has on regional economic activities, see Fornahl (2003).

Although these three processes were described separately one has to acknowledge the linkages between them. The access to resources is, for example, moderated by the information on the reliability and competence of business partners transferred via the network (see Shane and Cable 2002 for an application to venture capital) and on social obligations that might exist between the partners (Podolny 1994). Since all processes are linked to the transfer of information, in the following, what is called 'information exchange', refers only to information on technologies, markets and organizational structures and processes.

Besides the positive influences networks have, it should be noted that they also can have negative effects for members of the network as well as for outsiders, e.g. social networks which are a by-product of formal ones can lead to rigidity because the formal connections are not questioned, rearranged or terminated, even if better opportunities emerge or they can lead to increasing inefficiencies or lock-in, because old knowledge and procedures are used without a reaction to a changing environment which can deteriorate the competitive positions of the firms involved (Grabher 1993). While strong network connections facilitate the interaction inside the network, they can hinder exchange across networks and with outside agents. In general (at least closed) networks can be obstacles to change and creative development because they hinder the emergence of new mental models, the use or creation of new knowledge and information or a change in behavior. The result can be a lack of adaptation to changing environmental conditions resulting in a lock-in and a perspective biased to the information, resources and mental models present in the network (Birley 1985). Furthermore, these networks can be used for special arrangements between the involved firms that can lead to collusion and the establishment of market entry barriers.

Social networks structure exchange relations and are an important channel for information exchange, resource access as well as for the diffusion of role models along conduits laid by the social ties. They can enhance quality, quantity and pace of transfers by providing a framework for frequent interactions. In addition, the networks help to reduce uncertainty, risk and costs (Fritsch 1992, Sorenson & Audia 2000) because, for example, the information and resources transferred are regarded as reliable and the likelihood of opportunistic behavior is lower. Nevertheless, social networks can be afflicted with the described problems.

4. LOCALITIES AND THE EFFECT OF THE REGION ON SOCIAL NETWORKS

Based on the effects of networks described in the previous section, it should be analyzed how regional characteristics influence the formation and maintenance of social networks, and the resulting regional differences. For this the impact of geographic, cultural and social proximity on network formation and maintenance is presented.

A region is not a homogeneous mass with the same frequency of interaction between all agents. Inside one geographical region there exists a social network structure based on the described factors like work relations, family ties or friendship. The frequency of interaction of two agents depends on the network structure that they are part of, on the selective choice of partners in intended interactions, and not only on their co-location. The influence and diffusion of specific information and the frequency of interaction, communication and observation has to be analyzed with regard to their specific characteristics in these regional social networks.

Geographic proximity, the spatial distance between agents, strongly influences the formation, maintenance and use of networks. Many empirical studies have shown the importance of geographic proximity on the spatial boundary of social networks based on different reasons: On average the likelihood that people build social ties with other people is higher when they interact with them more frequently. Geographic proximity positively influences this frequency of (face-to-face) interaction and thus the likelihood of forming lasting social ties and networks in different fields of human life, like friendship, marriage, residential communities or workplaces (Festinger, Schacter and Back 1950, Stouffer 1940, Zipf 1949, Bossard 1932, Blau 1977). 'As the distance between two actors lengthens, the likelihood of an intervening opportunity – an equally preferred but closer contact – increases as well (Stouffer 1940)' (Cited from Sorenson, Rivkin and Fleming 2002, p. 15). Here two different issues have to be considered with regard to the formation of local social networks. On the one hand, the genesis of social networks is often based on unintended interactions and coincidental contacts. One agent meets another agent by chance, for example, in stores or churches as well as his neighbor on the street and by these constant and repeated contacts prepares the ground to build a social tie (Strambach 1995). Such a network has emergent properties and is not planned in advance. On the other hand, it is based on intended interactions that are more likely to occur with people in the same location. This might be the case in evening courses, sporting events, at dancing school, university or at work.

Additionally in order to maintain social networks the involved agents have to meet at least sometimes and interact with each other on a face-to-face basis. Since such interactions are more frequent, easier and less costly if the agents live in close geographic proximity to each other (Stouffer 1940, Zipf 1949, Boalt and Janson 1957), the likelihood that social networks connect different local agents and are bound locally is higher as well because they last longer.

Furthermore, the formation of functioning regional social networks is supported by the cultural and social context the agents are embedded in. In this case cultural and social proximity,[3] measured in shared experiences, world views, values and cultural traditions, support the formation of social networks because they provide common focal points, a common focus of selective attention and shared social norms as well as a higher comparability of agents and identification with other agents. These factors facilitate contacts and communication. These social and cultural proximities are not directly linked to the locality and geographic proximity, but it can be assumed that the local environmental context partly influences the emergence of specific local variants of these proximities.

Social networks do not have to be spatially bounded, but geographic, social and cultural proximity can facilitate the emergence and maintenance of networks. It was found that the density of local network relations and the number of regional network nodes is relatively high in comparison to cross-regional ones (Strambach 1995). Local networks structure the interaction of agents and provide a framework for information exchange, resource access and the diffusion of mental models.

Here only one direction, the impact of geographic, cultural and social proximity on network formation was presented, but these proximities are themselves subject to changes during the interaction process. Therefore, there is a strong connection between geographic, social and cultural proximity and regional social networks. Especially the existence of social networks and based on this the facilitation of continuous contacts inside these networks has a very strong link to social proximity. These interactions lead to the emergence of certain similarities inside networks building the basis for the mentioned social proximity.

As a result of this local boundedness of social networks some information, resources and mental models are (only) locally available which can explain region-specific behavior. Two features shall be noted here: content and diffusion. Apart from general information that might be collected by other means as well, it is especially region-specific information that is available and relevant in the local networks. This regional specificity includes information like know-who as well as technical, market and organizational information or gossip strongly determined by the past regional history and regional developmental trajectories. Furthermore, information diffuses through the local networks; agents not part of the network or located further away from the (geographic) center will receive this information later, if at all. The same holds for resources and mental models. The same regional specificity bias results and the access to resources and the diffusion of mental models are bound locally.

5. IMPACTS OF SOCIAL NETWORKS IN DIFFERENT STAGES OF THE FOUNDING PROCESS

After presenting the developmental process to become an entrepreneur and some main features of social networks, in this section the following two elements from the previous sections are taken up and integrated into one framework to get a more detailed picture: First, as was previously mentioned, the social networks influence the behavior of the agents in the different stages. Thus, the entrepreneurial development process is separated in four idealized stages: "active Search", "opportunity search / discovery"; "market / ability test and start-up decision" and the last stage is the "actual founding and the first planning". Second, in the following the main variables which are considered to affect the decision to start up a firm and which have an impact on the start-up process and the possible success are information exchanges and the resources (like knowledge, human capital, financial capital, capital goods) available to the agent as well as the mental model an agent holds as was presented in section 3. Based on these elements the question of which effects they have in the different stages and, thus, in the transition from one stage to the other, is addressed.

Before starting with the analysis of the stages, some general processes are addressed. In most cases, especially if the founder has never founded a firm before, the whole developmental process is characterized by high uncertainty. This uncertainty can be linked to factors like the own capabilities of the founder or the team, the market development, the technological feasibility of the idea, the quality of the personal to hire or the question of how to govern interactions with partners. This is especially true for firms in "new" markets where no reference or benchmark is given. Although most entrepreneurs have a tendency towards risk taking, it can be assumed that an important process in the development of starting-up a new firm is to try to reduce risk or to cope with uncertainty by different means. Networks can help to reduce these uncertainties not only for the entrepreneur but also for his employees and business partners, e.g. by the exchange of information about competences and reliability as was described above.

5.1 Transition from an economic agent to a potential entrepreneur

One impact social networks can have on this transition relates to the influence they have on the mental model of the agent.[4] The argument put forward here is that mental models are strongly influenced by positive examples, so-called role models, present in regions or especially in social networks the agent is involved in. Agents who observe the successful entrepreneurial activities of other agents take these as positive examples and may imitate these and reach the conclusion that they should start a business on their own. Thus, they develop the willingness to start a firm without having any concrete business ideas or perceived any opportunities yet. This willingness leads to a (re-)allocation of cognitive attention to the idea of founding in general and the active searching or the production of business opportunities. Such positive role models can be found especially in the close social (mother, father, friends and so on) (van Praag 1996, Kriegesmann 1999) or regional environment (Fornahl 2003). Klandt (1984) finds that frequent contacts with potential customers or collaborators in an incubator facility might trigger the decision to become an entrepreneur. Especially close and strong social networks support the recognition and acceptance of these role models.

For this transition to become a potential entrepreneur in most cases neither information on technologies or markets nor resources are needed. Since this is the case, networks providing these two factors are not strongly relevant for this transition.

5.2 Search and discovery of business opportunities

The opportunity discovery can originate from the potential entrepreneur as well as from the economic agent, although the latter is not actively searching. The perception and generation of opportunities is based on the (entrepreneurial) environment and the mental model the agents possess. Positive examples can have a twofold effect. First, positive examples make it easier to discover entrepreneurial opportunities because other (comparable and successful) business opportunities are known and serve as examples or references. Technological or market information are tested if they match known positive examples. Second, the examples lead to a (re-)allocation of cognitive attention to certain opportunities or business conceptions. The direction of active search, as well as the perception of opportunities is biased for example to the regionally or technologically 'common ones'. In general, the likelihood of discovering such biased opportunities is higher than discovering others (which is not only caused by prior knowledge or information access). In this stage positive models that are or were colleagues are of specific interest. This is due to the fact that many opportunities (especially in high tech industries) are discovered or developed by a team and not by an individual agent. Thus, the team members influence each other during the developing process and if one member of such a group successfully started a new firm, other colleagues might take him as a likely example.

Networks can serve as a screening device by providing information on markets, technologies and organizational arrangements. This keeps agents up-to-date on developing opportunities (Burt 1992). Of specific importance are networks to industry, other firms or founders in order to get information about markets, and to colleagues or, if the firm is technologically based, to other researchers to receive technological information.

Still the role of resources is not very high in this stage or at least the potential founder is not using huge amounts of it. If resources are needed these are provided by family, friends or the current employer. The latter strongly depends on the kind of employer and the new firm's business conception. Such a support will take place if the new firm is not a competitor and if the negative effect for the employer is low. It is more likely, for example that research institutes support spin-offs more willingly than private firms (Fornahl and Graf 2003).

5.3 Ability, market test and founding decision

The mental model and the comparison with other existing entrepreneurs influence the evaluation of business conceptions and the founding option. Although market tests should be based on objective facts in order to decide whether a business conception is worthy of putting it in action, the collection of data and especially its evaluation is subjective in the end. This is particularly true in markets that are just emerging and in which a prediction of the future development is not an easy task. The test of the own abilities to start a firm is as well a strongly subjective endeavor. Furthermore, the founding decision, including the willingness, is based on an evaluation of the option to found a firm and other alternatives. Positive examples can lead to a bias in these tests and the evaluation of alternatives and to an increase in the likelihood of starting up a firm. Since, for example, the mental model moderates the related threats and risks, the agent might underestimate them. In addition, the general attitude towards risk is not a fixed factor but can change over time by the influence of imitative learning. The same is true for the desire to be independent, an important element related to the actual founding decision (Kriegesmann 1999), which is also a variable developing over time and being influenced by mental models. For these processes especially connections to other founders (especially to those working in the same field) are important because the founders directly compare their own capabilities with those of other agents. Van Praag (1996) and Kriegesmann (1999), for example, found that the likelihood of an agent to start his own firm was positively influenced by self-employed people in his close social environment (e.g. the father).

In this phase the decision has to be made whether a whole team of founders will start-up the new firm. Furthermore, the start-up process has to be planned. Since this process and the composition of the team is of high importance for the future development of the firm, information is needed on what to do in order to start a firm and whom to choose for the founding team.

Mainly other founders or service and support organizations provide the former information. Networks consisting of family members, friends, colleagues or employers influence the latter. Note that the founding team constitutes an own network that is important for firm development. Littunen (2000), for example, analyses the impact of external and internal networks and comes to the conclusion that internal networks have a stronger impact on the development of the firm (Almus and Nerlinger (1999) were not able to support these findings). Furthermore, still information on markets and technologies are relevant and the networks described in the previous stage have an impact.

The networks do not only provide the information on the potential team members, but they also serve as a pool from which the team can be selected. Based on the information about these members, the risk to choose the wrong person is minimized. The role of resources is still small and if some are needed the close social environment provides them.

5.4 Actual founding process and first planning of the new firm

The importance of role models in this stage is small in comparison to the strong impact in the earlier stages of development but still former employers or other founders can serve as examples of how to organize and run a firm.

Many different decisions have to be made and, thus, many different kinds of information are relevant in this stage: Ranging from information on how to do a firm start-up including the legal steps or where to find financial and human capital to how to enter a market and find customers, how to organize a firm or how to build up a testing or production facility. This information and advice is provided by a whole magnitude of personal, service and business networks. Strambach (1995) found for example that networks are in the beginning helpful to find the first customers. Birley (1985) noticed that they are useful to find rooms and personal or to get information on how to organize the daily work. But in order to serve these functions a founder has to know which agent in the network offers which help, information or resource (Birley 1985). Information on resources like human capital is probably mainly provided by former colleagues and friends, on capital goods and machinery by former employers, other founders or service networks, on financial capital by other founders, associations or families.

Especially in this phase of the start-up resources are necessary because personnel has to be hired, machinery used, rooms rented and so on. Almus and Nerlinger (1999), for example, found that links to external firms have a positive influence on financial capital, know-how and the building of networks with suppliers and customers (see Cable and Shane 2002 for similar results on financial capital). In most cases the new founders themselves cannot provide the resources they need, but these resources have to be supplied by external sources. Networks can help because they provide opportunities to get access to specific resources, for example a specific machinery only available at a research institute where a founder was employed before. Or the networks might help to get these resources at a lower price, with higher quality or quicker. In addition the risk and uncertainty of the founder might be reduced because he does not have to invest a lot of capital in specific machinery or he already knows the quality of the resource, for example by employing workers with whom he worked together before. These effects on resource access and the reduction of uncertainty are important in this stage and the potential of involvement and commitment is especially high in strong social networks.

To sum up the argument: Besides the mere existence of information, role models and resources, the access and use of these factors by social networks strongly influences an agent and subsequently the likelihood of starting up a firm. By providing close contact with positive role models networks support the development through the stages and the related likelihood of discovering entrepreneurial opportunities and they increase the willingness to start a new firm. Furthermore, the direction of search for opportunities, business conceptions and firm organization is biased. Resources and information are provided by these networks as well and by this provision the networks increase the likelihood for an agent to found (successfully). In general networks reduce uncertainty in the entrepreneurial processes and can also lead to reduced transaction costs.

6. DISCUSSION OF THE IMPACT OF (REGIONAL) SOCIAL NETWORKS

6.1 Network usage and effects during the entrepreneurial development

From the described framework one can derive that the influence of role models, information exchange and resource access changes during the development to become an entrepreneur. As was pointed out resources are especially needed in the last phase of the start-up processes. Role models have an impact during the whole start-up process, but are of specific importance in the first stages in which the agents develop willingness and search for or discover opportunities. Later on the development is stronger linked to the necessities of the markets, own products and technologies. Information is necessary during the whole process as well. But the kind of information changes. In the beginning the general information on markets and technologies is mainly relevant. During the later development information on how to start a firm and how and where to find appropriate resources, business or research partners is more important. This could be tested empirically in two ways: which kind of information, resource and positive example are used in which part of the development process and how do these factors influence the further development?

It is assumed that different social networks have a different importance during the development from one stage to the other because, as was just described, the necessity of information, resources and mental models changes as well. In the beginning network connections to the own family, friends and close social environment are more important and in the end more formal networks play a role. For example networks that provide resources are primarily needed in the later stage while role models are relevant in the first stages. Other regional founders mainly provide these role models and thus networks in which regional founders are part of are relevant here. Information on markets and technologies are provided by loose industry connections or by colleagues. Advice what to do in order to found a firm is given by other founders or service organizations. If one differentiates networks just in two groups, the ones in which agents are part because of birth or by chance (e.g. families or friends), meaning those that are not purposefully build, and those which are purposefully build and in which agents try to enter (e.g. research or business partners), some further insights are possible. Particularly in the beginning the former ones are more important because they influence the agent in part unconsciously. If the agent is not in these networks, it is likely that he does not try to build them up purposefully because he does not know at all that he needs such networks. An agent not part of these networks might never find an opportunity or might never develop the willingness to start a firm because he does not get the necessary information or is not provided with a positive role model. Later on the relevance of purposefully designed networks increases. The founder can try to build or enter networks that provide the needed effects. Especially if the founders are already in a later stage of the development process and need resources for their firm, they can try to establish networks that can provide these resources. Important in this respect is the overlap of networks. Besides other effects, this might lead to the possibility that agents get to know other networks and enter them more easily when they think that this is necessary. For example family networks can open up other more formal networks. Such a perspective on the use of different networks in the development process could shed some light on the problem which networks are exogenous and which are endogenous to the entrepreneurial process. An empirical approach should analyze the change of network use with the hypothesis that the relevance of purposefully established networks increases. Furthermore, the change of the content of these network interactions to an increase of the relevance of access to resources, as was described in the former paragraph, can be tested for each individual network.

6.2 Structural characteristics of social networks

The various structural characteristics of the networks can strongly influence the effects of networks on the founding process. Here only some elements are discussed. With regard to the density of networks, Cowan and Jonard (1999) found by simulating the knowledge transfer in differently structured networks, that so-called 'small world' networks with a high degree of cliquishness and a short average path length, are most effective in the diffusion process. The same probably holds for the transfer of information and role models. But this quick diffusion does not imply that such networks have the best effect on all network effects. The strongest impact on the access to, especially scarce, resources have networks with very strong and direct links resulting in a cohesive structure, e.g. inside families or between close friends or colleagues (Løvås and Sorenson 2003, Lingblad 2004). Thus, financial and human capital cannot be substituted by a general increase in network activities (Brüderl and Preisendörfer 1998), but specific network activities are needed. In contrast a magnitude of indirect ties supports the variety of knowledge transfer and information access. Note that the complexity of knowledge can have an impact on the network processes (see e.g. Sorenson in this volume) with sparse networks between agents exchanging simple knowledge and dense, redundant and strong ties for members exchanging complex knowledge. It is a difficult task for an agent to build and organize social networks in such a way that all necessities for the different kinds of content exchanges are fulfilled, thus, to build a balanced mixture of strong, direct ties and of brokering ones (Hansen 1999). Concerning the impact of role models no such empirical tests have been conducted to far. The hypothesis is that both strong and weak ties are relevant for the adoption of mental models but that the agent has to accept the positive example as a behavioral model, e.g. the agent and the positive example must have some common characteristics.

The centrality of agents in the network has different impacts. First, the more central an agent is, the more likely it is that he receives a lot of information and that he gets access to the necessary resources which might favor his development to become an entrepreneur. On the other hand, centrality goes along with strong cohesion. Thus, if this cohesion favors non-entrepreneurial behavior and if the agent under consideration is not the leader or reference person of the network able to introduce new behavioral modes, it is likely that this person will not change his behavior towards a more entrepreneurial one. As Granovetter (1973) pointed out, first adopters of risky, controversial or deviant behavior are not central to the social network. The empirical question is which persons in a social network are the first to create or adopt role models and how the diffusion of mental models takes place.

6.3 Negative influence of social networks

In general a positive impact of involvement in networks on the likelihood of survival and growth of young firms in the first years after they started was found in many cases (e.g. Hansen 1995, Brüderl and Preisendörfer 1998 or Johannisson 1998). A negative impact of social networks nevertheless can be assumed because new ideas diffuse in the network and can be stolen, employees change from one firm to another by using information on job opportunities and thus reduce the human capital inside individual firms. The characteristics of the social networks can facilitate exchanges on but can also prevent other interaction, e.g. with agents outside the network. Disadvantages are that some opportunities might be neglected because the information exchanged inside the network is biased towards other opportunities, there are diminishing returns to searching activities in just one direction and the competition between the agents increases. Or, as was mentioned in the centrality debate, cohesive social networks might hinder the adoption of new behavior, like starting a firm, because such behavior deviate from the one present in the network. Thus, the membership in social networks can cause disadvantages for individual agents because they cannot adapt to a changing environment, get new information or change their behavior.

For agents outside the network disadvantages might results from the fact that barriers to entry to the network but also to information, resources and markets are established. For examples, so called "old-boys" networks can be defined as a kind of club with elitist character that establish hidden barriers to entry on the one hand but which offer support to their members on the other hand (Heald 1983).

Further theoretical and empirical research has to focus on this balance between advantages and disadvantages of social networks. This is especially true for the diffusion of mental models because they are strongly linked to the current behavior in the networks and to the norms leading to cohesive behavior (see Seri 2003 for an application to a regional context).

6.4 Social networks and regional factors

Regional disparities observed in the number of firm foundings and economic activity in general can be partly explained by the dependence on regional social networks (Sorenson 2003). The strongest impact results from an acceleration of already existing entrepreneurial tendencies that can lead to the emergence of localized industrial clusters based on the co-location of firms (Brenner 2003, Sørenson and Sorenson 2003). They based these results on the two aspects of information exchange and resource access, but their findings also go in-line with the impact of regional positive examples and their impact on mental models. Social networks cannot force an agent to become an entrepreneur, but they can support the social-cognitive learning processes by which one or more positive examples can change the mental model of the agents and the entrepreneurial attitude in the end. If such an attitude spreads in the whole regional population by these regional networks or other effects caused by different proximities, even a long-lasting positive regional entrepreneurial climate can emerge (Fornahl 2003). Besides the mere number of firm foundings, also the orientation of the business conceptions inside a region can be influenced by social networks via a region-specific mental model in combination with biased information transmission leading to a re-production of the industrial structure present in the regions (Sorenson 2003). Since these positive examples are mainly relevant in the beginning of the developmental process to become an entrepreneur, this would support the finding of Sorenson (2003) that the impact of regional networks decreases over time along with the development in the industry as well as the single firm. This would lead to de-concentration processes when the industry gets more mature, if not other processes hinder such a de-concentration.

Besides the positive effects on regional development, there also exist negative ones. As was described above networks can constitute barriers to entry and can lead to a region specific lock-in. Furthermore, an increase in the number of entrepreneurs in the region or in the network increases the competition on input- and output-markets.

There are further relevant questions that have to be investigated in the future. An important one relates to the findings of Sorenson and Audia 2000 that agglomerated regions with the highest failure rates can continue to experience high entry rates. The hypothesis is that the convergence of mental models leads to a high rate of firm foundings with similar business conceptions because of factors like over-confidence and other psychological factors that strengthen the impact of positive models but weaken the impact of negative ones.

7. CONCLUSIONS AND OUTLOOK

The facilitating effect of social networks on start-up activities was the core element of this paper. Linked to this was the question of how regional aspects influence the formation and effect of networks and, in turn, which impact these networks have for regional start-up activities. In order to get a detailed picture of the impact of social networks on firm foundings, a stage model containing opportunity perception, the willingness to found, the ability and market test as well as the founding decision and early operation was developed. Social networks that have effects on information exchange, resource access and mental model diffusion influence this development. In this paper, a framework was presented in order to show how different regional networks have the described effects and how they affect the development through the stages in different ways. In general networks and the associated effects can influence the occurring processes and lead to a successful or quicker development through the stages. It has to be noted that social networks are in many cases neither necessary nor sufficient; but nevertheless they can have a significant influence on the economic activities because if they are not present the effects they provide have to be at least partly substituted which might be impossible or costly.

Furthermore, some important issues are linked to the influence of social networks on described development process. First, different kinds of networks are relevant during the development. This has two implications: an overlap of different kinds of networks helps to bridge them and diffuse (new) information, models and resources between them. Furthermore, specific networks have different relevance during the stages; starting with not purposefully designed ones consisting of family members or friends and ending by more formal, goal-oriented networks. Since the start of the development process to become an entrepreneur is of high relevance, not purposefully established networks seem to play an important role. Second, the mixture of direct and indirect ties must be well balanced to gain the most effect. Third, although networks have some positive effects, the negative ones and possible problems cannot be left aside, because the costs of networking and possible lock-ins with negative implications for adaptability to changing environments can hinder the development. The region plays an important role, because geographic proximity significantly influences the development, maintenance and effect of social networks. This can lead to a high rate of start-ups, which are biased to the industrial structure present in the region, and the formation of industrial clusters. Since social networks support these processes, they can provide an explanation for the acceleration and high-rates of start-ups in regions. The explanatory power with regard to the explanation of initial differences between regions is lower, at least at the moment.

This has implications for political programs because the different factors that might support regional start-ups need different political measures to be supported. In addition to measures supporting the regional environment, policy makers should also focus on the development of entrepreneurs through the presented stages. The support of social networks can be one way of improving this. But policy makers have only limited possibilities to intervene and built social networks. Normally the structure, processes and resulting behavioral modes described above develop spontaneously - if at all - by self-organizing processes inside a region. The question of how the described networks can be built artificially or how the services provided by the networks can be provided by other organizations is not very well answered so far in the literature. Several political programs were launched in the past to support start-ups, e.g. EXIST in Germany. Such approaches had some success (Koschatzky 2003), but they could maybe gain from taking into consideration first stages of the processes and could be extended by supporting and activating already existing social networks.

In order to confirm the theoretical argument, empirical studies are needed. Since networks, their use and impact are not obvious, various case studies have to be conducted to find similarities and differences and to fit them into this framework. Other researchers already did this in the past and a next step is to check more of these case studies and their fit into the framework.

ACKNOWLEDGEMENTS

I want to thank Olav Sorenson, Anja Kettner, Thomas Brenner and Christian Zellner for helpful comments and discussions. The usual disclaimer applies.

NOTES

[1] According to Denzau and North (1994, p. 4) mental models '(...) are the internal representations that individual cognitive systems create to interpret the environment (...)' and '(...) a prescription as to how that environment should be structured (...)'.

[2] If the socialization and development in adolescence is region specific, this can have an effect on the likelihood of founding a firm and on the ability and propensity to build and use social networks.

[3] Social and cultural proximity both built on shared experiences and norms. The main difference between them is that social proximity entails continuous contact and common experiences, i.e. between work colleagues or friends, whereas cultural proximity does not need previous direct relations between the involved agents (Menzel 2003).

[4] It is stated here that during the development through the stages, the mental models of the agents change based on social-cognitive learning processes (for a more detailed analysis on this changes in mental models see Fornahl (2003)).

REFERENCES

Almus, M. and E.A. Nerlinger (1999). Wachstumsdeterminanaten junger innovativer Unternehmen – Empirische Ergebnisse für West-Deutschland, *Journal of Economics and Statistics* 218(3/4), 257-275.

Anderson, J.R. (2000). *Cognitive psychology and its implications,* 5ed, New York: Worth.

Audretsch, D.B. and A.R. Thurik (2000). Capitalism and democracy in the 21st century: From the managed to the entrepreneurial economy, *Journal of Evolutionary Economics* 10, 17–34.

Bade, F. J. and E.A. Nerlinger (2000). The spatial distribution of new technology-based firms: Empirical results for West-Germany, *Papers in Regional Science* 79, 155-176.

Bandura, A. (1986). *Social foundations of thought and action – A social cognitive theory,* Engelwood Cliffs: Prentice-Hall.

Barnett, W.P., A.-N. Swanson and O. Sorenson (2003). Asymmetric selection among organizations, *Industrial and Corporate Change* 12(4), 673-695.

Bednarzik, R.W. (2000). The role of entrepreneurship in U.S. and European job growth, *Monthly Labor Review* (July), 3–16.

Birley, S. (1985). The role of networks in the entrepreneurial process, *Journal of Business Venturing* 1, 107-117.

Blau, P.M. (1977). *Inequality and heterogeneity,* New York: Free Press.

Boalt, G. and C.G. Janson (1957). Distance and social relations, *Acta Sociologica* 2, 73-97.

Bossard, J.S. (1932). Residential propinquity as a factor in marriage selection, *American Journal of Sociology* 38, 219-224.

Brenner, T. (2004). *Local Industrial Clusters, Existence, Emergence and Evolution,* London: Routledge.

Brüderl, J. and P. Preisendörfer (1998). Network support and the success of newly founded business, *Small Business Economics* 10(3), 213-225.

Burt, R.S. (1992). *Structural holes: The social structure of competition,* Cambridge, MA: Harvard University Press.

Burt, R.S. (1997). The contingent value of social capital, *Administrative Science Quarterly* 42, 339-365.

Busenitz, L.W. and C.-M. Lau (1996). A cross-cultural cognitive model of new venture creation, *Entrepreneurship Theory and Practice* 20, 25–39.

Camerer, C. and D. Lavallo (1999). Overconfidence and excess entry: An experimental approach, *American Economic Review* 89, 306-318.

Castilla, E.J., H. Hwang, E. Granovetter and M. Granovetter (2000). Social networks in Silicon Valley, in: Lee, C.-M., Miller, W.F., Gong Hancock, M. and Rowen, H.S. (eds), *The Silicon Valley edge – A habitat for innovation and entrepreneurship.* Stanford University Press, Stanford, CA, 217-247.

Coleman, J.S. (1988). Social capital in the creation of human capital, *American Journal of Sociology* 94, 95-120.

Cooper, A. C. Woo and W. Dunkelberg (1988). Entrepreneurs perceived chances for success, *Journal of Business Venturing* 3, 97-108.

Cowan, R. and N. Jonard (1999). *Network structure and the diffusion of knowledge,* Discussion Paper No. 99028, MERIT, Maastricht University, The Netherlands.

Denzau, A.T. and D.C. North (1994). Shared mental models: Ideologies and institutions, *Kyklos* 47(1), 3-31.

Festinger, L., S. Schacter and K.W. Back (1950). *Social pressure in informal groups,* New York: Harper.

Fornahl, D. (2003). Entrepreneurial activities in a regional context, in D. Fornahl and T. Brenner (eds), *Cooperation, networks and institutions in regional innovation systems,* Edward Elgar, Cheltenham, UK, Northampton, MA, USA, pp.38-57.

Fornahl, D. and Menzel, M.-P. (2002). *Co-development of firm foundings and regional clusters.* mimeo, Max-Planck-Institut zur Erforschung von Wirtschaftssystemen Jena.

Fornahl, D. and H. Graf (2003). Standortfaktoren und Gründungsaktivitäten in Jena, in U. Cantner, R. Helm and R. Meckl (eds), *Strukturen und Strategien in einem Innovationssystem: Das Beispiel Jena,*. Stuttgart: Verlag Wissenschaft und Praxis, 97-123.

Foss, L. (1993). Resources, networks and entrepreneurship: a survey of 153 starters and 84 non-starters in the cod farming industry in Norway, in N.S. Churchill et al. (eds), *Frontiers of entrepreneurship research*, 355-369.

Fritsch, M. (1992). Unternehmens-"Netzwerke" im Lichte der Institutionenökonomik, *Jahrbuch für neue politische Ökonomie* 11, 89-102.

Grabher, G. (1993). The weakness of strong ties: the lock-in of regional development in the Ruhr area, in: G. Grabher (ed.): *The embedded firm – On the socioeconomics of industrial networks*. London, New York: Routledge, 255-277.

Granovetter, M. (1973). The strength of weak ties, *American Journal of Sociology* 78, 1360-1380.

Granovetter, M. (1985). Economic action and social structure: The problem of embeddedness, *American Journal of Sociology* 91, 481-510.

Hägerstrand, T. (1953). *Innovation diffusion as a spatial process*. Chicago: University of Chicago Press.

Hansen, E.L. (1995). Entrepreneurial networks and new organization growth, *Entrepreneurship Theory and Practice* (Summer), 7-19.

Hansen, M.T. (1999). The search-transfer problem: The role of weak ties in sharing knowledge across organization subunits, *Administrative Science Quarterly* 44, 82-111.

Heald, T. (1983). *Networks. Who we know and how we use them,* London.

Johannisson, B. (1998). Personal networking in emerging knowledge-based firms: Spatial and functional patterns, *Entrepreneurship and Regional Development* 10, 297-312.

Klandt, H. (1984). *Aktivität und Erfolg des Unternehmensgründers, eine empirische Analyse unter Einbeziehung des mikrosozialen Umfeldes*. Bergisch-Gladbach.

Koschatzky, K. (2003). Entrepreneurship stimulation in regional innovation systems – Public promotion of university-based start-ups in Germany, in D. Fornahl and T. Brenner (eds), *Cooperation, networks and institutions in regional innovation systems*, Edward Elgar, Cheltenham, UK, Northampton, MA, USA, pp.277-302.

Kriegesmann, B. (1999). Unternehmensgründungen aus der Wissenschaft – Eine empirische Analyse zu Stand, Entwicklungen und institutionellen Rahmenbedingungen in außeruniversitären Forschungseinrichtungen, *Zeitschrift für Betriebswirtschaft* 70, 397-414.

Lazarsfeld, P.F. and R.K. Merton (1954). Friendship as a social process: A substantive and methodological analysis, in M. Berger, T. Abel and C.H. Page (eds), *Freedom and control in modern society*, New York: Van Nostrand, pp. 18-66.

Liebeskind, J.P., A.L. Oliver, L.G. Zucker, M.B. Brewer (1995). *Social networks, learning and flexibility: Sourcing scientific knowledge in new biotechnology firms*, NBER Working Paper 5320. National Bureau of Economic Research.

Lingblad, M. (2004). *The external social network of innovation project managers and project performance*, Paper presented at the DRUID Summer Conference 2004, Elsinore, Denmark.

Littunen, H. (2000). Networks and local environmental characteristics in the survival of new firms, *Small Business Economics* 15, 59-71.

Løvås, B. and O. Sorenson (2003). *Social capital, competition and reource mobilization*, mimeo.

McPherson, M. L. Smith-Lovin and J.M. Cook (2001). Birds of a feather: homophily in social networks, *Annual Review of Sociology* 27, 415-444.

Marsden, P.V. and N.E. Friedkin (1993). Network studies of social influence, *Sociological Methods and Research* 22, 127-151.

Maskell, P. and A. Malmberg (1999). Localised learning and industrial competitiveness, *Cambridge Journal of Economics* 23, 167-185.

Menzel, M.-P. (2003). *Networks and technologies in an emerging cluster: The case of Bioinstruments in Jena*, mimeo.

Podolny, J. (1994). Market uncertainty and the social character of economic exchange, *Administrative Science Quarterly* 39, 458-483.

Reynolds, P.D, B. Miller and W.R. Maki (1995). Explaining regional variation in business birth and deaths: U.S. 1976-1988, *Small Business Economics* 7, 389-407.

Rosegrant, S. and Lampe D.R. (1992). *Route 128 – Lessons from Boston's high-tech community*. Basic Books, New York.

Saxenian, A.-L. (1994). *Regional advantage*. Harvard University Press, Cambridge.

Saxenian, A.-L. (2000). Networks of immigrant entrepreneurs, in: Lee, C.-M., Miller, W.F., Gong Hancock, M. and Rowen, H.S. (eds), *The Silicon Valley edge – A habitat for innovation and entrepreneurship*. Stanford University Press, Stanford, CA, 248-268.

Seri, P. (2003). Learning pathologies in losing areas: Towards a definition of the cognitive obstacles to local development, in D. Fornahl and T. Brenner (eds), *Cooperation, networks and institutions in regional innovation systems*, Cheltenham, UK and Northampton, MA, USA: Edward Elgar, pp. 128-148.

Shane, S. (2000). Prior knowledge and the discovery of entrepreneurial Opportunities, *Organization Science* 11, 448–69.

Shane, S. and D. Cable (2002). Network ties, reputation, and the financing of new ventures, *Management Science* 48(3), 364-381.

Simonton, D.K. (1975). Sociocultural context of individual creativity: A transhistorical timeseries analysis, *Journal of Personality and Social Psychology* 32, 1119–33.

Sørenson, J.B. and O. Sorenson (2003). From conception to birth: Opportunity perception and resource mobilization in entrepreneurship, *Advances in Strategic Management* 20 (J.A.C. Baum and O. Sorenson, eds), 71-99.

Sorenson, O. (2003). Social networks and industrial geography, *Journal of Evolutionary Economics* 12, 513-527.

Sorenson, O. and T. Stuart (2001). Syndication networks and the spatial distribution of venture capital investments, *American Journal of Sociology* 106(6), 1546-1588.

Sorenson, O. and. P.G. Audia (2000). The social structure of entrepreneurial activity: Geographic concentration of footwear production in the United States, 1940-1989, *American Journal of Sociology* 106(2), 424-462.

Sorenson, O, J. Rivkin and L. Fleming (2003). Complexity, networks and knowledge flow, *Harvard Business School, Strategy Working Paper Series*, Working Paper Number: 02-09.

Stouffer, S.A. (1940). Intervening opportunities: A theory relating mobility and distance, *American Journal of Sociology* 99, 614-639.

Strambach, S. (1995). *Wissensintensive unternehmensorientierte Dienstleistungsnetzwerke und –interaktion. Am Beispiel des Rhein-Neacker-Raumes,* Wirtschaftsgeographie Band 6, Münster.

Stuart, T. and O. Sorenson (2003). The geography of opportunity: Spatial Heterogeneity in founding rates and the performance of biotechnology firms, *Research Policy* 32, 229-253.

Sugden, R. (1995). A theory of focal points, *The Economic Journal* 105, 533–50.

Van Praag, M. (1996). *Determinants of successful entrepreneurship*, Thesis Publishers: Amsterdam.

Witt, U. (1999). Do entrepreneurs need firms? A contribution to a missing chapter in Austrian Economics, *Review of Austrian Economics* 11, 99–109.

Zellner, C. and Fornahl, D. (2002). Scientific knowledge and implications for its diffusion, *Journal of Knowledge Management* 6(2), 190-198.

Zipf, G.K. (1949). *Human behavior and the principle of least effort*, Reading, MA: Addison-Wesley.

CHAPTER 5

SOCIAL NETWORKS, INFORMATIONAL COMPLEXITY AND INDUSTRIAL GEOGRAPHY[*]

Olav Sorenson

University of California, Los Angeles

1. INTRODUCTION

Why do some industries reside in a limited number of highly clustered geographic locations while others spread across the landscape more broadly? Traditional explanations for variation in the spatial distribution of industrial production have focused o n examining differences in the transportation costs associated with obtaining important inputs and with distributing finished goods to consumers. These transportation cost based arguments fail, however, to account for the concentration of a variety of light manufacturing and service industries, such as high technology or entertainment, where these costs make up a negligible fraction of the value of the good. Attempts to explain the clustering of these industries has led researchers to revisit the agglomeration economies proposed by Alfred Marshall (1920). Thus, recent work has elucidated the potential benefits of an extended division of labor (Romer, 1990), labor pooling (Diamond and Simon, 1990; Rotemberg and Saloner, 1990) and information spillovers (Arrow, 1962).

Although these factors undoubtedly play a role in the maintenance of many industrial districts, geographic concentration can persist even when economic efficiency (at least in production) does not support it. The explanation for this phenomenon comes from a more nuanced consideration of the process of entrepreneurship – specifically, the importance of social networks to it. Two factors must converge for a nascent entrepreneur to found a new firm. First, the potential entrepreneur must perceive an opportunity for profit in a particular segment, or market niche, of the economy. Since much of the relevant information only exists privately, awareness of potentially profitable opportunities requires connections to those with the pertinent knowledge, typically those currently engaged in business in a particular industry. Second, the individual that perceives an opportunity must build a firm – assemble the necessary capital, skilled labor and knowledge – to exploit it. Again, social relationships play a crucial role in acquiring tacit information and in convincing resource holders to join the fledgling venture, whether as employees or investors. Because the social ties that facilitate both of these antecedents rarely extend beyond the regions in which these relevant resources and knowledge reside, entrepreneurs within a given industry most frequently arise in close proximity to industry incumbents. This regularity implies that industries can remain geographically concentrated even when co-location disadvantages firms.

Though recent studies provide support for this social network based explanation (e.g., Sorenson and Audia, 2000; Klepper, 2001; Stuart and Sorenson, 2003), it suffers from a critical shortcoming: it predicts that all industries should cluster into industrial districts. Consistent with the gradual diffusion of social networks over time, some of the variation in the degree of geographic concentration stems from differences in the maturity (or age) of industries. Nevertheless, even among established industries, sectors vary in the degree to which they cluster into a small number of productive regions. Why do some industries continue to agglomerate while others spread?

This paper seeks to address this issue by answering the more focused question: when do social networks play a vital role in structuring industrial geography? This extension focuses on the interaction of social networks with the characteristics of the knowledge flowing through them – in particular, its degree of complexity. I argue that social networks become increasingly important for the transmission of knowledge as the complexity of the underlying knowledge increases. This expectation emerges from recognizing that the assimilation of information may require the receiver to engage in a process of search to fill in gaps, or correct transmission errors, in the knowledge received – a difficult task when dealing with complex knowledge. Dense social networks can diminish the need for search by facilitating high fidelity knowledge transfer: complete information with negligible noise. On the other hand, when relatively sparse social networks – such as one might find spanning the borders of salient social groups – connect the receiver to the sender, search plays an increasingly important role in transmission. Under such conditions, simple knowledge flows easily both within and across social boundaries because search can easily substitute for imperfect transmission (Rivkin, 2000). These dynamics lead us to expect that industries based on more complex knowledge will concentrate geographically to a greater degree.

This paper engages in two types of analysis to corroborate this hypothesis. First, it investigates patent data to confirm the micro-dynamics of knowledge flows. Citation patterns across patents offer something like a fossil record of the flow of knowledge. To assess our argument, we estimate the effect of knowledge complexity on the geographic dispersion of future citations using a case-control logistic analysis. Consistent with the thesis proposed, the results show that knowledge complexity plays an important role in limiting the rate at which knowledge diffuses across geographic boundaries. Next, the paper investigates the industry-level correlation between the knowledge complexity in an economic sector and its degree of geographic concentration. Again, the results show a significant relationship between the average level of informational complexity embodied in the patents associated with an industry and its spatial concentration in employment.

2. SOCIAL NETWORKS AND INDUSTRIAL GEOGRAPHY

Social networks affect the degree of geographic industrial concentration because they do not connect individuals at random. People interact most commonly with others living in the same geographic regions and with whom they share backgrounds, interests and affiliations. These spatial patterns arise from the likelihood of having an opportunity to form a tie. To begin a relation, two individuals usually must meet one another. Because geography, interests and affiliations strongly influence daily activities, similarity on these dimensions increases the probability that two individuals will meet by chance (Festinger, Schacter and Back, 1950; Blau, 1977; Sorenson and Stuart, 2001). Even after a contact has been made, these factors continue to affect the probability of developing and maintaining a tie. Empirical research consistently reveals that individuals appear to prefer to pursue and sustain social contacts with those from similar backgrounds and with related interests (Lazarsfeld and Merton, 1954; for a review of recent research, see McPherson, Smith-Lovin and Cook, 2001). Geographic proximity also has a strong influence on the longevity of ties, as it decreases the cost of continuing a relationship. The frequent and intense interaction required to maintain a close tie can incur substantial direct costs, especially when considerable distance separates the two parties (Zipf, 1949). The opportunity costs of a tie also increase with distance as the number of equally preferred but more proximate individuals rises (Stouffer, 1940).[1] Therefore, social networks primarily connect like individuals that live in close proximity to each other.

These social networks play an important role in structuring both who engages in entrepreneurship and what regions and industries they enter. By shaping both the awareness of opportunities and the ability to capitalize on those prospects, these networks tend to reify the existing distribution of industry (Sorenson and Audia, 2000). Consider the first stage in the entrepreneurial process: identifying an opportunity. Evaluating market potential often requires access to private information. Incumbents prefer to conceal, for instance, their positioning and profitability to prevent others from entering munificent market niches. Regardless, many individuals do have access to this valuable data, notably employees of incumbent firms as well as their contacts – a group that, given the local structure of social networks, likely includes others in the same industry and in the same local communities in which existing firms operate.

Once an opportunity has been identified, social networks also constrain where individuals can successfully build new firms. Even in an emerging industry, firms require capital and labor. As industries mature, firm efficiency rises as a result of investments in physical and human capital, and through the accretion of valuable knowledge. Fledging firms need access to each of these three elements – (1) financial capital, (2) human capital, and (3) knowledge capital – to compete effectively against incumbents. Social networks facilitate access to each of these resources.

In the absence of social networks, nascent entrepreneurs may find it difficult to garner sufficient financial and human capital. All new firms face substantial and fundamental uncertainty – not only does the venture entail substantial risk, but actors even find it difficult to assess the level of risk involved. Both potential backers and recruits likely approach opportunities to join new firms with substantial suspicion. Moreover, those considering an investment in the new venture face a potential information asymmetry problem: The nascent entrepreneur probably has a better understanding of the probable success of the proposed venture than the prospective financial supporters and employees that she attempts to recruit, an asymmetry that can lead to market failure (Akerlof, 1970). These factors create a friction in the movement of financial and human resources that social networks can help lubricate.

Social relations elevate the likelihood of mobilizing financial capital by dampening the perceived risk of the new venture. Two factors drive this effect. First, people typically consider information gathered from known parties more reliable; hence, investors more likely trust the projections of entrepreneurs with whom they share a social relation. For example, Fried and Hisrich (1994) report that venture capitalists prefer to fund companies referred to them by close contacts. Second, in the absence of a close contact, triangulating information from multiple sources might afford potential investors a greater deal of confidence regarding the reliability of their information on the prospective target (Sorensen and Stuart, 2001). The effectiveness of these close social ties in fostering the acquisition of financial capital tends to bind entrepreneurs to the regions in which they have contacts, even if other locations might seem more attractive.

Prospective entrepreneurs also need to bring human capital into the nascent firm. In industries requiring skilled labor, the largest pool of available labor frequently resides in incumbent firms of like kind (Sorenson and Audia, 2000). Considering the risks involved, entrepreneurs likely find it difficult to convince potential employees to leave their secure jobs to join an uncertain new venture. To recruit personnel at early stages, entrepreneurs frequently must use their networks of contacts within the industry to convince workers to join the fledgling firm. Particularly in the managerial and professional ranks, employees will not likely leave behind their stable positions if they do not trust the company founders and their abilities. Here also, strong social ties engender the trust necessary to recruit these scarce human resources. The need to draw on these networks, together with the workers' likely preferences to remain near family and friends, again acts to bind entrepreneurs to the regions in which they have previously lived and worked.

Finally, and most importantly for this paper's argument, social networks play a critical role in directing the flows of knowledge across firms. In a wide range of industries, knowledge of particular operating routines and technologies probably accounts for a large proportion of the heterogeneity across firms in profitability; these differences likely arise when rival firms find it difficult, for one reason or another, to replicate this scarce and valuable knowledge. Entrants with access to this information, then, potentially enjoy a large advantage over other firms (Klepper and Sleeper, 2000; Klepper, 2001). Such industry-specific knowledge resides almost entirely within the incumbents in an industry. Hence, nascent entrepreneurs require strong social ties to individuals that work in the industry, a condition that nearly requires that entrepreneurs in an industry arise from the ranks of its current employees (Sorenson and Audia, 2000). Though the odds of any tie erode with geographic and social distance, the frequency of the strong ties necessary to access this knowledge probably declines very rapidly. Developing and sustaining these strong ties entails repeated and intensive interaction, a circumstance unlikely to occur except among co-workers and close, personal friends.

All three factors, therefore, imply that entrepreneurs will find it difficult to start new ventures successfully without strong contacts to other participants in the industry they wish to enter. Moreover, due to the localized nature of social networks, only those individuals that live in close proximity to industry incumbents – and probably only those that have previously worked for one or more of these incumbents – will likely have the required connections. As a result, entry acts as a centralizing force: even in the absence of agglomeration externalities, the distribution of new entrants tends to replicate the existing distribution of production in the industry, diffusing only slowly away from the locations of the first successful entrants (Sorenson and Audia, 2000).

3. SOCIAL NETWORKS, INFORMATIONAL COMPLEXITY AND KNOWLEDGE FLOW

Although these centripetal forces likely operate to some degree in all sectors, it seems probable that at least some of these factors act more strongly in some industries than in others. Industries vary in their degree of concentration. The factors described in the previous section, however, offer little explanation for why such heterogeneity might arise across populations of firms, except as a result of differences in their ages (slow diffusion processes can accrete over time). Although other factors relevant to the strength of centripetal and centrifugal forces may vary from one industry to the next, this section focuses on one element that might explain a portion of these industry-level differences: the characteristics of the knowledge capital necessary for success in an industry.

Certain characteristics of knowledge may reduce the ease with which it travels spatially by increasing the difficulty of transferring it. For example, even those that possess the knowledge may find it difficult to specify and communicate it precisely. As a result of causal ambiguity, the knowledge holder might lack a clear understanding of the connection between actions and outcomes (Lippman and Rumelt, 1982). Or, the use of such knowledge might call on tacit personal skills or interactions among multiple parties that the participants themselves do not fully appreciate (Polanyi, 1966; von Hippel, 1988, 1994), or that elude codification (Zander and Kogut, 1995). These factors essentially increase the incompleteness of knowledge transfer over distances (Sorenson, Rivkin and Fleming, 2002). The complexity of the information itself can also hinder knowledge transfer across space by reducing the likelihood that a recipient of the information can fill these gaps and correct transmission errors successfully.[2]

Informational complexity refers to the degree to which pieces of information interact to produce a desired outcome. Think of knowledge as a set of (somewhat discrete) chunks of information. Sometimes the routines represented by these chunks operate relatively independently to produce an outcome. Other times, these pieces interact in important ways. Simon (1962), thus, identifies complex knowledge as that which comprises many elements that interact richly. Similarly, scholars of information science define the complexity of knowledge according to the length of the string required to describe it completely (Kolmogorov, 1965) – a direct function of the number of chunks and their intensity of interaction.

Complex knowledge evades easy replication. The interactions among components generate two effects that undermine copying. First, small errors in replication produce large differences in outcomes in tightly coupled systems; getting it 'a little wrong' does not mean having routines nearly as effective as the original – rather, such errors frequently lead to substantial degradations in performance. As a result, those attempting to replicate the original knowledge need to correct these errors to achieve anything close to the performance of the original code. The second effect, however, stymies these efforts: Interdependence also produces a rapid increase in the number of 'local peaks' – internally consistent, though not optimal combinations of components that thwart improvement through incremental search because altering any single component degrades the efficacy of the whole (Kauffman, 1993; Rivkin, 2000). Not only do copying errors substantially degrade the value of the knowledge, but also correcting these errors becomes increasingly difficult, as the complexity of the knowledge increases.

Social networks, therefore, become even more important to effective knowledge transfer under these conditions. These relationships can facilitate the transfer process in at least two ways. First, they may allow the actor trying to replicate the knowledge to begin with a better facsimile – either because fewer errors arose in the transmission itself or because they began working with a more complete set of information – thereby beginning their attempts to replicate and improve on the original knowledge closer to the target. Second, social networks may allow the knowledge recipient to refer back to the source of the original knowledge when problems arise with understanding and deploying it. Strong ties thus mitigate both of the factors that frustrate the flow of complex information.

Empirical corroboration

Patent data allow me to corroborate my basic argument empirically. In particular, I estimate the effect of informational complexity on the rate at which knowledge diffuses for a sample of 17,264 patents.[3] Patents and their citations offer a useful setting to test these ideas. The U.S. Patent Office requires applicants to cite prior knowledge where relevant. Patent examiners review this citation data for accuracy ensuring that these data offer more objective and consistent information than one would typically find in bibliometric studies. In addition, Fleming and Sorenson (2001) have developed a means of measuring the degree of interdependence among the knowledge components that make up patents, a measure that would be difficult to replicate in other types of data. The MicroPatent database, which reports information from the U.S. Patent and Trademark Office (USPTO), provides the bulk of the data.

Fleming and Sorenson (2001) proposed an interdependence measure that entails two stages of calculation. Intuitively, interdependent pieces of knowledge should prove difficult to combine, as interactions impede the process of invention. In developing this measure, they use patent subclasses to represent knowledge components.[4] In the first stage, they calculate the ease with which each component recombines – the inverse of interdependence (see the first equation for subclass i used in patent j). This measure identifies every appearance of the subclass i in previous patents from 1790 to 1990.[5] The total number of previous occurrences provides the denominator. For the numerator, Fleming and Sorenson tally the number of different subclasses appearing with subclass i on previous patents. The measure, therefore, increases when a subclass combines with a wider variety of other subclasses, controlling for the total number of applications. To generate a patent-level measure of interdependence, they take the mean of the inverted ease of recombination scores for all subclasses to which a patent belongs (the second equation below). Though some might reasonably question whether this measure successfully proxies for interdependence, Fleming and Sorenson (2004) have shown that it accords well with inventors' own perceptions of the degree of coupling (i.e. level of interaction) among the components in their inventions. As prior research has revealed a non-monotonic relationship between this measure and the likelihood of future citations, I include both the interdependence measure and its square in the models as controls.

$$\text{Ease of recombination of subclass } i \equiv E_i = \frac{\text{Count of subclasses previously combined with sublass } i}{\text{Count of previous patents in subclass } i}$$

$$\text{Interdependence of patent } j \equiv K_j = \frac{\text{Count of subclasses on patent } j}{\sum_{i\in j} E_i}$$

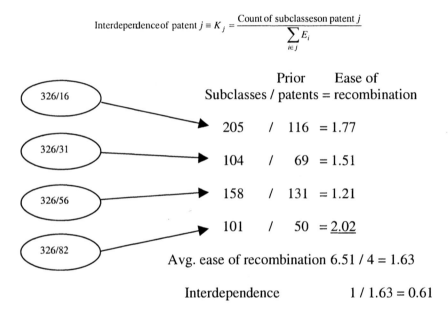

Figure 5.1. Calculation of interdependence measure

Figure 5.1 illustrates an example of this calculation for one specific patent (#5,136,185). The electronic device described by this patent belongs to four subclasses: 326/16, 326/31, 326/56, and 326/82. Each of these subclasses corresponds to a component of the circuit. For instance, subclass 326/16 refers to the test facilitate feature, a standard feature in digital design which implements a testing mode within the semiconductor chip (McCluskey, 1986). Prior to its appearance on this patent, this subclass had been combined with 205 different subclasses across 116 patents. Hence, the ease of recombination for this subclass is 205/116 = 1.77. Similar calculations can be made for each of the other components: 326/31 has appeared on 69 patents with 104 different subclasses (104/69 = 1.51); 326/56 combined with 158 different subclasses on 131 prior inventions (158/131 = 1.21); and 326/82 has been coupled with 101 different components in 50 patents ($101/50 = 2.02$). The average of these ease of recombination scores is 1.63; since interdependence relates inversely to the ease of recombination, inverting this score provides us with a measure of the degree of interdependence, or coupling.

Analyzing the dispersion of future citations also necessitates a measure of distance. Since patents list the inventor's address, we can locate patents according to where their inventors live, matching 3-digit zip codes[6] to the latitudes and longitudes of the centroids of these postal codes. The distance separating two points, i and j, on a sphere is:

$$d_{ij} = C\left[\arccos\left(\sin(lat_i)\sin(lat_j) + \cos(lat_i)\cos(lat_j)\cos\left(\left|long_i - long_j\right|\right)\right)\right]$$

with latitude (*lat*) and longitude (*long*) measured in radians. C translates the result into linear units; $C = 3437$ corresponds to miles. Taking the natural log of this measure generates a functional form consistent with theoretical expectations (Stouffer, 1940; Zipf, 1959; cf. Sorenson and Stuart, 2001, for empirical results). Interacting this term with the interdependence measure allows a test of our thesis; if social networks play an especially strong role in structuring the diffusion of complex knowledge, patents with a high degree of interdependence should diffuse even more slowly.

To explore the diffusion of knowledge, we estimate the likelihood that a future patent cites a focal patent conditional on its distance from the focal patent, the complexity of the information embodied in the focal patent, and several control variables. This procedure corresponds to an analysis of tie formation. Although many researchers approach such data by generating a matrix of all potential dyads (i.e. a case for every future patent that could have cited a focal patent), using logistic regression to estimate the effects of covariates, this approach has two weaknesses. First, it fails to account correctly for non-independence across cases. This weakness could prove particularly problematic here, as it would tend to underestimate the standard errors for properties of the patent (e.g., complexity). Second, generating and manipulating such a large matrix can prove unwieldy. For example, analyzing all potential dyads in our sample would require the generation of a data matrix with more than eleven billion cells. Sampling from this set offers one potential solution; however, this approach fails to account for the fact that the citations (as opposed to the non-citations) provide most of the information in the estimation of the likelihood function (Coslett, 1981; Imbens, 1992). This analysis approaches the problem by using a matched sample design. All 70,271 citations that actually occur enter the data, along with a comparison set of four[7] randomly selected patents that did not cite each focal patent. Although this sampling yielded 139,487 dyads, the analyses only consider the 76,807 cases where both inventors reside in the U.S.

Since focal patents still enter the data multiple times, the tables report Huber-White robust standard errors. As logistic regression can yield biased estimates when the sample design correlates with the dependent variable (as it does here), the models correct for this effect using the method proposed by King and Zeng (2001).[8]

Table 5.1 reports the results of these models. The first model, which includes only the covariates of interest, reveals that the likelihood of a future patent citing a focal patent declines with distance; moreover, as expected, the strength of this effect increases with the interdependence of the technology embodied in the focal patent. Interdependence also exhibited its expected non-monotonic relationship to the likelihood of future citation.

Model 2 introduces a variety of control variables: *Same assignee* takes a value of one if both the focal patent and the potential citing patent have the same assignee listed (i.e. a self-citation); though studies of patent citations typically find higher rates of self-citation, these effects do not appear robust to the fine-grained controls for technological similarity used here.

Table 5.1. Rare events logit models of future citations*

	Model 1	Model 2	Model 3	Model 4 No self cites
Distance (logged miles)	-.453•• (.012)	-.464•• (.051)	-.492•• (.057)	-.431•• (.056)
Distance X Interdependence	-.118•• (.011)	-.109• (.052)	-.108• (.051)	-.098• (.048)
Interdependence	1.27•• (.143)	1.28• (.646)	1.23 (.648)	1.28•• (.714)
Interdependence^2	-.185•• (.045)	-.176 (.185)	-.177 (.184)	-.232 (.196)
Same assignee		.335 (.242)	.381 (.248)	
Same class		3.63•• (.469)	3.62•• (.459)	3.64•• (.486)
Subclass overlap		4.85•• (.761)	4.82•• (.734)	4.75•• (.764)
Activity control		.736• (.348)	.727• (.348)	.723• (.356)
Distance control			-.192 (.163)	
Distance control X Distance			.026 (.025)	
Constant	-4.50•• (.083)	-6.39•• (.357)	-6.16•• (.409)	-6.57•• (.394)
Log-likelihood	-49064.5	-22848.5	-22804.7	-20549.5
Pseudo R^2	.076	.562	.562	.552

* 76,807 cases, 51.7% represent ties (vs. .00059% in population) • $p \leq .05$ •• $p \leq .01$; Standard errors shown in parentheses

Same class is a dummy variable with a value of one if both patents belong to the same primary technological class; patents in the same class cite one another with much greater frequency than those in different classes. *Subclass overlap*, the proportion of subclasses on the potentially citing patent that appears on the focal patent, provides a much finer-grained measure of the technological similarity between two patents; this measure also reveals a strong relationship between the technological similarity of two patents and the likelihood of a citation. Finally, the *activity control* accounts for the total degree of activity in the technology classes to which the focal patent belongs – essentially, it amounts to a weighted average of the number of citations received by a typical patent in each of the classes in which the focal patent falls. As one would expect, patents in more active technological areas receive future citations at a higher rate. Regardless, the effects of distance and the interaction between interdependence and distance still hold: interdependence retards the geographic dispersion of future citations.

Despite these strong results, the distribution of research activity in a technological area might explain these results. In other words, industries characterized by highly complex knowledge might concentrate more intensely. Though the argument being made here suggests precisely such a relationship, the direction of causality could run in the opposite direction of the one proposed here: co-location might lead to the development of more complex technologies, rather than informational complexity limiting the geographic flow of the diffusion of knowledge. To account for such an effect, the models incorporate a *distance control*. The distance control averages the natural log of the distance between all pairs of patents, granted in 1990, in the same primary class as the focal patent; in essence, it captures the average distance that one would expect to see between citing patents in a technological field if geography did not influence who cited whom. Model 3 includes both this variable and its interaction with the distance term as controls; however, these controls neither have significant effects on the likelihood of a citation, nor do they affect the estimates for the interaction between distance and interdependence.

The final column, model 4, reports an estimate without self-citations. Since the process described in section 2 would require the movement of knowledge across firms, this model restricts the analysis to these cases. Once again, the results appear robust to this alternative specification of the model: interdependence depresses the likelihood that a distant patent cites the focal patent. Figure 5.2 displays this effect graphically. A patent of average interdependence is more than four times more likely to receive a citation from another patent in the same zip code as from one 100 miles away; by comparison, a patent with an interdependence score one standard deviation above the mean is six times more likely to be built on by a local patent than one 100 miles distant. Hence, the figure illustrates that informational complexity intensifies the localization of spillovers.

One might notice that the expected main effects of interdependence on the likelihood of a citation falls below traditional levels of significance. Though this fact appears inconsistent with the baseline relationship between interdependence and future citations proposed by Fleming and Sorenson (2001), a careful look at the models reveals that the lack of significance stems from an increase in the size of the standard errors, rather than a decline in the point estimates of the effect size. Hence, multi-collinearity may well account for this result, by reducing the model's statistical power.

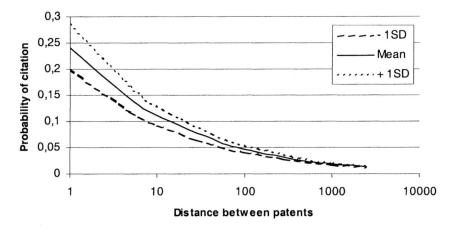

The lines illustrate effects at the mean level of interdependence, as well as at one standard deviation above and below this mean.

Figure 5.2. The likelihood of a within class citation by complexity and distance

4. COMPLEXITY AND INDUSTRIAL GEOGRAPHY

Pushing this mechanism up to the industry level of analysis generates a fairly straightforward set of predictions. Consider the following premises: a) Knowledge capital represents an important resource necessary for successfully entering an industry; b) Incumbents form the primary repository for this information; c) Particularly when this knowledge is complex – containing many elements that depend sensitively on each other – entrepreneurs require strong social networks to access this information effectively; and d) Social networks tend to localize in geographic and social space. Taken together, these factors imply that social networks should matter most in industries with relatively complex technologies at their core; as a result, industries based on these technologies should diffuse more slowly in space.

Ideally, one would like longitudinal information on the spatial dispersion of a variety of industries. The data requirements, however, make such information infeasible. The evidence presented here relies on a cross-section instead. In particular, I compare the dispersion of industry to the average level of interdependence found in the patents related to that industry.

The measure of industrial dispersion comes from the figures reported in the appendix of Krugman (1991). These statistics purport to describe the level of geographic dispersion in employment across US states using a Herfindahl measure for 106 3-digit SIC industries. The highest possible score on this measure (one) would correspond to an industry in which all employees worked in a single state. A score of zero (or near zero) suggests that production spreads across all states in a manner roughly proportional to the populations in those states.

Relating the characteristics of patents to industries involves some assumptions. In the US, patents themselves to not include SIC codes. The aggregation to industries here makes use of a concordance between USPTO classes and SIC codes developed by Brian Silverman (1999). In its first step, this concordance uses data from Canadian patents to assign USPTO classes to a probability distribution of International Patent Codes (IPC; i.e. if all patents from a USPTO class fell in the same IPC class it would translate one-to-one, but if only 50% fell in a particular IPC class, it would receive a weight of .5 in translating from one system to the other). The second step involved relating the IPC classes to industries; since Canadian patents include information on both, this entailed the relatively straightforward process of generating a probability distribution of likely industry applications associated with each IPC. To return back to the US system, the concordance takes the third step of relating Canadian industry codes to US SIC codes (for details on this measure, see Silverman, 1999). The concordance provides a noisy, though unbiased, means of associating the characteristics of patents with industries. To generate the industry level measures of interdependence, I averaged the level of interdependence across all patents within a particular technological class. To arrive at industry level measures, I averaged these scores across the technological class weights indicated by the concordance.

Figure 5.3 depicts the correlation between Krugman's geographic concentration measure and the average level of informational complexity for these 106 3-digit SIC industries. As the figure illustrates, industries based on more complex knowledge appear more likely to remain tightly clustered in a small number of regions. These results fit quite nicely with the expected pattern. In total, informational complexity can account for roughly 15% of the degree of dispersion across industries ($p < .001$). Though that number might seem low, one must remember that a large number of other factors likely influence the degree of geographic concentration within an industry, including the location of keys inputs, transportation costs, and the age of the industry itself (since diffusion processes take time).

Even a cursory perusal of the chart, however, suggests that two outliers may play a heavy role in educing this correlation. To verify that these cases do not account for the results, I reran the analysis excluding them. Although the strength of the relationship declines somewhat – without the two outliers, informational complexity only explains 10% of the variation in the geographic concentration of industries – the association remains significant (p < .005). Thus, the results appear broadly consistent with the thesis that social networks matter most in industries drawing on relatively complex information.

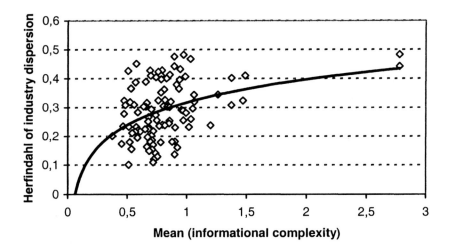

Figure 5.3. Industry dispersion by informational complexity

Though my account emphasizes the importance of access to information in the entrepreneurial process, clustering as a result of informational complexity might also reflect a type of agglomeration economy. To the extent that the knowledge concerned improves firm performance, firms that can access this information without incurring the full cost of acquiring it will benefit relative to those that cannot. Firms might therefore cluster so that they can 'share' the costs of acquiring valuable information (Arrow, 1962), or alternatively the labor efficiency embedded in employees with access to this difficult-to-transfer knowledge.

Note, however, that this account still assumes that informational complexity curtails the flow of knowledge through social networks. It simply does not imply any social inefficiency to this outcome. Though beyond the scope of this chapter, one means of differentiating between these two accounts might entail examining the distribution of *de novo* and *de alio* entrants separately. Whereas all firms would benefit from these externalities, the constraints described in sections 2 and 3 should primarily affect entrepreneurs (and hence the localization of *de novo* firms).

5. CONCLUSION

Social networks matter to industrial geography. In particular, these networks play an important role in determining who can successfully start a new venture in an industry, and where they can start it. Potential entrepreneurs need access to a variety of resources – including knowledge of the key technologies in the industry – to begin operations and to compete successfully; social networks facilitate access to these resources, a notion supported by several recent studies (e.g., Sorenson and Audia, 2000; Klepper, 2001; Stuart and Sorenson, 2003).

Industries do not always agglomerate, however. If social networks strongly structure this process, all industries should exhibit clustering. Nevertheless, industries vary substantially in the degree to which they concentrate geographically, begging the question: Why do some industries concentrate while others spread? Put differently, one might ask: When do social networks play a vital role in structuring industrial geography?

The paper maintains that the characteristics of the knowledge underlying the key technologies in the industry determine the ease with which distant entrepreneurs can attempt entry. Social networks become increasingly important for the knowledge transmission as the complexity of the information increases. Entrepreneurs trying to replicate the success of incumbents must successfully mimic their understanding of key technologies, a process that involves trial-and-error learning if the entrepreneur does not begin with a perfect understanding of this knowledge. Such trial-and-error learning proves difficult, however, with complex knowledge. Dense social networks can diminish the need for search though, by facilitating high fidelity information transfer: complete information with little noise. Hence, networks prove most important to entrepreneurship, and most limiting to the diffusion of industry, when complex knowledge contributes importantly to success in the industry.

To corroborate this thesis, the paper offers two types of evidence. At the micro-level, analysis of patent citations reveals that these citations bridge more extensive geographic expanses when the underlying knowledge contains a low level of interdependence, or coupling, between its components. Moving to the industry-level, a cross-sectional analysis of the geographic dispersion of production across industries shows that the degree of informational complexity (measured using the average level of interdependence for patents related to an industry) explains a significant portion of this cross-industry variation. Hence, the evidence appears to support the notion that the complexity of the information flowing through a network has some bearing on its relevance for the geographic distribution of economic activity.

NOTES

* This paper reports research that builds substantially on work that the author has done in conjunction with Lee Fleming and Jan Rivkin. Though faults in this piece remain the responsibility of the author, Lee and Jan deserve credit for many of its merits. I also thank Brian Silverman for generously providing access to his patent class-SIC code concordance. Guido Bünstorf and the participants of the Max Planck Institute workshop on "The role of labor mobility and informal networks for knowledge transfer" provided many comments that proved useful in the development of this paper.

1 Stouffer (1940) and Zipf (1949) both derive formal models to predict the functional relationship between distance and the probability of interaction – opportunity costs drive Stouffer's model while direct costs play a larger role in Zipf's approach. Both expect that the probability of a tie should vary in proportion to the reciprocal of the distance between two actors.

2 Sorenson, Rivkin and Fleming (2002) provide an extended discussion and analysis of this process.

3 The focal data include information on May and June of 1990 (see Fleming and Sorenson, 2001). We selected the year to make maximal use of the data, since we needed several years of data following the sample to follow citations, while still retaining recency. We chose the start month for 1990 at random and limited the set to two months of data to maintain a manageable computational burden – even so, the computation of the interdependence independent variable required roughly 50 billion calculations.

4 The USPTO classifies each patent into one or more fine-grained subclasses (nearly 100,000).

5 Although some might question the stability of this measure over time, all of the results remain robust to the use of a second interdependence measure based only on the data from 1980 to 1990.

6 Although the USPTO reports the 5-digit zip, the cleaned data, available from CHI, which called every patent holder to verify inventor location, only provides these data at the 3-digit level.

7 The inclusion of four patents ensures that the 'control' group has roughly the same size as the set of realized ties.

8 The traditional logistic regression model treats the dichotomous outcome variable as a Bernoulli probability function that takes a value 1 with the probability π:

$$\pi_i = \frac{1}{1 + e^{-X_i\beta}},$$

where X represents a vector of covariates and β denotes a vector of parameters. King and Zeng (2001) show that the following weighted least squares expression estimates the bias in β from over-sampling rare events:

$$\text{bias}(\hat{\beta}) = (X'WX)^{-1} X'W\xi,$$

where $\xi = 0.5 Q_{ii}[(1+w_1)\pi_i - w_1]$, the Q are the diagonal elements of $Q = X(X'WX)^{-1}X'$, $W = \text{diag}[\pi_i(1-\pi_i)w_i]$, and w_1 represents the fraction of ones (events) in the sample relative to the fraction in the population. Essentially, one regresses the independent variables on the residuals using W as the weighting factor. Tomz (1999) has developed a Stata command, relogit, which corrects for this bias.

REFERENCES

Akerlof, G.A. (1970). The market for 'lemons': qualitative uncertainty and the market mechanism. *Quarterly Journal of Economics, 84*, 488-500.

Arrow, K.J. (1962). The economic implications of learning by doing. *Review of Economic Studies, 29*, 155-173.

Blau, P.M. (1977). *Inequality and heterogeneity*. New York, Free Press.

Coslett, S.R. (1981). Maximum likelihood estimator for choice-based samples. *Econometrica, 49*, 1289-1316.

Diamond, C. and Simon, C. (1990). Industrial specialization and increasing returns to labor. *Journal of Labor Economics, 8*, 175-201.

Festinger, L., Schacter, S. and Back, K.W. (1950). *Social pressures in informal groups*. New York, Harper.

Fleming, L. and Sorenson, O. (2001). Technology as a complex adaptive system: evidence from patent data. *Research Policy, 30*, 1019-1039.

Fleming, L. and Sorenson, O. (2004). Science as a map in technological search. *Strategic Management Journal, 25*, forthcoming.

Fried, V.H. and Hisrich, R.D. (1994). Toward a model of venture capital investment decision-making. *Financial Management, 23*, 28-37.

Imbens, G. (1992). An efficient method of moments estimator for discrete choice models with choice-based sampling. *Econometrica, 60*, 1187-1214.

King, G. and Zeng, L. (2001). Logistic regression in rare events data. *Political Analysis, 9*, 137-163.

Klepper, S. (2001). Employee startups in high-tech industries. *Industrial and Corporate Change, 10*, 639-674.

Klepper, S. and Sleeper, S. (2000). Entry by spinoffs. Mimeo

Kolmogorov, A.N. (1965). Three approaches to the quantitative definition of information. *Problems of Information Transmission, 1*, 1-17.

Krugman, P. (1991). *Geography and Trade*. Cambridge, MA, MIT Press.

Lazarsfeld, P.F. and Merton, R.K. (1954). Friendship as a social process: a substantive and methodological analysis. In: Berger, M., Abel, T. and Page, C.H. (Eds.). *Freedom and control in modern society*. New York, Van Nostrand.

Lippman, S. and Rumelt, R. (1982). Uncertain imitability: an analysis of interfirm differences in efficiency under competition. *Bell Journal of Economics, 13*, 418-438.

Marshall, A. (1890). *Principles of economics*. London, MacMillan.

McCluskey, E. (1986). *Logic design principles with emphasis on testable semi-custom circuits*. Englewood Cliffs, NJ, Prentice Hall.

McPherson, M., Smith-Lovin, L. and Cook, J.M. (2001). Birds of a feather: homophily in social networks. *Annual Review of Sociology, 27*, 415-444.

Polanyi, M. (1966). *The tacit dimension*. New York: Anchor Day.

Rivkin, J.W. (2000). Imitation of complex strategies. *Management Science, 46*, 824-844.

Romer, P. (1987). Growth based on increasing returns to specialization. *American Economic Review, 77*, 56-62.

Rotemberg, J.J. and Saloner, G. (1990). Competition and human capital accumulation: a theory of interregional specialization and trade. Mimeo

Simon, H.A. (1962). The architecture of complexity. *Proceedings of the American Philosophical Association, 106*, 467-482.

Silverman, B.S. (1999) Technological resources and the direction of corporate diversification: toward an integration of the resource-based view and transaction cost economics. *Management Science, 45*, 1109-1124.

Sorenson, O. and Audia, P.G. (2000). The social structure of entrepreneurial opportunity: geographic concentration of footwear production in the United States, 1940-1989. *American Journal of Sociology, 106*, 424-462.

Sorenson, O., Rivkin, J.W. and Fleming, L. (2002). Complexity, networks and knowledge flow. Mimeo.

Sorenson, O., Stuart, T.E. (2001). Syndication networks and the spatial distribution of venture capital financing. *American Journal of Sociology, 106*, 1546-1588.

Stouffer, S.A. (1940). Intervening opportunities: a theory relating mobility and distance. *American Sociological Review, 5*, 845-867.

Stuart, T.E. and Sorenson, O. (2003). The geography of opportunity: spatial heterogeneity in founding rates and the performance of biotechnology firms. *Research Policy, 32*, 229-253.

Tomz, M. (1999). relogit (Stata ado file). Available at http://gking.harvard.edu/stats.shtml

von Hippel, E. (1988). *The sources of innovation.* New York, Oxford University.

von Hippel, E. (1994). Sticky information and the locus of problem solving: Implications for innovation. *Management Science, 40*, 429-439.

Zander, U. and Kogut, B. (1995). Knowledge and the speed of transfer and imitation of organizational capabilities: an empirical test. *Organization Science, 6*, 76-92.

Zipf, G.K. (1949). *Human behavior and the principle of least effort.* Reading, MA, Addison-Wesley.

CHAPTER 6

TRANSNATIONAL NETWORKS AND THE EVOLUTION OF THE INDIAN SOFTWARE INDUSTRY:
The Role of Culture and Ethnicity

Florian A. Täube

Johann Wolfgang Goethe-University, Frankfurt/ Main

1. INTRODUCTION

How can the Indian success in IT, especially software, be explained? Is it an eventual consequence of the liberalization in the 1990s? Why, then, have other sectors not produced such an impressive performance? And why do we find an uneven record of growth and development between Indian states with the South being more successful in these industries? Is it rather influenced by other factors, probably generated – or released – through this liberalization, e.g. a regional culture of entrepreneurship and innovation? Or might there even be a predisposition towards the so-called knowledge economy? And what is the relevance of transnational network connections, with Silicon Valley (SV) in particular?

The Indian IT industry mainly consists of a broad spectrum of software development enterprises. The figures for software exports show an astonishing annual growth of roughly 50 % for the 1990s. Having started with basic programming India now delivers services, less products, on a globally competitive level that has not been seen in any other industry since independence. There are several factors contributing to this extraordinary development and there is no doubt about the purely economic ones. Over the last few years there have been many studies on the Indian software industry analyzing it from different angles ranging from general perspectives (Arora et al. 2001) to others more focused on innovative capabilities (Fromhold-Eisebith 1999; D'Costa 2002) and quality considerations (Banerjee & Duflo 2000) to the involvement of multi-national firms and domestic linkages or spillovers (Basant et al. 2001; Patibandla & Petersen 2002), and an eventual development impact (Arora & Athreye 2002).

Although its involvement is criticized as 'benign neglect' (Arora et al. 2001) rather than active stimulation of business, the Indian Government did recognize the importance of supporting the software sector in general, and exports in particular – as early as 1972 with the establishment of an export processing zone (Evans 1992). Other supportive policies like establishing the prestigious Indian Institutes of Technology (IIT) have been of critical value to the evolution of the software industry. Subsequently, the first Software Technology Parks (STP) were established in 1990 (Bajpai & Shastri 1998). The quality of software-exporting firms is assessed at high levels. India has more than half of ISO 9000 certified companies and the largest number of enterprises assessed at Level 5 of Carnegie Mellon University's Software Engineering Institute Capability Maturity Model worldwide (Arora et al. 2001). Nevertheless, the innovative capabilities of the Indian software industry are viewed rather skeptically as being still rather low in the value chain (Arora et al. 2001; D'Costa 2002). The relatively unimportant domestic market is identified as another major shortcoming (Bajpai & Shastri 1998). In spite of this, more recently almost all multinational companies (MNCs) increasingly locate not only low-level tasks but also research and development (R & D) centers or laboratories in India; many already have more than one research lab. However, the most advanced research continues to cluster in Bangalore. Generally, one finds an uneven distribution of the software industry locations, which is clustered in the South (Bangalore, Hyderabad and Chennai), West (Mumbai and Pune), and around the capital New Delhi in the North. Thus, the question addressed here is why some regions are more successful than others. More recently, there is a growing number of works on the spatial concentration in South Indian centers (D'Costa 2003; Balasubramanyam & Balasubramanyam 2000; Vijayabaskar & Krishnaswamy 2003) and emphasizing the influence of international networks (Dossani 2002; Kapur & McHale 2002; Saxenian et al. 2002).

The novelty of this chapter is the incorporation of culture and ethnicity as independent variables in order to explain the regional concentration of the Indian software industry predominantly in the South. These primarily non-economic variables translate into human capital through social capital and networks, and into foreign investment in India promoted by non-resident Indians (NRIs). Thus, the central hypotheses of this paper are that, firstly, some ethnic and cultural groups in India are more apt to socio-economic development in knowledge-intensive industries due to their higher appreciation of learning. Apparently there are diverse culturally rooted attitudes towards education and technological or economic change. It seems to be fruitful in order to understand the evolution of the Indian software industry, which appears to be dominated by South Indians and *Brahmins*. Secondly, it is argued that geographical distance can, at least partly, be bridged by other forms of proximity – in this case socio-cultural – through transnational networks given the socio-cultural dimensions of the actors in this industry and their network connections. Eventually, these particular groups from South India have developed the strongest transnational network ties between India and SV. It is important to note that the actors in these transnational networks are mainly individuals, often groups, but usually not firms – even when analyzing multinational companies (MNCs). On the one hand these networks appear to stimulate the growth of the Indian software industry. But on the other they are also influenced by developments within India. Notably the higher inclination of some groups to migrate abroad, in particular the better educated Indians from the South and West. Partly, this higher propensity stems from the expectation of higher rewards from their education. Hence, a positive feedback mechanism is in place here but, in order to simplify, the two phenomena will be examined separately. Firstly, the background for South India will be assessed, and then the transnational network channels are examined.

It is one of the first attempts to add socio-cultural factors as explanatory variables for the geographic concentration of the Indian software industry. The roles of culture and ethnicity, reflected through social and human capital, are analyzed because many requirements necessary for a successful economic development like basic physical infrastructure are lacking in India. The rest of this chapter is structured as follows. Section II discusses theoretically the issue of transnational labor mobility through ethnic networks. Section III outlines a South Indian regional culture and section IV extends the discussion to the background of Indian immigrants in high-tech industries. Section V supports the findings with evidence from existing interview-based works. Section VI examines three different channels of transnational ethnic networks, Indian employees of multinational firms, Indian Venture capitalists and Indian entrepreneurs in SV. Section VII concludes.

2. THE RELEVANCE OF ETHNIC NETWORKS FOR TRANSNATIONAL LABOUR MOBILITY AND KNOWLEDGE SPILLOVERS

Knowledge spillovers are considered to be one of the most important factors for economic growth (Lucas 1988, Romer 1990). Most research is centered on spillovers transmitted between economic agents in a local or regional setting like cities or metropolitan areas. But in a globalising economy, internationally or translocally linked actors steadily increase in importance. This chapter aims to identify various aspects of such transnational labor mobility through linkages of transnational *ethnic* networks and the eventual influence on the Indian economy.

There are two lines of research on how knowledge spills over. One looks at the firm as the main source of spillovers. In particular, MNCs are often perceived as a source of technology or knowledge spillovers through their co-presence with local firms. Theoretically, spillovers can occur through local firms copying MNC technology, enhanced competition leading to more efficient use of existing technology and search for more efficient technologies on the part of local firms, or through backward or forward linkages of MNCs with local firms (*e.g.* Patibandla & Petersen 2002). Secondly, there is a growing body of literature concerned with individuals and their mobility (Glaeser 1999; Klepper 2001; Storper & Venables 2002). In industries with attrition rates of 20-25% like the Indian software industry (Saxenian 1999) the mechanism of knowledge spillovers seems to be perfectly in place. For example, in Glaeser (1999) people learn randomly through contact with more skilled neighbors. Thus, those living in cities learn faster given the higher probability to meet people they can learn from. Other studies examine more deliberate spillovers like spin-offs. Franco & Filson (2000) and Klepper (2001) examine spin-offs in high-technology industries. The main finding is that entrepreneurs with experience from successful incumbents are more likely to run a start-up successfully. Emphasis of this paper is clearly placed on the influence on spillovers through mobility of individuals, even in the case of multinational companies.

In most cases knowledge spillovers are seen as a rather localized phenomenon, therefore labor mobility is usually analyzed in a local setting (Saxenian 1994). The reasoning behind this is that a large part of knowledge is not easily codifiable, but tacit. In order to transmit such knowledge – deliberately or unintended – between economic agents proximity is a crucial element. Usually, proximity is conceived of as a geographical construct. However, Lundvall (1992) argues that there is more than one kind of proximity and proposes a taxonomy with four dimensions of space, economic, organizational, geographical, and cultural.[1] Moreover, he argues that organizational proximity can be a substitute for geographical and cultural proximity. This paper examines whether cultural proximity can be a substitute for geographical proximity in order to ensure and allow for knowledge spillovers in a setting not geographically bound. A key feature of social or ethnic networks is that they provide a high degree of trust or social capital stemming from a common socio-cultural background and, hence, sharing the same language, customs, norms etc. This kind of trust can substitute for the trust present in face-to-face contacts. There is some evidence for labor mobility beyond geographical boundaries. Agrawal et al. (2003) find patent citations occurring to a large extent in locations where the inventor lived before the issue of the patent. Their interpretation is that there has been investment in social capital in expectance of future mobility. It appears to be the case for high profile knowledge-intensive activities that professional and social networks tend to be more spatially dispersed than in routine tasks (Storper & Venables 2002).

Through the international movement of US-educated individuals with Indian background a spatial extension of the localized SV model comes into existence. The immigrants open up their local networks and merge them with international contacts in order to become central nodes in a *global* value chain by providing the links for small firms in the US and India. Thus, the framework of analysis could be a 'Spatial Innovation System' (Malecki & Oinas 1999) connecting SV and Bangalore and forming a multi-regional entity with co-connection partly substituting for co-location in a 'Virtual Diamond' (Kapur & Ramamurti 2001). In this context, Appadurai's concept of an 'ethnoscape' is appealing. He defines it as 'the landscape of persons who constitute the shifting world in which we live: tourists, immigrants, refugees, exiles, guest workers, and other moving groups and individuals constitute an essential feature of the world and appear to affect the politics of (and between) nations to a hitherto unprecedented degree' (Appadurai 1996).

Thus, the term ethnoscape can be interpreted as representing translocal communities, i.e., groups of people who are bound not by geographical proximity, but by some form of shared, although mediated culture which resembles Lundvall's (1992) notion of a cultural space. Kotkin (1993) has identified such an ethnoscape for India as being one of the five global 'tribes' in terms of an ethnic group spread throughout the world, and likely to dominate business in the new global economy. The key features of these global tribes are a resurgence of 'age-old ethnic ties' demonstrated through tribal trust as the basis for a global network, and a passion for and belief in science and technological advancement, which bind together this ethnic identity (Kotkin 1993; see also Ballard 2001, Das 2001, Lachaier 2003).

3. REGIONAL CULTURE OF SOUTH INDIA

This section is a brief outline of the basic *economic* features of a culture that can be derived from a *Brahmin* and South Indian background, respectively. The central question is, whether there exists a regional culture of innovation resembling to some extent the one of Silicon Valley (Saxenian 1994). Economists arrived at the conclusion that the 'Hindu' attitude towards modernization and innovation impedes the modernization of the Indian economy (Akerlof 1976; Lal 1988), which is a misconception, since they were not acknowledging anthropological fieldwork (for a more detailed review see Taeube 2004). Recently, there is more than anecdotal evidence that new Indian enterprises are dominated even by the formerly priestly *Brahmin* caste rather than *Vaishyas*, the traditional merchant caste. It might result from the fact that *Brahmins* have been involved more generally with activities relating to knowledge. Earlier *Brahmins* had a much more negative attitude towards business, trade and commerce in general (Evans 1992).

With regard to South India there are a few notable deviations. Primarily, there have always been high-caste non-*Brahmins* pertaining to the indigenous population who were not only engaged with the learning of their texts but 'who were adept in Sanskrit learning as well' (Stein 1999: 52; Lachaier 2003). Hence, the foundations for a knowledge-based society have existed in South India ever since and, moreover, have been much more diffused throughout the broader society. Secondly, the population of the South is said to be much more homogenous than in the North. Thus, political movements in favor of backward groups started much earlier in South India and led to a more equal pattern compared to the still traditionally dominated, hierarchically oriented North (Jaffrelot 2002). Altogether, the Southern part of India seems to exhibit a more distinct regional culture of learning, not only in the sense of the regional development literature (Gertler 1997) but also literally. Apparently, this attitude is a solid foundation for the absorptive capacity necessary in order to adapt to new technologies (Lateef 1997). Although institutions of higher education have been allocated evenly over the whole country, there is a more than proportionate share of colleges, especially for engineering, and enrolment in the South (see table 6.1).

Table 6.1. Number of engineering colleges and enrolment compared to population

Region	Engineering colleges[1]		Enrolment[1]		Population[II]
	No.	National share	Capacity (no. of students)	National share	National share
Central	50	7,54%	9,470	6,05%	-
East	25	3,77%	4,812	3,07%	25,8%
North	140	21,12%	25,449	16,26%	31,3%
West	140	21,12%	34,165	21,83%	19,6%
South	308	46,46%	82,597	52,78%	23,2%
Total	663	100,00%	156,493	100,00%	100,00%

[1] *Source: Arora & Athreye (2002)*
[II] *Source: Dossani (2002)*

Some features in South Indian cultures, in particular with regard to education do not only provide a foundation for a broader and more pronounced human capital base, but also increase the intensity of interaction in social networks. Moreover, the South Indian type of marriage on average leads to family circles becoming more close-knit from one generation to the next (Lachaier 2003). Thus, 'cultural proximity' is presumably more distinct in the South, thereby increasing the level of trust that exists in these communities (Taeube 2004). This, in turn, enhances the potential for knowledge-intensive industries by facilitating the required communication, especially without geographical proximity by means of ICTs. This potential seems to be further nurtured by the immigration patterns to be found among Indians in the US, which triggers the positive feedback mechanism mentioned earlier.

4. INDIAN IMMIGRANTS IN HIGH-TECHNOLOGY INDUSTRIES

There is a lot of anecdotal evidence suggesting certain layers of the Indian society to particularly suit science-related and research-oriented activities (Das 2001). This translates into the dominance of the leading scientific institutions by these particular groups. Given that key actors in the Indian IT industry, both domestic and overseas, are graduates of graduates of the prestigious Indian Institutes of Technology or the Indian Institute of Science (IISc), the process of network building begins already in India. Except for one (Gowahati), all the other institutes (Bombay, Delhi, Kanpur, Kharagpur, Madras) maintain alumni associations.[2] Since many of those graduates migrated to the US there are now regular alumni meetings both in India and in the US. The common educational background appears to be a major force uniting NRIs in the US high-tech industry and upholding the link to and identification with their home country (Saxenian 1999; Tschang 2001). The underlying rationale for the establishment of hundreds of first-class educational institutions was the policy goal of self-reliance, which meant a great commitment to science and technology. Typically, Indians do their first degree, mostly a Bachelor, in India before they go to the US for higher studies; even scientists with master degrees or PhDs pursue further studies abroad. In 1998/ 99 Indian students accounted for 8 % of international students in US higher education. Among science and engineering graduates, India accounts for the biggest portion with more than 30 % of all the international students (Khadria 2001).

Regarding the focus of this paper the most important destination of Indian emigrants is the US, particularly Silicon Valley. Earlier Indian immigrants to California 30-40 % were mostly North Indians (Sikhs) who represent merely 2 % of the Indian population. Today India accounts for over 40 % of all H1-B visas, including more than 25 % of *worldwide* H1-B visa applications coming from South India (Xiang 2002). Estimates suggest that 25-50 % of Indian software engineers in the US are South Indians. In a similar vein, a survey among 10,000 members of Indian and Chinese software professionals' associations in SV finds that 36,5 % of the Indian respondents come from the South while this region accounts for only 23,2 % of the Indian population.

The Western part of India is also over represented (Dossani 2002). A plausible explanation for the dominance of South Indians is the localization of sensitive national research institutes. Bangalore has been an optimal location for the scientific research institutes established after independence for two reasons. First and most important, following the argument laid out in the previous section, the traditional standing of (higher) education and science. This is exemplified by the Indian Institute of Science, which has been established before independence and is deemed India's best research university (Dossani & Kenney 2002). Second, its mild and dry climate shows the necessary features required for this kind of research. Furthermore, the Hindustan Aeronautics Limited or the Indian Space Research Organization in Bangalore, the Defense Electronics Research Laboratory or the Defense Research and Development Laboratory in Hyderabad are critical for national security. Hence, they have been strategically established far away from the borders to both China and Pakistan (Lateef 1997).

The other interesting characteristic is that many of the IT professionals, and probably the students too, apparently have a *Brahmin* background (Xiang 2002). A study on technical and scientific manpower in the four South Indian states indicates that lower castes are represented much below their share in the population (Deshpande 2000). While it seems plausible that there is a high percentage of *Brahmins* in the industry workforce the industry leadership seems to be dominated by South Indian *Brahmins* too (Fromhold-Eisebith 1999). This is insofar fascinating as South Indians as a social group used to be excluded from the entrepreneurial pool of the Indian business houses (Kapur & Ramamurti 2001).

To sum up, in contrast to earlier rather low-skilled Indian migrants those working in knowledge-intensive high-tech sectors generally, and particularly in software, are among the best educated in the host economy (U.S. Census 1993; Saxenian 1999). Their Indian background is most often to be found in a South Indian *Brahmin* family and upbringing.

5. SOUTH INDIAN ECONOMIC CULTURE

The situation depicted for a South Indian economic culture together with the observations made among Indian immigrants to the SV are reinforced by the empirical perspective on the software industry in India. This section supports the findings of the previous one that the dominant pattern of socio-cultural background observed in the US seems to apply also to India or, better, has its origins in India. It is an analysis of four interview-based studies on the Indian software industry for spatial and socio-cultural clustering.

5.1 Data description

The hypothesis is that beyond economic and geographical aspects socio-cultural influences come into play and have a not negligible impact upon the economy. These socio-cultural influences, ethnicity and culture, are approximated through the variables geographical and social origin of the persons interviewed. The approach is qualitative looking at the interview data of previous empirical studies on the Indian software industry. Summarizing, all the interview partners are key entrepreneurs, managers or administrative staff. The information provided in the appendices is not uniform, thus the total number of the sample is not the same for all distributions. However, altogether there are more than 200 entries with nearly 200 mentioning also the name of the interview partner, which is crucial to my findings. Usually, Indian names can be ascribed to a certain caste and region of origin which are taken as approximations for culture and ethnicity. The categorization of these names has been accomplished by the use of anthropological literature. The significance of the numbers differs enormously between the Indian data and that from SV indicating an interesting possible development for future research. The studies analyzed are Arora et al. (2001), Bajpai & Shastri (1998), Saxenian (1999) and Tschang (2001). Their research methodologies differ to a certain degree, but there is also some commonality. Unfortunately, one commonality is that none of the studies provide detailed information about how the people interviewed were chosen. But the impression is that they share the methodology employed by Arora et al. (2001) in being not randomly chosen.

Bajpai & Shastri (1998) have conducted 30 interviews with both company and government representatives in India alone. The information given in the appendix covers names and organizations of the persons interviewed. They use the information gathered through the interviews to supplement their case study. The basic intention is the formulation of policy recommendations supported by the industry sentiment.

Saxenian (1999) has conducted 167 interviews with a focus on immigrant entrepreneurs in SV. Therefore 100 interviews with engineers, entrepreneurs, venture capitalists, policy makers and other key actors have taken place in SV, of which 42 with Indians and the rest with Chinese. Moreover, 42 interviews with Indians have been carried out in the three Indian regions of Bangalore, Bombay and Delhi (and 25 in two regions in Taiwan) with local and national policymakers and business representatives. She provides information on name, function, organization and location of the interview partners.

Tschang (2001) uses case studies and secondary data to analyze the state of three types of firms within the Indian software industry: Indian offshore development centers, MNC development centers; and start-ups. The case studies are looking at skills and organizational capabilities of these firms through empirical interviews. He has interviewed 19 people active in the software industry, but the only information regards the function of the interviewees and a distinction between Government and Education, and Firms, but he does neither provide the names nor the location.

The most comprehensive information is found in Arora et al. (2001). After extensive literature research, data collection, a survey with over 100 Indian software firms, and discussions with industry experts, they chose various companies for their interviews. These firms included MNCs, large and small software exporters, and firms focusing on the domestic market and others innovative software producers. They had 94 interviews with people from over 60 organizations in the Indian software industry, of which 70 in India and 24 in the US, at three points of time, between fall 1997 and summer 1999. They provide not only the names of the people interviewed for this project, but also the designation, firm and location. The interviews took place in Bangalore, Bombay and Hyderabad, each twice, plus Delhi, Pune and Madras. Interestingly, the only interviews regarding quality certification issues were in Bangalore and Bombay. Table 6.2 summarizes the different methodologies.

Table 6.2. Methodology of Studies on Indian Software Industry

Study	No. of interviews	Research Methodology	Purpose of interviews
Bajpai/ Shastri (1998)	30	Industry survey; no explicit interview methodology	Supplement for case study
Saxenian (1999)	167	Interviews in SV and 3 Indian cities to balance other primary data sources	Role of immigrants in SV and linkages to India, China
Tschang (2001)	19	Case studies of 3 firm types	Scenarios for organizational strategies
Arora et al. (2001)	94	5 firm types in 6 Indian cities selected after careful research	Industry overview; international linkages; quality and HR aspects

5.2 Results

Almost all studies claim to cover the entire software industry and do not specify a certain regional focus. However, analyzing the interview data of these studies one finds a bias towards South Indian (and, to a lesser extent, West Indian) locations as the major centers of this industry. More than 90% of the interview partners came from firms or authorities in South or West India and more than 50% were from Bangalore and its surrounding state Karnataka. Such a concentration is supported by the number of firms registered with the industry association NASSCOM, which has around 40% of its members coming from South and 25% from West India over the last few years (see table 6.3). This is confirmed by the findings of some researchers (Heeks 1998; D'Costa 2003). But there are also others asserting that Bangalore is not the center of the software industry, rather losing its former status as 'the Silicon Valley of India' (Arora et al. 2001).

Table 6.3. Top locations of Indian software companies (Source: Nasscom)

City	No. of Software company headquarters		
	2000	2002	2003
Bangalore	122	160	182
Chennai	55	72	92
Delhi and surroundings	111	106	182
Hyderabad	64	61	78
Kolkata	25	32	32
Mumbai	131	148	152
Pune	23	48	57
Other	69	73	79
Total	600	700	854

But if one takes a closer look at the names of the interview partners there is another remarkable finding. The findings for the Indian section of the interviews show that almost 70% of the interview partners are *Brahmins*, irrespective of the location within India (see table 6.4). Over the last decades the proportion of Brahmins among the population has been ranging between 4%-6%. Thus even taking into account the limitations of the data, and possible flaws, the discrepancy is quite substantial. Apparently, within India the traditionally assigned occupations are losing their importance.

Table 6.4. Distribution of interview partners according to cultural background

Caste affiliation	Share of interviews in India (in %)
Brahmin	69
Vaishya	19
Ksatriya	7
Other	5

(Own calculations, based on Tschang [2001], Saxenian [1999], Bajpai & Shastri [1998] and Arora *et al.* [2001])

The ethnic background is somewhat less clear with roughly 50% of the people interviewed being from south India and one additional quarter from the otherwise underrepresented Hindi speaking heartland in the Center North. According to Dossani (2002), the share of the South Indian population is only 23,2%, whereas more than 55% come from the North or the East of the country (see table 6.5). Again the composition of the software industry differs enormously from the usual pattern of the Indian society. These results need to be qualified for the small size of the sample. Also, there might be an ex-post selection bias stemming from the concentration of the most successful software firms in the South, overlooking developments taking place in other regions. However, they indicate worthwhile directions for further research.

Table 6.5. Distribution of software professionals according to ethnicity/birthplace

Region	Share of software industry[I]	Share of Immigration to US[II]	Share of national population[II]
South India	49	36,5	23,2
West India	7	29,6	19,6
North India	24	24,1	31,3
East India	8	10,3	25,8
Other	12	-	-

[I] *Own calculations, based on Tschang (2001), Saxenian (1999), Bajpai & Shastri (1998) and Arora et al. (2001)*
[II] *Source: Dossani (2002)*

However, in the context of SV the result is quite different. Only a minor fraction, roughly 30 %, of the people interviewed could be ascribed to a particular caste. On the one hand this is not very significant a result, but on the other hand it supports the findings of Saxenian (1999, et al. 2002) that Indians in SV share a common Indian identity that transcends the boundaries of caste or ethnicity. The ethnic background of SV Indians is somewhat clearer, with one third coming from the Northern Hindi-speaking states. Again, this subset does not exhibit many entries, thus is to be handled with even more care. A possible explanation might be that it is exactly those people to emigrate who do not find accession to the Bangalore cluster being dominated by other groups.[3] There is evidence of non-economic factors determining migration decisions in the context of a socio-culturally embedded setting in three regions of rural India (Gidwani & Sivaramakrishnan 2003).

To summarize, the findings are that the majority of the key people of the Indian software industry are located in South India, are *Brahmins* and come from a South Indian background in terms of ethnicity. These findings are supported by Saxenian et al. (2002) who highlight the importance of the South as a destination for investments and returns to their home country by SV Indians.

5.3 Discussion

Before I would venture into a discussion of the results I should repeat that they need to be interpreted very carefully. The reason is that the data is only covering four samples and sometimes is not entirely consistent. However the strength of the result allows for some provisional interpretations that call for further research into this direction.

The regional distribution seems to be influenced by historical and geographical factors, at least to a certain extent. There are explanations like university-industry linkages with the premier research institutes, the establishment of STPs close to the IITs and the IISc, as well as historical circumstances that led to the initial localizations. The historical factors rest in the early localization of science and technology related research and teaching institutions in Bangalore as an ideal place in terms of climate and infrastructure to conduct scientific research in strategic areas like defense and electronics. Moreover, the five states most prominent in software are those, which are considered to be most reform-oriented.

What is more surprising, however, is the distribution of socio-cultural and ethnic background. There have never in Indian history been so many entrepreneurial and managerial *Brahmins* as are seen in the software industry now, and especially there have been few entrepreneurs from South India (Fromhold-Eisebith 1999; Kapur & Ramamurti 2001).

Generally speaking, *Brahmins* were rather associated with priestly tasks, government jobs, all sorts of administration and landholding (Adams 2001). On the other hand, *Brahmins* as members of the priestly caste were always connected to all sorts of scholarly activities being related to knowledge, learning and teaching, like mathematics, but the *brahminical* education includes other sciences like grammar, geometry and logic (Sen 1997). Hence, there are many disciplines that are very useful for intellectually challenging professions like sciences or research related pharmaceuticals, biotechnology or software. Moreover, the combination of the subjects emphasized by a *brahminical* syllabus seems to be especially apt for software, which requires not only mathematics but also language or grammar. Being handed down from one generation to the next for decades or even centuries would place descendants in a privileged position regarding such professions and, thus, be an example for a regional culture. Eventually, this has been compounded by land ownership and political power. Deshpande (2000) calls a cumulative advantage that the upper castes today are in such a strong position that in order to retain their privilege they do not need the customary inheritance of status anymore. However, a dominant position in administration could have been used in order to assure a more than proportionate share of Brahmins in high schools and universities (Adams 2001). But even if *Brahmin*s have monopolized learning there might be a positive impact on the Indian economy in the 'knowledge age' (Das 2001).

In addition what is unexpected is the relative under-representation of *Vaishyas*, the traditional group of entrepreneurs, although recent studies do not show a significant change in this occupation pattern (Deshpande 2000; Adams 2001). They have always been the entrepreneurial castes of the Hindu population providing economic services like trading, money lending (Rutten 2002). One explanation resides in the attitude of the traditional merchants and trader class towards risk and quick profits. They often prefer the latter and avoid taking risks, thus foregoing higher profits in the longer term (Frederking 2002).

In the same vein, what follows for the ethnic background might simply be an eventual consequence – a path dependent process that resulted in a lock-in in South India. However, as has been argued above, these Southern states exhibit not only a higher appreciation of learning but also a more hospitable climate towards change, both technological and social. Consequently, the higher degree of tertiary education and reform orientation

What remains is the fact that in SV socio-economic factors among Indians do not seem to play a role since a pan-Indian identity overrides sub-national differences. This is a highly interesting direction for further research, since it is the actual transfer of not only technological knowledge but also social and business norms and practices that apparently originates from SV. Thus the question would be if there might occur a change in social relations in India too, at least in the medium to long run?

6. ETHNIC INDIAN TRANSNATIONAL NETWORKS

For developing countries opportunities to participate in a commodity chain based on a global division of labor have existed for a long time. However, such tasks do not leave much of the value added for the developing country, although such a division of labor can be the (necessary) initial step in a process of upgrading developing country firms' capabilities through international cooperation (Lateef 1997). The rise of the SV model with a network of highly specialized companies over the vertically integrated firm of earlier decades gives entrepreneurs the opportunity to venture into niche markets, and outsource a large part of the global value chain to their home country (Saxenian et al. 2002). Moreover, in this case the migration of skilled labor through transnational networks can be beneficial to the developing country. The importance of international networks for the development of the Indian software industry is examined from various perspectives. Firstly, MNCs and their Indian executives, secondly NRI venture capitalists and, thirdly, (non-resident) Indian entrepreneurs. In theory, another category would be the international migration of students, but practically Indian students in the US prefer to stay there after having completed their studies.

The contributions highly skilled Indians made to the rise of SV, either as entrepreneurs or managers of high-technology firms is astonishing. According to Saxenian (1999), one fourth of CEOs in SV is Indian or Chinese. While Chinese are more present in engineering professions, Indians venture more into management and entrepreneurship. For example, in an internet-based survey among foreign-born professionals in high-technology industries in the San Francisco Bay Area, 60% of Indian-born respondents have been involved in founding a company in SV, most of them full-time, as compared to 32 % and 51 % among Mainland Chinese and Taiwanese, respectively (Saxenian et al. 2002). However, these numbers tend to overstate the actual participation in startups, since the survey has been conducted among immigrants from ethnic professional associations, who are plausibly the most active immigrants.

The following sections give an account of the following three channels of transnational networks: MNCs and their Indian executives, NRI venture capitalists, and (non-resident) Indian entrepreneurs. Unfortunately, the information on these different types is neither equally available nor uniform. Whereas there is some qualitative and, more limited quantitative, evidence of MNCs' activities in India, there is only little data on NRI Venture Capitalists and almost only anecdotal evidence on returning Indian entrepreneurs. Evidence on MNCs is provided by the National Association of Software and Service Companies (NASSCOM) and Department of IT and Biotechnology, Govt. of Karnataka websites, and previous field studies (Basant et al. 2001; Patibandla & Petersen 2002). Additional information is taken from company and association websites, especially TIE (Bangalore), which lists biographies of invited speakers at their networking events as examples for successful entrepreneurship. Further information has been compiled from various financial dailies and weeklies, both Indian as well as international. Finally, there is some qualitative evidence from 16 semi-structured interviews with senior executives of small, medium and large Indian companies in Frankfurt conducted in October and November 2002.

6.1 Multinational Companies

In the case of India as in other developing countries, MNCs are a source of technological know-how since they are usually based in technologically advanced economies. There is evidence that MNCs are a critical source for emerging economy firms to enter the global software market (Giarratana et al. 2003). Knowledge spillovers from MNCs occur in various ways. Firstly, they happen through local linkages, viz. in the developing country itself or rather in a sub-national region thereof. For example, if a MNC localizes an R & D center in Bangalore, there are typically backward linkages with indigenous companies in the region depending on the sensitivity of the research undertaken often realized through outsourcing less critical work. In order to supply inputs for a MNC, the local firm ought to have some knowledge about the product. Hence, there must a knowledge transfer from the technologically advanced MNC to the relatively backward local supplier to have some professional and technological proximity. A drawback for developing countries is that many MNCs do not disclose their critical knowledge whether accumulated at home or in an expatriate research lab. Therefore, even in the case of co-location of the MNC and a local company, the kind of knowledge transferred is typically codified and not tacit. A case in which the knowledge transferred is more of a tacit type is through spin-offs (Franco & Filson 2000). Even if they do not consider MNCs in an emerging economy setting explicitly, they offer useful insights for the Indian context. As mentioned above, spin-offs with experience from successful incumbents tend to have a higher probability to survive than those without such experience. Since many start-ups in the Indian software industry come directly or indirectly from SV firms, there is a lot of industry experience.

The set-up of Indian operations by MNCs has typically been triggered by senior executives of Indian origin (Tschang 2001). This is well documented in the case of Nortel Networks (Basant et al. 2001) as well as Texas Instruments (TI), the first MNC to invest in India after early liberalization efforts in 1985, and Hewlett Packard (Patibandla & Petersen 2002). Interestingly, Nortel executives wanted to establish long-term relationships with India and, therefore, asked people they knew in TI and HP, probably also of Indian origin, about their experiences (Basant et al. 2001). Through Nortel's initiative to also enter the Indian market the Indian partner firms benefited a lot, since they were closely interacting on a local level with a global technological leader, producing not only for the global but also for the domestic market. Moreover there are demonstration effects both by Nortel's commitment and the presence of the Indian partners in a strategic alliance.

And, although Nortel tried to minimize the interaction amongst their four Indian partner firms, there are also spillover effects through employee mobility, which is about 25 % in the Indian software industry. Altogether the case of Nortel collaborating with domestic firms is different from MNCs who merely want to profit from an abundant, cheap labor reservoir. Especially knowledge of advanced technologies and business know-how can be best learned in an international firm, since it requires both contact with latest technologies and foreign markets (Tschang 2001). A motivation for such collaboration was the small technology gap between Indian and foreign software firms; also the competency in telecom was crucial which made Bangalore with two important public sector firms suitable (Basant et al. 2001). To summarize, most of the MNCs investments in India have been realized after NRIs were successfully working in the US operations of these companies and reached senior positions. Such positive experience had broad reputation effects, which were then leveraged by the Indian managers many of whom subsequently headed the Indian offices. In Bangalore, for instance, at 71 out of 75 MNCs this was the case (Kapur & McHale 2002).

Another source for spillover originating from MNCs is through international (intra-firm) transfer of personnel. By going to the US or other advanced economies the Indian staff gets exposed to global technological leaders. However, this kind of labor mobility is not only to be found within MNCs but also, maybe much more, at the (in-) famous 'body shops'. These are small to medium intermediary firms specialized in sending qualified software engineers from India to the US on H1-B visas to work on an assigned project at the client's site, quite often hired by Indian companies' US branches (Kapur & McHale 2002). Eventually it has become quite common that programmers returning from the US quit their job and start their own business. In doing so they expose another batch of professionals to the knowledge they obtained abroad, hence initiating a diffusion process (Tschang 2001).

6.2 Ethnic Entrepreneurship

In SV strong ethnic networking among Indians is found to be highly concentrated in one association, The IndUS Entrepreneur (TiE) and, to a lower extent in the Silicon Valley Indian Professional Association (SIPA) (Dossani 2002). Its main purpose is to foster and support entrepreneurship, particularly in the early steps of a start-up through angel investing. The benefits for minorities like SV Indians of sticking to an ethnic network, and how long they last for members before they eventually leave it for the 'mainstream' are analyzed by Dossani (2002) in order to find out more about the sustainability of ethnic networks. This interpretation suggests an ethnic network being merely a response to difficulties faced by immigrants in the labor market, and not posing entry barriers to individuals outside the ethnic target group. It is highly fascinating to discern the composition of these ethnic Indian networks, because these immigrants cluster not within their ethnic, sub-national group but rather share an 'Indian' identity: 'Bengalis, Punjabis, Tamil, and Gujaratis tend to stick together. But in Silicon Valley it seems that the Indian identity has become more powerful than these regional distinctions. [...]. This feeling of community could override religion and caste.' (Saxenian 1999)

This distinction of the SV immigrant community's behavior is insofar important as it differs from traditional immigrant settings like London, where immigrants showed a higher tendency to stay among their co-ethnic people (Frederking 2002). This might stem from the fact that SV is perceived to have a very flexible structure and open culture which is cited among the organizational advantages of SV in its evolution as the dominant high-tech cluster (Saxenian 1994). Tschang (2001) finds a similar openness in terms of labor market flows in India indicating that the SV business culture has already been partly transferred.

It is particularly important for India that this networking transcends the boundaries of SV and goes back to Asia. In their recent survey Saxenian et al. (2002) find that 74 % of Indians plan to start their own business, and 76 % out of that even think of locating it in India; the survey by Dossani (2002) reports 76% for locating a business in India. Interestingly, when asked directly, only 45% of the Indian respondents answered they will probably return home in the near future (Saxenian et al. 2002). Obviously, none of these numbers will necessarily materialize, since they usually include some overstating. But there seems to be an indication of a reversed brain drain with the highest impact yet to come. The immigrant entrepreneurs have quickly adapted to SV business culture, which they hopefully would carry with them. They mention the 'culture and lifestyle in the country of birth' as the most important factor followed by the desire to contribute to economic development. Unfortunately, it is not specified what they mean by 'culture'.

Nevertheless, many SV Indians have already been instrumental in starting a business through counseling or lobbying, or even investing their own money in India (Saxenian et al. 2002), for example through venture capital (Dossani & Kenney 2002). TIE has spread to India through the opening of local chapters; the first one was opened in Bangalore in 1999 signaling the importance of Bangalore as a destination for the Indian entrepreneurs in the US.[4] However, the transnational contacts of this ethnic Indian network display an uneven distribution. Apparently regarding both inward and outward linkages there is a concentration in the South. Interestingly, most NRIs attracted by the opportunities of the software business in India are looking towards Bangalore (28 %), with another 52 % concentrated in four other metropolitan centers in South and West India (Saxenian et al. 2002), thereby reinforcing the agglomerative tendencies; again (Dossani 2002) reports similar figures with 27% for Bangalore and 54% for other South and West India.

With the liberalization of the Indian economy in the early 1990s many of the US-trained Indians were more inclined to return to India, which now offered ample opportunities that did not exist before for these highly qualified professionals (Lateef 1997). An example of the firms established by returning Indian migrants is Satyam Computer. Founded as late as 1987, it is number 4 in India in terms of turnover, much of it software exports. After receiving his higher education (MBA) in the US, Ramalinga Raju returned to India. Having studied and learned business in an environment different from the Indian one, he brought back home not modern technology but rather western business culture. Many other engineers or managers working in American companies experience a different organization of work, usually much more flexible and open, especially in high-tech companies in SV. A major difference is the less hierarchical structure with more freedom and responsibility. Eventually he established a very untypical modern organizational structure at his company modeled after what he had seen in the US.

Another important characteristic of returning NRIs is that they take their personal networks with them. That means, once they are back in India they do not necessarily forego business opportunities with their US-American contacts, on the contrary, these might actually increase. The industry or management experience they gained enables them to become an entrepreneur. The network of contacts they make during their stay abroad often supports this. Actually, one ought to know people and the market abroad to be internationally successful (Tschang 2001). An example for a very successful continuation of such a network is the case of Infosys whose founders have all worked in the US before starting their own company in India (Lateef 1997). Eventually Indian companies set up offices in the US to take advantage of the large (professional) Indian community with know-how on the US market (Tschang 2001). Similarly, what we heard from executives in Frankfurt branches is that Indian firms continuously rotate their labor force in Europe in order to get a larger percentage accustomed to this environment. By working in this climate with European clients, they learn not only project skill but also, more importantly, managing capabilities and dealing with customers culturally different from US-American ones. They are trained through learning-by-doing in an intercultural environment in order to obtain some cultural proximity, beyond the professional and organizational they have while working in a medium to large Indian company, and to avoid misunderstandings based on different cultural contexts (Grote et al. 2002). However, in the Indian case there are pessimistic appraisals due to little institutionalization efforts by the Indian Government and hence an underutilized network potential (cf. Saxenian et al. 2002).

6.3 Transnational Venture Capital

Another mode for NRIs to contribute to the Indian economy is through capital remittances. In fact this is a common observation for many decades now. However, the novelty regarding the software industry is that much of this investment comes via venture capital (VC). Why is VC different from other forms of capital? And why is it particularly important for IT? Since these questions are related to each other, I will deal with them jointly.

Venture capital is different from other forms of investment in that it is risk capital. It is used for seed financing to get firm start-ups going; hence it is closely connected to entrepreneurship, which has been discouraged in India through most of the period after independence. Usually an important characteristic of VC is the high geographic proximity between entrepreneurs and the VC firm (Zook 2002). Since it is one of the most risky investments, banks usually refuse to lend to newly established companies or those in the way of setting up. The risk is even higher when new and unknown technologies, or more generally innovations are involved. Typically this kind of start-up requires substantial investments before the first profits can be obtained; the need for upfront investment is lower in the case of software which is more human capital-intensive. The link between VC and high-tech has been evident from the US and Israel. And, without positing any causation, Mani and Bartzokas (2002) find for India the highest correlation between the two among 9 high-technology exporting Asian countries. In the Indian case 48 % of VC has gone towards the high-tech sector, substantially more than in China, though much less than in other East-Asian countries. The two factors are complementary, for sufficient investment opportunities are necessary for a for a successful VC industry to evolve.

The interesting link to the international networks is the geographical breakdown of VC sources in 1999. In India, 60 % of the funds came from non-Asian sources, third after Vietnam and Hong Kong, but about 50 % more than in China, Indonesia, Singapore and Thailand. However, in absolute terms India lags behind many East-Asian countries both regarding VC investments and sourcing from abroad (Mani & Bartzokas 2002). One example of a successful firm founded and funded through VC by (returned) Indian expatriates is Mindtree (Das 2001). Many other examples of NRI entrepreneur-turned-Venture Capitalists are mentioned in Saxenian (1999) or Dossani & Kenney (2002). Actually some of the experienced entrepreneurs from SV assisted the Securities and Exchange Board of India (SEBI) to draft a white paper for the VC industry in India. Later also the privately organized Indian Venture Capital Association was established in Bangalore. This was a historical event that gave way to a path-dependent evolution of a 'technology-related' VC cluster resembling the US counterparts in SV or Boston. On the other hand Bombay recently attracts a larger number of VC firms that, however, provide much less capital than do the Bangalore ones. The importance for the development of the software industry stems from the fact that much of the capital flowing through these VC funds has been raised in SV. Thus the know-how of high-tech industries the NRI entrepreneurs obtained in the US regarding the financing of such start-up companies has been transferred to the Indian setting, both through the active involvement of retired entrepreneurs and those who became venture capitalists and through counseling government agencies like SEBI (Dossani & Kenney 2002).

Without going into detail, an interesting feature regarding this flow of venture capital should be mentioned, that it has been increasing without the spatial proximity typically seen in the VC industry. It is in this context that the issue of cultural proximity (Grote et al. 2002) assumes greater importance. The question is whether cultural proximity can be a substitute for geographical proximity in the VC industry, too, where the latter is particularly important? [5] Apparently that is the case, the ethnoscape of an 'Indian' tribe providing the basis for the degree of trust necessary for a transnational dispersion of VC.

7. CONCLUSIONS

This paper has looked at the Indian success in the global IT industry from a new perspective. The view taken here suggests that beyond economic and geographic factors there is an important role played by socio-cultural aspects, epitomized by the key actors in the industry and their transnational linkages or networks. This has been approximated through a pair of variables: 'caste' as a proxy for culture and regional origin taken as ethnicity. Two kinds of conclusions follow, one theoretical and one empirical.

Theoretically, the incorporation of a cultural space allows for the analysis of knowledge spillovers through labor mobility over geographical distance. The spatial proximity necessary for the exchange of tacit knowledge through face-to-face contact seems to be substitutable through cultural proximity to be found in ethnic networks, even in a transnational setting. Such networks have been examined in various instances, MNCs, transnational entrepreneurship and venture capital. However, this study has only been a first step in this direction. Therefore, it requires further analysis in order to substantiate the findings and the mechanisms at work in ethnic networks. In particular, it is necessary to further develop the theoretical argument and distinguish between the various channels of transnational networks. Furthermore, other kinds of proximity or spaces could be assessed for similar substitution effects, like organizational proximity through vertical integration can overcome geographical and cultural distance.

Empirically, a key finding of the socio-cultural background of the Indian software industry is that the once dominant group of entrepreneurs has not retained its customary share in business. At least for the situation in India the software industry seems to be dominated by South Indians mostly of *Brahmin* origin, which, in turn, has some additional explanatory power regarding the spatial concentration of this industry. Although the results seem to be very clear I must reiterate that one has to be very careful with interpretation of these results, especially in terms of political interpretations. One implication for policy makers in India and the developing world would be to make education and technological change better accepted among the population. This is not a new result for development policy, especially when looking at East Asia, but its relevance cannot be overemphasized. Another important implication is to create a milieu hospitable for the return of emigrants and actively encourage entrepreneurship.

That the situation is less clear in SV might be explained by the more open regional culture. It can be hypothesized that with the 'brain circulation' of returning SV Indians or through the transnational networks these features will be transferred to the Indian clusters and might further dissolve customary patterns of occupation. With Indians in the SV trying to integrate into the US business mainstream ethnicity in the narrow sense loses its importance, while at the most an identification with an 'Indian culture' remains and probably continues to play an important role in transnational networks. But so far, the geographical origin or ethnicity seems to play a very important role, since most of the flows through the transnational networks are directed towards South India. Hence, this positive feedback process increases the regional concentration of the Indian software industry. This process seems to be already well under way providing in particular Bangalore, and to a lesser extent Hyderabad and Madras, with the competitive advantage for research-intensive industries in a knowledge economy.

NOTES

[1]   For other forms of proximity see the *Cambridge Journal of Economics*, 23 (2), March 1999 (Special Issue on Learning, Proximity and Industrial Performance) or the *Journal of Economic Geography*, 4 (1), January 2004 (Special Issue on Physical and organizational proximity in territorial innovation systems).

[2]   See e.g. the links section of the IIT Alumni Association Canada, http://www.iitalumnicanada.com/iitlinks.htm.

[3]   Thanks are due to Robin Cowan for introducing this issue.

[4]   The internet address of the *Bangalore* chapter is www.tieindia.org.

[5]   This is crucial regarding the operation of transnational VC that will be examined as part of a following research project.

REFERENCES

Adams, J. (2001). Culture and Economic Development in South Asia. *Annals of the American Association of Political and Social Sciences, 573, January*, 152-175.

Agrawal, A, I. Cockburn & J. McHale (2003). *Gone but not forgotten: Labor Flows, Knowledge Spillovers, and enduring Social Capital.* NBER Working Paper 9950.

Akerlof, G. A. (1976). The economics of Caste, of the Rat Race and other woeful tales. *Quarterly Journal of Economics, 90*, 599-617.

Appadurai, A. (1996). *Modernity at Large: Cultural Dimensions of Globalization.* Minneapolis: Univ. of Minnesota Press.

Arora, A. & S. Athreye (2002). The Software Industry and India's Economic Development. *Information Economics and Policy, 14, Issue 2*, 253-273.

Arora, A., V.S. Arunachalam, J. Asundi & R. Fernandes (2001). *The Globalization of software: The Case of the Indian Software Industry.* A Report submitted to the Sloan foundation, Carnegie Mellon.

Bajpai, N. & Shastri, V. (1998). *Software Industry in India: A Case Study.* Discussion Paper No. 667, Harvard Institute for International Development.

Balasubramanyam, V.N. & A. Balasubramanyam (2000). The Software Cluster in Bangalore. In: J.H. Dunning (ed.). *Regions, Globalization, and the Knowledge-Based Economy.* Oxford, Oxford University Press, 349-363.

Ballard, R. (2001). *The impact of Kinship on the Economic Dynamics of Transnational Networks: Reflections on South Asian Developments.* Paper prepared for the Workshop on Transnational Migration, Princeton University, June 29 – July 1.

Banerjee, A.V. & E.Duflo (2000). Reputation Effects and the Limits of Contracting: A Study of the Indian Software Industry. *Quarterly Journal of Economics, August*, 989-1017.

Basant, R., P. Chandra & L. Mytelka (2001). *Inter-Firm Linkages and Development of Capabilities in the Indian Telecom Software Sector.* Working Paper No. 14, East-West Center, Honululu, Hawai.

Das, G. (2001). *India Unbound – The Social and Economic Revolution from Independence to the Global Information Age.* New York: Anchor.

D'Costa, A. (2002). Export Growth and Path Dependence: The Locking-in of Innovations in the Software Industry. *Science, Technology & Society, 7, No. 1*, 13-49.

___ (2003). Uneven and Combined Development: Understanding India's Software Exports. *World Development, 31, No. 1*, 211-226.

Deshpande, A. (2000). Recasting Economic Inequality. *Review of Social Economy, LVIII (3), September*, 381-399.

Dossani, R. (2002). *Chinese and Indian Engineers and their Networks in Silicon Valley.* Asia/Pacific Research Center, Stanford.

___ & M. Kenney (2002). Creating an Environment for Venture Capital in India. *World Development, 30, No. 2*, 227-253.

Evans, P. (1992). Indian Informatics in the 1980s: The Changing Character of State Involvement. *World Development, 20, No. 1*, 1-18.

Franco, A. & D. Filson (2000). *Knowledge Diffusion through Employee Mobility.* Research Department Staff Report 272, Federal Reserve Bank of Minneapolis.

Frederking, L. (2002). Is there an endogenous relationship between culture and economic development? *Journal of Economic Behavior & Organization 48*, 105-26.

Fromhold-Eisebith, M. (1999). Bangalore: A Network Model for Innovation-Oriented Regional Development in NICs? In: E. Malecki & P. Oinas (eds), *Making connections: Technological learning and regional economic change.* Aldershot, U.K.; Brookfield, Vt. and Sydney: Ashgate, 231-260.

Gertler, M. (1997). The Invention of Regional Culture. In: R. Lee & J. Wills (eds.). *Geographies of Economies*, London *et al.*: Arnold, 47-58.

Giarratana, M., U. Pagano & Torrisi, S (2003). *Links between multinational firms and domestic firms: a comparison of software in India, Ireland and Israel.* 9th International Conference of the Regional Studies Association: Reinventing Regions in a Global Economy, Pisa.

Gidwani, V. & K.Sivaramakrishnan (2003). Circular Migration and the Spaces of Cultural Assertion. *Annals of the Association of American Geographers 93(1),* 186-213.

Glaeser, E. (1999). Learning in Cities. *Journal of Urban Economics, 46,* 254-277.

Grote, M., V. Lo & S. Harrschar-Ehrnborg (2002). A Value Chain Approach to Financial Centres – The Case of Frankfurt. *Journal of Economic and Social Geography, 93, No. 4,* 412-423.

Heeks, R. (1998). *The Uneven Profile of Indian Software Exports.* Working Paper No. 3, Institute for Development Policy and Management, Manchester.

Jaffrelot, C. (2002). The subordinate caste revolution. In: A. Ayres & P. Oldenburg (eds.). *India Briefing: Quickening the pace of change.* Armonk, NY: M.E. Sharpe, 121-158.

Kapur, D. & R. Ramamurti (2001). India's emerging competitive advantage in services. *Academy of Management Executive, 15,* No. 2, 20-32.

Kapur, D. & J. McHale (2002). *Sojourns and Software: Internationally Mobile Human Capital and High-Tech Industry Development in India, Ireland, and Israel.* Harvard University: mimeo.

Khadria, B. (2001). Shifting Paradigms of Globalization: The Twenty-first Century Transition towards Generics in Skilled Migration from India. *International Migration, 39 (5),* 45-69.

Klepper, S. (2001). Employee Startups in High-Tech Industries. *Industrial and Corporate Change, 10, No. 3,* 639-674.

Kotkin, J. (1993). *Tribes: How Race, Religion, and Identity Determine Success in the New Global Economy.* New York: Random House.

Lachaier, P. (2003). The socio-cultural world. family, community, 'value-concepts'. In: B. Dorin (ed.). *The Indian Entrepreneur. A sociological profile of businessmen and their practices.* New Delhi: Manohar, 19-64.

Lal, D. (1988). *The Hindu Equilibrium: Cultural Stability and Economic Stagnation.* New York: Oxford University Press.

Lateef, A. (1997). *Linking up with the global economy: A case study of the Bangalore Software Industry.* Discussion paper 96/1997, Geneva: International Institute for Labour Studies.

Lucas, R. (1988). On the Mechanics of Economic Development. *Journal of Monetary Economics 22,* 3-39.

Lundvall, B.-A. (1992). User-Producer Relationships, National Systems of Innovation and Internationalisation. In: Lundvall, B.-A. (ed.). *National Systems of Innovation: Towards a Theory of Innovation and Interactive Learning.* London: Pinter, 45-67.

Malecki, E. & P. Oinas (1999). *Technological Trajectories in Space: From 'National' and 'Regional' to 'Spatial' Innovation Systems.* Regional Science Association, North American Meeting, Montréal.

Mani, S. and Bartzokas, A. (2002). *Institutional Support for Investment in New Technologies: the Role of Venture Capital Institutions in Developing Countries.* Discussion Paper 2002-4, UNU/ Intech.

Patibandla, M. & B. Petersen (2002). Role of Transnational Corporations in the Evolution of a High-Tech Industry: The Case of India's Software Industry, *World Development, 30, No. 9,* 1561-1577.

Pieterse, J. (2003). Social capital and migration, beyond ethnic economies. *Ethnicities, 3(1),* 5-34.

Romer, P. (1990). Endogenous Technological Change. *Journal of Political Economy, 98(5),* 71-101.

Rutten, M. (2002). A Historical and Comparative View on the Study of Indian Entrepreneurship. *Economic Sociology, 3, No. 2 (February),* 3-16.

Saxenian, A. (1994). *Regional Advantage: culture and competition in Silicon Valley and Route 128.* Cambridge (MA): Harvard University Press.

__ (1999). *Silicon Valley's New Immigrant Entrepreneurs*. Public Policy Institute of California.

__, Y. Motoyama & X. Quan (2002). *Local and Global Networks of Immigrant Professionals in Silicon Valley*. Public Policy Institute of California.

Sen, A. (1997). Indian Traditions and the Western Imagination. *Daedalus, 126*, 1-26.

Stein, B. (1999). *Peasant state and society in medieval South India*. New Delhi: Oxford University Press.

Storper, M. & A. Venables (2002). *Buzz: The Economic Force of the City*. DRUID Summer Conference, Copenhagen.

Taeube, F. (2004, *forthcoming*). Culture, Innovation and Economic Development: The Case of the South Indian ICT Clusters. In: S. Mani & H. Romijn (eds.). *Innovation, Learning and Technological Dynamism of Developing Countries*, Tokyo: UNU Press.

Tschang, T. (2001). *The Basic Characteristics of Skills and Organizational Capabilities in the Indian Software Industry*. ADB Working Paper 13, Manila: Asian Development Bank.

U.S. Census (1993). *We the Americans: Asians*. Department of Commerce, Washington, D.C.

Vijayabaskar, M. & G. Krishnaswamy (2003). Understanding Growth Dynamism and its Constraints in High-Tech Clusters in Developing Countries: A Study of Bangalore. In: S. Mani & H. Romijn (eds.). *Innovation, Learning and Technological Dynamism of Developing Countries*, Tokyo: UNU Press.

Xiang, B. (2002). *Ethnic Transnational Middle Classes in formation – A Case Study of Indian Information Technology Professionals*. 52nd Annual Conference of Political Studies Association (UK), University of Aberdeen.

Zook, M. (2002). Grounded Capital: venture financing and the geography of the Internet industry, 1994-2000. *Journal of Economic Geography, 2*, 151-177.

PART II

Scientific knowledge flows and labour mobility

CHAPTER 7

FIRM PLACEMENTS OF NEW PHDS
Implications for Knowledge Transfer

Paula. E. Stephan, Albert J. Sumell

Andrew Young School of Policy Studies, Georgia State University

James D. Adams

Rensselaer Polytechnic Institute and National Bureau of Economic Research

Grant C. Black

School of Business and Economics, Indiana University South Bend

1. INTRODUCTION

PhDs increasingly work in industry. While for some the first industrial job occurs several years after receipt of the degree, for many it occurs upon completion of the PhD. To date we know very little about these initial placements despite the fact that graduate students play a role in transmitting knowledge from the university sector to the industrial sector. This means of knowledge transfer is especially important because it facilitates the movement of tacit knowledge, which is not readily transferable via codified sources.

This paper takes a first step at rectifying this deficiency, using a newly created source of information regarding the placement of new PhDs with firms. Of particular interest is placement of students with a top 200 R&D company or a subsidiary of a top 200 R&D firm, given the important role such firms play in research and development.[1] Data for the paper are drawn from the Survey of Earned Doctorates (SED), administered by Science Resources Statistics (SRS) of the National Science Foundation to all doctoral recipients in the United States. The survey has a response rate of over 98% and thus provides a comprehensive view of the career plans of virtually all U.S. PhD recipients. While the SED has always asked graduates to provide information concerning industrial placements, the identity of the firm has only become available to researchers since 1997 and then only in verbatim form.

We have recently used these verbatim files to code the identity of the firm and determine whether the new PhD was placed at a top 200 R&D firm (or one of its subsidiaries). This paper is exploratory in nature, presenting our initial findings using this unique data.

The paper is organized into four sections. The first section provides an introduction to the role that new PhDs play in knowledge transfer. The second section provides an overview of the SED data, examining characteristics of the firms employing new PhDs, the educational providence of the PhDs working in these firms, and the top 30 destination firms of new hires by SIC classification. The third section focuses on the role of geography by examining the regional location of PhD institutions making industrial placements and then comparing this distribution to the distribution of R&D expenditures. Comparisons are drawn between region of training and region of placement. The top 25 destination cities employing new PhDs in industry are examined with an eye to determining the number who are locally trained as well as the proportion of those trained within the city who stay in the city. The distribution of distances traveled is also investigated. Conclusions are drawn in the last section.

Our research shows that PhDs hired by top R&D firms differ from those hired by other firms; to wit, they are educated at higher-ranked institutions and travel longer distances to accept industrial employment. Our research also informs the discussion concerning the role geography plays in innovation, showing that public knowledge sources, as measured by industrial hires of new PhDs, are concentrated in different geographical centers than university research and development data would suggest. The geography story is also one of a mismatch of training and hiring locations, with significant outflows of PhDs trained in the Midwest and significant inflows of PhDs going to work in the Pacific and Northeast regions of the country.

2. THE ROLE OF NEW PHDS IN KNOWLEDGE TRANSFER

A common theme in the work of Mowery and Rosenberg (1998) is the key role that universities play in fostering innovation in the United States. The transmission mechanism by which knowledge flows from universities to firms is varied, involving formal means, such as publications, and less formal mechanisms, such as discussions between faculty and industrial scientists at professional meetings. Graduate students are one component of the formal means by which knowledge is transferred. Much of a graduate student's training is of a tacit nature, acquired while working in their mentor's lab in graduate school. These new techniques, which cannot be codified, can be transmitted to the R&D labs through the hiring of recently trained scientists and engineers. New hires can also establish and reinforce existing networks between firms and university faculty whereby the firm can acquire more ready access to new knowledge being created in the university.[2]

The recent Carnegie Mellon Survey of R&D labs in manufacturing located in the U.S. asked respondents to rank the importance of ten possible sources of information concerning public knowledge for a recently completed "major" R&D project (Cohen, Nelson and Walsh, 2002). A four-point Likert scale was used. The ten sources included patents, publications/reports, meetings or conferences, informal interaction, recently hired graduates, licenses, cooperative/JVs, contract research, consulting and personal exchange. The findings show that across all industries publications/reports are the dominant means by which R&D facilities obtained knowledge from the public sector. Next in importance are informal information exchange, public meetings or conferences, and consulting. Recently- hired graduates show up in the second cluster, which, in the overall rankings, is lower than the first cluster of sources of public knowledge. In certain industries, however, 30 percent or more of the respondents to the Carnegie Mellon Survey indicate that recently hired graduates played at least a "moderately important" role in knowledge transfer. These industries are: drugs, mineral products, glass, concrete, cement, lime, computers, semiconductors and related equipment and TV/radio. This finding likely relates to the relative importance of tacit knowledge in certain fields and the key role that graduate students play in the transmission of tacit knowledge.[3]

In a related study, Agrawal and Henderson (2002) interviewed 68 engineers at MIT, all of whom had patented and licensed at least one invention, asking them to "estimate the portion of the influence your research has had on industry activities, including research, development, and production" that was transmitted through a number of channels. Consulting headed the list, with a weight of 25.1 percent, followed by publication at 18.5 percent. Recruitment of MIT graduates was a close third at 16.8 percent.

Despite the fact that placements of new PhDs play a role in the university-industry interface, empirical studies of knowledge transfer between the public and private sectors consistently use other measures as proxies for knowledge transfer or the potential of knowledge transfer. Early work by Jaffe (1989), for example, used university research and development expenditures as a proxy for knowledge spillovers as did work by Audretsch and Feldman (1996a, 1996b). More recent work by Feldman and Audretsch (1999), Anselin, Varga, and Acs (1997, 2000), and Black (forthcoming) has followed suit, shifting the analysis, however, from the state to the MSA. Other studies of knowledge transfer between the public and private sectors focus on flows of codified knowledge, using, for example, article counts or patent citations to articles written in the academic sector. Adams (1990) finds the effects of publications to be important to productivity in the manufacturing sector, though in the case of publications coming from basic sciences the lag is approximately 20 years.

Deng, Lev and Narin (1999) report a strong connection between a firm's patent citations to articles written in the academic sector and the firm's market-to-book value. Narin, Hamilton, and Olivastro (1997) show that over 70 percent of papers cited in U.S. industry patents come from public science.

One of the few papers to focus specifically on scientists as a measure of spillovers was written by Audretsch and Stephan (1996) and examined academic scientists affiliated with a biotech company. Because the authors knew the location of both the scientist and the firm, they were able to establish the geographic origins of spillovers embodied in this knowledge transfer process. Their research shows that although proximity matters in establishing formal ties between university-based scientists and companies, its influence is anything but overwhelming. Approximately 70 percent of the links between biotech companies and university-based scientists in their study were non-local. Audretsch and Stephan hypothesize that this is because companies, knowing their needs and having well-established networks, seek specific expertise regardless of the geographic location of the scientist. Firms are then able to interact face to face with these scientists at prearranged times and benefit in this manner from tacit knowledge embodied in the scientists.

Here we extend the Audretsch-Stephan framework, examining recent graduates as a source of knowledge transmission. Although our work is descriptive in nature, we are particularly interested in the extent to which PhD training can inform our understanding of the process by which knowledge is transmitted as well as the role that geography plays in this process.

3. DEPLOYMENT OF NEW PHDS IN INDUSTRY

We begin our analysis by examining characteristics of firms employing new PhDs and then examine the providence of new PhDs working in these firms and thus the source of the knowledge spillovers. We continue by examining the distribution of new PhDs by industrial classification.

We choose to focus on new PhDs because of the key role they play in knowledge transfer and the availability of data permitting such a study. The specific data come from the SED, which asks PhD recipients to "name the organization and geographic location where you will work or study." Although this question has been asked for many years, for those going to industry the name of the firm has only become readily available in verbatim form since 1997.[4] Prior to that date, information concerning the location of the industrial placement was not recorded. As part of a larger project, we have undertaken the not inconsiderable task of coding the verbatim records by firm name and location. Here we present our initial findings from this research.

This approach is not without its limitations. Two are particularly notable. First, a sizeable number of PhD recipients do not have definite plans at the time they complete the Survey of Earned Doctorates and thus do not list a destination. In 1999, for example, approximately 35 percent of scientists and engineers were without definite plans at the time they completed the survey (Sanderson, Dugoni, Hoffer and Myers, 2000). This means that the SED undercounts firm placements, as well as all other types of placements, at time of graduation.[5] Second, initial placements with firms undercount placements of PhDs in the industrial sector. The primary reason for this is the heavy incidence of postdoctoral appointments in academe immediately following receipt of the degree. Some indication of this undercount is given by comparing the percent of PhDs who report working in industry four years after completion of their PhD to the percent of PhDs with definite plans to work in industry at the time of receipt of the PhD.[6] Such a comparison shows that although there is variation by field, approximately three times as many doctorates end up working in industry as those who initially specify a firm. Despite these limitations, and as we have argued above, much can be learned from analyzing firm placement data contained in the Survey of Earned Doctorates.

Table 7.1. Firm Placements of New S&E PhDs: 1997-99

Field	Percent of All PhDs Awarded that Identified a Firm	Percent of Those Identifying a Firm Going to a Top 200 R&D Firm
All S&E fields	14.5%	38.2%
All Engineering	30.7%	44.7%
Agriculture	9.0%	14.9%
Astronomy	7.8%	36.4%
Biology	3.8%	23.2%
Chemistry	18.7%	45.0%
Computer Science	28.4%	50.3%
Earth Science	12.3%	39.7%
Math	12.5%	32.3%
Medicine	5.0%	20.0%
Other*	8.3%	10.7%
Physics	16.1%	33.2%

*Includes PhDs that earned their degree in economics and psychology.

Analysis shows that for the 1997-1999 period, 17,382 PhDs in S&E planned to work in industry; 10,932 recipients identified the specific name of the firm.[7] Table 7.1 presents a summary of our findings, showing (1) those who identified a firm as a percent of all new PhDs in the field and (2) those who identified a top 200 R&D firm or subsidiary[8] of a top 200 firm as a percent of all those who identified a firm.

As indicated in Table 7.1, 14.5 percent of the new PhDs in science and engineering during this period identified a specific firm. Approximately 40 percent of these were going to a top 200 R&D firm. The fields with the highest initial industrial placement were engineering and computer science, followed by chemistry.[9] The field with the lowest percent going to industry was biology. This is not surprising given the extraordinarily high prevalence of academic postdoctoral positions in the life sciences and the relatively small percent of seasoned biologists working in industry. Approximately half of the 763 computer scientists going to industry were headed to a top 200 firm and about 45 percent of the engineers destined for industry were going to a top R&D placement. By way of contrast, only one in seven of those trained in agriculture who had accepted employment in industry was headed to a top R&D firm. These patterns undoubtedly reflect the distribution of firms by R&D status, suggesting, for example, that a large portion of computer and engineering related R&D occurs at top 200 R&D firms.

Table 7.2 examines the field of training of scientists and engineers hired by firms by R&D status. Firms are divided into five categories: top 20 R&D firms, top 21-50, top 51-200 and "other," including firms that engage in little or no R&D. Across the board, engineers make up by far the largest proportion of industrial S&E hires, regardless of R&D classification.

Table 7.2. Field of Training of Firm Placements by R&D Classification: 1997-99

Field	All (n=10,932)	Other Firms (n=(6,754)	Top 51-200 (n=999)	Top 21-50 (n=1,184)	Top 1-20 (n=1,995)
Engineering	49.1%	43.9%	58.3%	57.7%	56.9%
Agriculture	2.8%	3.9%	1.5%	S	0.5%
Biology	5.6%	6.9%	2.9%	2.9%	3.9%
Chemistry	11.1%	9.9%	14.1%	13.4%	12.4%
Computer Sci.	7.0%	5.6%	7.6%	6.2%	11.7%
Earth Sci.	2.3%	2.3%	5.0%	S	0.4%
Math	4.4%	4.8%	2.5%	3.7%	4.3%
Medicine	4.0%	5.2%	1.3%	2.4%	2.3%
Other*	7.8%	11.1%	1.8%	2.6%	2.7%
Physics	6.0%	6.5%	5.0%	5.7%	5.0%
All Fields	100.0%	100.0%	100.0%	100.0%	100.0%

*Includes PhDs that earned their degree in economics, psychology or astronomy.
s=suppressed. Counts of 6 or less not reported at the request of Science Resources Statistics, National Science Foundation. Counts also not displayed if a specific firm contributes half or more of the counts in a cell.

This is partly an artifact of the data, reflecting the exclusion of individuals who take postdoctoral appointments in academe before going to industry. But it is consistent with the fact that engineers make up the largest percent of all seasoned S&E PhD recipients working in industry.[10]

Differences in mix of hires exist based on the R&D classification of the firm, and a Chi-square test that the distributions are the same can be rejected at the .01 level of significance. For example, and perhaps not surprisingly, we see that, compared to the top 200 R&D firms, "other" firms are more likely to hire from the fields of agriculture, biology, and medicine. This reflects the role that small firms play in these fields, especially in biotechnology, a likely employer of new PhDs in agriculture, biology and medicine. By way of contrast, top 200 R&D firms hire a higher proportion of engineers than do "other" firms. We also see that the top R&D firms are more likely to hire computer scientists than are "other" firms and this computer science intensity is even more concentrated among the top 20. The high intensity of computer science hires reflects in part the importance and size of companies doing research that is computer related. To wit, 48 firms (24 percent) of the top 200 are computer related.[11]

Table 7.3 indicates by R&D classification the percent of placements trained at a top-rated doctoral program.[12] We see that firms are reasonably selective in their hiring, recruiting two-thirds of their new PhDs from top-rated programs.

Table 7.3. Firm Placements Trained at Top Rated Doctoral Programs by R&D Classification of Hiring Firm: 1997-99

	All	Other Firms	Top 51-200	Top 21-50	Top 1-20
Top Engineering	72.0%	69.2%	69.9%	75.8%	78.0%
Top Agriculture	80.5%	79.4%	86.7%	90.5%	80.0%
Top Biology	69.8%	68.2%	69.0%	85.3%	73.1%
Top Chemistry	60.8%	54.9%	66.7%	74.8%	64.4%
Top Computer Sci.	66.1%	62.5%	64.5%	69.9%	71.4%
Top Earth Sci.	67.5%	64.5%	62.0%	*s*	*s*
Top Math	55.8%	56.3%	36.0%	50.0%	62.4%
Top Medicine	52.0%	47.1%	76.9%	72.4%	68.9%
Top Other*	46.3%	47.5%	38.9%	35.5%	38.9%
Top Physics	61.9%	57.7%	72.0%	67.2%	72.0%
All S&E	66.2%	62.7%	67.7%	73.6%	73.1%

*Includes PhDs that earned their degree in economics, psychology or astronomy.
s=suppressed. Counts of 6 or less not reported at the request of Science Resources Statistics, National Science Foundation. Counts also not displayed if a specific firm contributes half or more of the counts in a cell.

Moreover, there is a relatively well-defined pecking order of selectivity, which is especially noticeable (and significant) for all S&E fields combined.[13] The distributions, in terms of selectivity, are also significantly different for the field of engineering at the 5 percent level of significance but not for the other fields. If we narrow our focus, however, and compare the top 20 with "other" firms we find that top 20 R&D firms are significantly more selective than are "other" firms in the fields of engineering, chemistry, medicine and physics.[14]

Table 7.4. Industry Classification of Top 30 Firms and Subsidiaries Employing New PhDs: 1997-99

Industry	All	AllEng	Biol	Chem	Comp	Math	Medi	Phys	Other
SIC Code 28: Chemicals, including pharmaceuticals	479	104	70	197	s	61	35	s	s
SIC Code 371: Motor vehicles and motor vehicle parts	190	154	s	s	s	s	s	s	s
SIC Code 372 and 376: Aircraft, including engines and parts and space equipment	241	180	0	s	10	s	s	s	s
SIC Code 737: Computer programming, data processing and prepackaged software	630	361	s	s	166	s	s	44	s
SIC Codes 35 and 36: Industrial machinery, equipment including computers, computer storage devices, communications equipment, and semiconductors	733	569	s	s	54	7	0	57	s
SIC Codes 26, 29, 33, 38, 48, and 99: OTHER	561	338	s	79	s	24	s	35	s
SUM TOP 30	2834	1706	82	326	266	124	43	165	122

s=suppressed. At the request of Science Resources Statistics, National Science Foundation, counts not reported if 6 or less, if reporting permits the inference of counts of 6 or less, or if a specific firm contributes half or more of the count in a cell.
All = All Fields Combined; AllEng = All Engineering; Biol = Biology; Chem = Chemistry; Comp = Computer Science; Math = Mathematics; Medi = Medicine; Phys = Physics and Astronomy; Other = Economics, Psychology, Agriculture and Earth Science.

PhD placements by field are given in Table 7.4 for the top 30 hiring firms, grouped by industrial classification. In accordance with SRS guidelines, all cells contain three or more firms with no firm hiring 50 percent or more of the new PhDs. Together, these 30 firms hire 26 percent of all new PhDs going to industry during the period studied and 68 percent of those working at a top 200 firm.

Among the top 30, the firms making the largest number of hires were located in computer programming, data processing, and prepackaged software (SIC 737); industrial machinery, equipment including computers and computer storage devices (SIC code 35), communications equipment, and semiconductors (SIC 36); chemicals, including pharmaceuticals (SIC 28); motor vehicles and motor vehicle parts (SIC 371); aircraft, including engines and parts, and space equipment (SIC 372, 376) and other.[15]

The top 30 are interesting on several counts. First, although we do not have earlier years to use as a benchmark for comparison, we suspect that the pattern reflects the dominance of IT during the late 1990s. Moreover, the dominance of Firms in these fields clearly affected the rate at which engineers and computer scientists were being hired by industry, relative to other fields. The table also shows that pharmaceuticals and other chemical companies were actively hiring new PhDs, especially in the fields of chemistry, math and biology. When pharmaceuticals are examined by themselves, we find that 15 percent of the hires were in math, undoubtedly reflecting the importance of modeling in drug discovery.

The table also shows that although most industries hire disproportionately from one or two fields, almost all hire from four or more fields. Furthermore, when we display the data at the firm level (not shown), we find the distinction to be even finer, with almost all of the top 30 firms hiring from five or more fields.

The degree to which the PhD hire rate proxies the R&D expenditure rate is investigated by comparing the two rankings. Not surprisingly, we find some differences. For example, 6 of the top 10 hiring firms rank in the top 10 in terms of R&D expenditure and 18 of the top 25 hiring firms are among the top 25 in terms of expenditures.[16] Clearly the PhD hiring variable is related to the R&D expenditure variable but also captures a somewhat different dimension of innovation. This is consistent with work done by Stephan (2002), which demonstrates that human resource data can provide a means of analyzing innovative patterns embedded in firms outside traditional R&D labs.

4. THE ROLE OF GEOGRAPHY

Measures of innovation consistently show extreme geographic concentration. For example, Black (forthcoming) reports patent counts to be highly skewed geographically and Small Business Innovation Research (SBIR) awards to be even more highly skewed. Moreover, patents and SBIR awards are heavily concentrated in the Northeast and California. For example, approximately one-third of all utility patents are issued in five cities. Four of the five are located in either California or the Northeast. (The five, in order of total counts, are New York, San Francisco, Los Angeles, Chicago, and Boston.) SBIR phase II awards are even more heavily concentrated, with approximately one in two being awarded to firms located in San Francisco, Boston, Los Angeles, the District of Columbia and New York.

A common explanation for the geographic concentration of innovation in a small number of coastal cities is that innovative activity flourishes in an environment where external knowledge sources are present. And these sources are themselves geographically concentrated. For example, university R&D expenditures, a common measure of knowledge sources, are heavily concentrated in a handful of states, which, with the exception of Texas, are located in the extreme west or extreme east (California, New York, Texas, Massachusetts and Pennsylvania, in descending order of total R&D expenditures). Taken together, expenditures in these five states constituted 37.9 percent of all university R&D expenditures in 1999 (National Science Foundation, 2001).

The regional distribution of PhD production is given in Table 7.5.[17] Three categories are presented: share of all S&E PhDs produced, share of PhDs produced that are hired by industry, and share hired by top 200 R&D firms. The largest proportion of S&E PhDs is produced in the East North Central region, closely followed by the South Atlantic, Pacific and the Mid Atlantic. Taken together these regions produce approximately two-thirds of all PhDs in the United States. The region with the lowest proportion is the East South Central. A fairly similar, although slightly more regionally concentrated story emerges when we focus on PhDs hired by industry. The same four regions dominate, led again by the East North Central. The distribution is even more concentrated when we look at the regional origins of those destined to work at a top 200 R&D firm. Here we find that 22.2 percent were trained at an East North Central institution. Heading the list is the University of Illinois-Urbana/Champaign, which graduated 177 S&E PhDs during this period going to a top 200 R&D firm. A close second is Purdue University, which graduated 141 PhDs headed to a top 200 firm during the time period. The table also indicates that certain regions have a higher propensity of sending the PhDs they train to industry, with the Mid Atlantic taking the lead. By way of contrast, the East South Central not only trains the smallest share of PhDs but among those trained it has the lowest rate going to industry.

Table 7.5 shows that PhDs destined to work in firms are educated in certain geographic centers often associated with innovation. For example, we find that a fourth of those destined to go to a top 200 R&D firm are educated in New England and the Mid Atlantic (25.3 percent); about one sixth (16.6 percent) are educated in the Pacific states of California, Oregon or Washington. But the headline here is the extraordinarily strong role Midwest institutions (East North Central and West North Central) play, educating 29.2 percent of all top 200 R&D placements. The picture is similar when the focus shifts to "all firms." The New England and Mid Atlantic states again educate a fourth (26.2 percent) of all placements; the Pacific states educate one sixth (16.6 percent) of the hires; the Midwest states educate 26.1 percent.

As indicated earlier, public knowledge sources are often measured in terms of university R&D expenditure data. Column 7 shows the distribution of these expenditures by region. A comparison of column 7 with column 3 indicates that public knowledge sources as measured by human capital flows to industry are concentrated in different geographic regions than are university R&D expenditure data and the differences are statistically significant. For example, the South Atlantic region produces about one-eighth of all PhDs going to a top 200 R&D firm, but accounts for close to one-fifth of all university R&D expenditures. By contrast, the East North Central region trains 22.2 percent of PhDs destined for a top 200 firm but accounts for only 14.4 percent of university R&D expenditures. A Chi-square test indicates that the hypothesis that the PhD distribution is the same as the expenditure distribution can be rejected at the 1 percent level of significance. We also find that the regional distribution of PhD hires by industry, regardless of R&D status (column 2), is statistically different from the distribution of university R&D expenditures, again at the 1 percent level of significance. We conclude that the spatial distribution of knowledge sources embodied in newly minted talent is distributed differently than the distribution of knowledge sources stemming from university research, as measured by university R&D expenditures.

Table 7.5 also presents data on the regional distribution of new PhDs by location of hiring firm. The table tells a striking story of significant outflows from the Midwest and significant inflows to the Pacific and North East regions of the country. Once again, the headline here is the Midwest story, where approximately 30 percent of all PhDs destined to work at a top R&D firm are trained, but which hires only 18.1 percent of PhDs working at a top 200 R&D firm (column 5). By way of contrast, the Pacific region trains 16.6 percent of top 200 R&D hires but actually hires 26.4 percent of them. A Chi-square test shows that the hiring distribution differs from the training distribution at the 1 percent level of significance. This finding is consistent with the research of Audretsch and Stephan (1996) that shows for the case of academic scientists working with biotech firms that proximity matters but its influence is anything but overwhelming.

Earlier work by Stephan (2002) makes the case that R&D expenditure data fail to capture certain dimensions of innovation that can be better measured by human resource data. A comparison of the spatial distribution of new hires (columns 4 and 5) with the spatial distribution of R&D industrial expenditures (column 6) is consistent with this argument, showing that regardless of whether one measures placement for all firms, or only for top 200 R&D firms, the distributions are spatially (and significantly) different. For example, the Mid Atlantic region hires 23.5 percent of PhDs going to a top 200 R&D firms but its regional share of industrial R&D expenditures is but 18.0 percent; likewise, the West South Central hires 11.9 percent of the new PhDs but accounts for only 5.8 percent of all R&D expenditures. While some of these differences are undoubtedly due to our inability to fully measure PhD flows to industry, the differences are provocative and suggest that R&D expenditures alone fail to capture regional differences.

Table 7.5. Regional Distributions: PhD Production,
PhD Placements, and R&D Expenditures, 1997-99

	PRODUCTION			PLACEMENTS		EXPENDITURES	
Region	Region's Share of PhDs in S&E (1)	Region's Share of PhDs Hired by Industry (2)	Region's Share of PhDs Hired by Top 200 Firms (3)	Region's Share of New PhD Industrial Placements (4)	Region's Share of New PhD Placements at Top 200 Firm (5)	Region's Share of Industrial R&D Expenditures* (6)	Region's Share of University R&D Expenditures* (7)
New England	8.2	8.9	7.5	8.8	6.6	9.5	8.2
Mid Atlantic	15.5	17.3	17.8	19.4	23.5	18.0	14.7
East North Central	18.0	19.2	22.2	13.1	13.4	17.2	14.4
West North Central	7.2	6.9	7.0	4.9	4.7	4.1	6.7
South Atlantic	16.5	15.1	14.2	12.4	8.3	9.5	19.0
East South Central	4.2	2.8	1.9	1.9	1.2	1.8	4.4
West South Central	8.8	8.2	8.1	10.2	11.9	5.8	9.3
Mountain	6.0	5.1	4.8	4.6	4.0	6.0	6.3
Pacific	15.7	16.6	16.6	24.6	26.4	28.1	17.0
Sum	100.0	100.0	100.0	100.0	100.0	100.0	100.0
N	74791	11502**	4171	10281	4112	na	na

*Based on 1996 constant dollars for 1997-99. Source: National Science Board (2002).
**11,502 PhDs had definite plans to work in industry. Of these, 10,932 had written a legible firm name on their SED.

Table 7.5 raises the question of the degree to which firms recruit from their own backyard or hire from outside their immediate area. We take a first look at that question here, examining in Table 7.6 the top 25 metropolitan statistical area (MSA) destinations of new PhDs hired by firms. We restrict our analysis to those placements educated by the 110 universities that account for most of the academic research conducted in the United States.[18] We are able to determine location because respondents to the SED are requested to give the city and state location of the firm.[19] This allows us to examine the geographic distribution of the hires and the extent to which the placements are "local," where local is defined as receiving one's PhD at a research university in the same MSA.

The data are striking on several counts. First, 66 percent of the placements educated at research universities go to one of the top 25 MSAs.[20] Second, there is incredible disparity in counts between the top-ranked MSA and all other MSAs, with San Jose employing 2.2 times more scientists and engineers than Boston, the second most popular destination. Third, and related, California has high prevalence in the counts. Six of the top 25 destinations are in California. Combined, these six MSAs capture approximately one-third of those going to a top 25 MSA and slightly more than one-fifth of those going to any MSA. Fourth, as in other measures of innovation, the coasts play a special role; approximately 60 percent of those headed to a top 25 MSA go to a coastal MSA.

As suggested by Table 7.6, the proclivity of firms to hire local talent is not high. Indeed, approximately 75 percent of the top 25 MSA industrial hires from research universities were educated outside the MSA area where the firm is located. The minimal role that local research institutions play in educating the local work force suggests that knowledge spillovers embedded in new hires are less geographically bounded than one might expect. There are several reasons for this, including but not limited to the insufficiency of local supply,[21] the desire to diversify one's knowledge portfolio by hiring from a large number of institutions, and the establishment of traditional networks.

There is also the fact that these outcomes represent the investment decisions of firms and individuals engaged in a job-search process. While the initial contact between firm and scientist in that process may be facilitated by proximity, the investment nature of the decision means that alternatives outside the local area are likely to enter the choice set. In this respect, the finding is reminiscent of that of Audretsch and Stephan that while proximity matters in the case of academics working with biotech companies, it does not matter that much.

This is not to totally dismiss the role that proximity plays. For many MSAs the local research university is often the top supplier of PhDs. Stanford, for example, is the dominant supplier to San Jose, training 175 of the 862 hires trained at a top research university. The University of Minnesota trained 86 of the new hires in the Minneapolis-St. Paul MSA, the University of Texas at Austin trained 67 of the hires in the Austin MSA area and the Georgia Institute of Technology trained 61 of the new PhD hires in Atlanta.

If we cast a larger net and look at those trained at research institutions within the state instead of those trained in the destination MSA, we see a somewhat different story with regard to geography, with slightly over 40 percent being trained in the state or states in which the MSA lies.[22] Especially striking are the cities of Anaheim, Atlanta and Los Angeles, all hiring 60 percent or more of their new PhDs from within the state.

Table 7.6. Top 25 MSA Locations of Industrial Hires from Research Universities: 1997-99

MSA NAME	Num. Hired from Univ.	Num. Hired from Local Univ.	% Hired from Local Univ.	Num. from In-State Univ.	% from In-state Univ.	Num. of PhDs Trained Locally	% of Locally Trained Hired Locally
San Jose, CA	862	175	20.3%	391	45.4%	330	53.0%
Boston, MA	389	145	37.3%	175	45.0%	438	33.1%
New York, NY	346	86	24.9%	120	34.7%	198	43.4%
Los Angeles-Long Beach, CA	287	141	49.1%	177	61.7%	392	36.0%
Portland-Seattle, OR-WA	286	56	19.6%	69	24.1%	139	40.3%
Chicago, IL	275	91	33.1%	114	41.5%	228	39.9%
Washington, DC-MD-VA	273	36	13.2%	95	34.8%	168	21.4%
Newark, NJ	252	s	s	37	14.7%	s	S
Houston, TX	247	30	12.1%	88	35.6%	86	34.9%
Minneapolis-St. Paul, MN-WI	216	86	39.8%	96	44.4%	235	36.6%
San Francisco, CA	210	s	s	117	55.7%	18	33.3%
Dallas, TX	171	s	s	35	20.5%	s	S
Austin, TX	170	67	39.4%	78	45.9%	257	26.1%
Oakland, CA	158	44	27.8%	84	53.2%	271	16.2%
Philadelphia, PA-NJ	155	24	15.5%	38	24.5%	118	20.3%
Detroit, MI	151	34	22.5%	80	53.0%	53	64.2%
Raleigh-Durham, NC	138	52	37.7%	74	53.6%	175	29.7%
San Diego, CA	130	44	33.8%	70	53.8%	81	54.3%
Atlanta, GA	116	66	56.9%	79	68.1%	248	26.6%
Anaheim-Santa Ana, CA	106	18	17.0%	70	66.0%	52	34.6%
Phoenix, AZ	106	35	33.0%	47	44.3%	66	53.0%
Middlesex-Somerset-Hunterdon, NJ	105	21	20.0%	27	25.7%	111	18.9%
Trenton, NJ	99	13	13.1%	21	21.2%	112	11.6%
Pittsburgh, PA	94	42	44.7%	51	54.3%	198	21.2%
Cincinnati, OH-KY-IN	89	25	28.1%	37	41.6%	82	30.5%
SUM Top25/Average	5431	1339	24.7%	2270	41.8%	4064	32.9%
Not Top 25 Receiving MSA	2474	403	16.3%			3535	11.4%
Not To MSA	305	39	12.8%			427	9.1%

s=suppressed. At the request of Science Resources Statistics, National Science Foundation, counts not reported if 6 or less or if a specific firm contributes half or more of a cell count.

By way of contrast, five cities hired fewer than 25 percent of their new PhDs from research institutions within the state.

A first cut at the insufficiency-of-local-supply hypothesis is taken by examining the number of PhDs trained locally at a top 110 program, headed to industry, and the percent of them hired locally (columns 6 and 7). We see that four cities (San Jose, Detroit, San Diego, and Phoenix) hire more than 50 percent of local trainees going to industry. In nine cities, local industry hires fewer than 30 percent of the locally trained going to industry.

Table 7.7 provides added insight concerning the role of geography, giving information on the average distance traveled by new PhDs. as well as the percent that came from within 50 miles away and the percent who came from further than 1000 miles away.[23] The data are arranged by R&D classification as well as by institutional classification in terms of research university status. Significant differences exist between "other" and top 200 R&D firms in terms of distance traveled and the distributions. More than one in three hires of "other" firms are trained within 50 miles of where they go to work, while fewer than one in four of the top 200 R&D hires come from the local area. Likewise, and not surprisingly, we find that three in ten of the top 200 R&D hires traveled more than 1000 miles to take a job, while fewer than one in five of the "other" hires took a job more than 1000 miles away.[24] Average distance also varies.

Table 7.7. Distance between Institution of Training and Firm of Placement

	N	Average	<=50 Miles	>1000 Miles
All Industrial Hires	10018	623.4	31.8%	23.1%
Top 200 R&D Hires	4012	764.9	23.7%	29.8%
"Other" Hires	6006	528.9	37.2%	18.6%
Trained at Top 110 Institution	8210	646.4	30.5%	24.1%
Trained at Non-Top 110 Institution	1808	519.1	37.6%	18.5%
Top 200 Employed from Top 110 Institution	3426	792	22.3%	31.0%
Top 200 Employed from Non-top110 Institution	586	606.5	32.1%	22.4%

Those going to a top 200 firm move on average 765 miles, while those going to non-top 200 R&D firm move 529 miles. Those educated at a research university also take positions located further away than those trained at an institution not ranked in the top 110.[25]

5. CONCLUSION

This paper takes a first look at using human resource data to track knowledge transfers from public science to the private sector. Using data from the Survey of Earned Doctorates, we are able to track the firm placement and MSA destination of S&E PhDs in the late 1990s who specified a firm. Of particular interest are placements at top 200 R&D expenditure firms. Although the database has limitations, especially for fields where the postdoc position is common, the results provide a first look at mapping knowledge flows through the placement of students.

We find that firms hiring new PhDs are heavily concentrated in communication equipment, computers, semiconductors, pharmaceuticals, electronics, and transportation. These findings dovetail reasonably well with the findings of the Carnegie Mellon survey, which reports that recent hires play at least a moderately important role in knowledge transfer in drugs, mineral products, glass, concrete, cement, lime, computers, semiconductors and related equipment, and TV/radio.

Computer scientists and engineers were the most likely to head to industry, and industry was more likely to hire engineers than any other field of training. But we also find that most of the large R&D firms hired across disciplines, rather than focusing on one discipline. This suggests that care must be taken in matching industries with fields of science, a practice that is common in relating innovation to knowledge spillovers.

This research suggests that human resource data provide a different lens for viewing innovation than do traditional measures of innovation, such as industrial R&D expenditures. We find, for example, that the correlation between R&D rank and hiring rank is far from perfect. We also find that the location of PhDs hired by industry follows a different regional distribution than that of industrial R&D expenditures. This is consistent with earlier work of Stephan (2002) that argues that R&D expenditure data fail to capture certain dimensions of innovation that can be better measured by human resource data.

The providence and location of firm hires is of interest. We find, for example, that top R&D firms are more selective in their hiring than are "other" firms, overwhelmingly recruiting talent from programs ranked highly by the most recent National Research Council rankings. We also find that, compared to those headed to "other" firms, individuals hired by top 200 R&D firms are less likely to have been trained within 50 miles of where they are hired and more likely to have been trained more than 1000 miles away. Thus, in terms both of intellectual origins and geographic mobility those destined to work at top research firms differ from those working at lower-ranked R&D firms.

The spatial distribution of the institutions where the industrial hires receive their PhD training is striking, particularly in light of the fact that new PhDs provide one means by which knowledge spills over from universities to firms. Our work shows that public knowledge sources, as measured by human capital flows to industry, are concentrated in different geographic centers than university R&D expenditure data would suggest and the differences are statistically significant. Especially striking is the important role the Midwest plays, educating 30 percent of all S&E PhDs who headed directly to industry during the period 1997-1999 but contributing only 21 percent of university R&D expenditures during the same time interval.

The geography story does not end here. A comparison of region of training with region of employment shows significant outflows from the Midwest and significant inflows to the Pacific and Northeast regions of the country. The geography story continues when we focus on the origins of new PhDs going to the top 25 cities hiring new PhDs working at a firm. Our research shows that 75 percent were trained outside the MSA; 60 percent were trained outside the state. We conclude, in a manner reminiscent of Audretsch and Stephan, that, when the source of knowledge is embodied in scientists and engineers having formal ties with a firm, proximity matters—but it does not matter that much.

States often invest in higher education with the conviction that it stimulates local economic development. And certainly research supports this conviction. Our work, however, casts doubt on the benefits states realize from one piece of this investment, the education of a PhD scientific workforce, and suggests that states capture but a portion of the knowledge spillovers embedded in newly trained PhDs. What we don't investigate here is *why* states are able and willing to educate PhDs who leave after graduation. Are the knowledge spillovers produced while students are in graduate school sufficient to justify the expenditure? Is the halo generated from having a top-rated program beneficial in attracting industry to the state? Or, is what we observe an indication of disequilibrium, which bleak budget prospects may hasten to adjust as state budgets for higher education are slashed?

We would be remiss and naïve not to point out the limitations of the exploratory nature of this study. Heading the list is the limited time period of analysis coupled with the fact that the years (1997-1999) coincide with the boom period in information technology. Clearly there is a need to extend the analysis to later years, as the data become available. A close second is the limitations of the data, which eliminate PhDs who do not specify a firm and which do not include PhDs who eventually go to industry after first taking a postdoc position. Third, the role that geography plays is examined here in a very rudimentary way, focusing on regions and top 25 MSA distributions and making inferences based only on distributions. Much work remains to be done to more fully understand the role that geography plays and the degree to which knowledge sources embedded in firm placements are geographically bounded.

Shortcomings and future research agendas aside, the Survey of Earned Doctorates provides a powerful lens for examining spillovers embedded in the PhD workforce and the role that geography plays in this process. Here we have taken a first step toward demonstrating that private placements provide new insights into public sources of knowledge.

APPENDIX: STATES BY REGION

New England
Connecticut
  Maine
  Massachusetts
  New Hampshire
  Rhode Island
  Vermont

Middle Atlantic
  New Jersey
  New York
  Pennsylvania

East North Central
  Illinois
  Indiana
  Michigan
  Ohio
  Wisconsin

West North Central
  Iowa
  Kansas
  Minnesota
  Missouri
  Nebraska
  North Dakota
  South Dakota

South Atlantic
  Delaware
  District of Columbia
  Florida
  Georgia
  Maryland

East South Central
Alabama
Kentucky
Mississippi
Tennessee

West South Central
Arkansas
Louisiana
Oklahoma
Texas

Mountain
Arizona
Colorado
Idaho
Montana
New Mexico
Nevada
Utah
Wyoming

Pacific
Alaska
California
Hawaii
Oregon
Washington

Virginia
West Virginia
North Carolina
South Carolina

NOTES

Work on this project was supported in part by a grant from the Andrew W. Mellon Foundation. We would like to acknowledge the considerable contribution of Roger Clemmons. Asmaa El-Ganainy worked on creating the MSA codes. Participants at the conference "The Role of Labor Mobility and Informal Networks for Knowledge Transfer" provided useful comments on an earlier draft of this paper, as did two referees and participants at a seminar presented at CRNS-IDEFI. We have also benefited from discussions with Julie Hotchkiss, Robert Moore, and Mary Beth Walker. Bill Amis, as always, provided useful comments on all drafts of this paper. The authors also wish to thank Science Resources Statistics of the National Science Foundation for their data assistance.

[1]   The top 200 R&D firms, ranked in terms of 1998 R&D expenditures, perform 66 percent of all industrial R&D in the United States. Within the top 200 the distribution is extremely skewed. The top firm performs close to 5 percent of all R&D; the 200th firm performs less than .04 percent. We limit our analysis to the top 200 for data manageability and because of their dominant role in R&D.

[2]   Networks have been found to relate to firm performance (Powell, Koput, Smith-Doerr, and Own-Smith, 1998; Zucker and Darby, 1997).

[3]   The second tier ranking of graduates as a means of knowledge transfer reflects in part the fact that graduate students contribute indirectly through networking to several pathways of knowledge transfer (such as informal information exchange, public meetings or conferences, and consulting) that are listed separately on the questionnaire.

[4]   By way of contrast, for those going to academe, the institution of higher education has been coded for many years.

[5]   This undercounting does not affect our conclusions unless those with definite plans differ significantly from those without definite plans. In the future we will investigate this possibility.

[6]   The actual comparison made was between the percent of 1995 PhDs who report working in industry in 1999 (using the Survey of Doctorate Recipients weighted data) and the percent of 1997, 1998, and 1999 PhD placements in industry.

[7]   The 10,932 had signed a contract or made a definite commitment, or were returning to or continuing predoctoral employment.

[8]   Sources such as The Directory of Corporate Affiliations and One Source were used to establish ownership.

[9]   Slightly more than 50 percent of seasoned PhDs in chemistry worked in industry in 1999. By comparison, Table 7.1 shows that only 18.7 percent of new PhD chemists identified a firm. The lower placement rate for new PhD chemists undoubtedly relates to the somewhat common practice in chemistry of taking a postdoctoral position upon receipt of the PhD.

[10] In 1999, engineers constituted 33.5 percent of all S&E PhDs working in industry.

[11] As noted in the introduction, our focus is on the top 200 R&D firms, defined in terms of expenditures. There are other ways to define top R&D firms, such as R&D expenditures per employee. While we have not ranked all firms in such a manner, we have ranked the top 200 R&D expenditure firms on the measure of expenditures per dollar of sales and expenditures per employee. In the distributions generated by these two measures, firms at the top of the distribution hire a smaller proportion of engineers than do firms further down the distribution. By way of contrast, firms that have high R&D expenditures per employee and per dollar of sales hire a larger proportion of computer scientists than do firms lying further down in these distributions.

[12] Top programs are based on the 1992 National Research Council rankings (1995) for all fields except medicine and agriculture. The rankings for the majority of fields are based on the "scholarly quality" scores in the NRC rankings for each relevant program at institutions. For field definitions that were broader than the program definitions in the NRC rankings

(such as biology), we calculated the mean for each rated program applicable to our broader field for each institution. For the fields of medicine and agriculture, we used the 1998 NSF CASPAR data to rank institutions, due to the absence of data for these fields in the NRC rankings. Institutions in these fields were ranked by total federal R&D expenditures at each institution. In the case of biology and medicine, which have a very large number of PhD programs, 75 institutions were included among the top programs. For smaller fields, such as astronomy, top includes the top 25 programs. In most other instances, top refers to the top 50 programs in the field.

[13] Using a Chi-square test, we can reject the hypothesis that the selectivity distributions, across R&D status, are the same at the .01 level of significance in favor of the alternate hypothesis that they are different.

[14] The differences, using a Chi-square test, are significant at the .01 level in all cases except medicine, where the difference is significant at the .05 level.

[15] The SIC patterns extend beyond the top 30 to the top 200 R&D firms. Seventeen percent of the top 200 hires were in SIC 737; 28 percent were in SIC codes 35 and 36; 20 percent were in SIC 28 and 12 percent in SIC codes 371 and 372.

[16] Overall the correlation coefficient between placement rank and expenditure rank for the top 200 firms is .65.

[17] The regions are defined in the appendix. Alaska and Wyoming are excluded due to the absence of R&D data.

[18] These 110 research institutions are the focus of our larger study and are the institutions that ISI includes in its Science Watch database.

[19] We are able to determine the MSA location of 8210 of the 8936 new PhDs indicating a firm who were educated at a top 110 institution.

[20] 3571 of the top 200 R&D placements were educated at one of the 110 institutions.

[21] Recall that we are focusing only on hires from the top 110 research universities and that certain cities do not have a top 110 institution.

[22] MSAs in some instances extend across state lines. In these cases, we report the percent of PhDs trained within the states encompassed by the MSA.

[23] Distance is calculated using the latitude and longitude coordinates for each doctorate's PhD institution and reported city of employment. We first calculate the angle in radians between the two areas on a unit sphere, and convert this distance to miles on a sphere with the size of the earth. We are able to calculate distance for 10,018 of the 10,932 PhDs, with 914 PhDs either reporting an unreadable city location or locating outside the U.S.

[24] Using a Chi-square test, we can reject the hypothesis that the distribution of the top 200 is the same as the distribution of the "other" at the .01 level of significance.

[25] In both instances we can reject, at the .01 level of significance, the hypothesis that the means are the same.

REFERENCES

Adams, J. D. (1990). Fundamental stocks of knowledge and productivity growth. *Journal of Political Economy, 98*, 673-702.

Agrawal, A. and Henderson, R. (2002). Putting patents in context: Exploring knowledge Transfer from MIT. *Management Science 48(1)*, 44-60.

Anselin, L, Varga, A. and Acs, Z. (1997). Local geographic spillovers between university research and high technology innovations. *Journal of Urban Economics, 42*, 422-48.

Anselin, L., Varga, A. and Acs., Z. (2000). Geographic and sectoral characteristics of academic knowledge externalities. *Papers in Regional Science 79(4)*, 435-43.

Audretsch, D. and Feldman, M. (1996a). Innovation clusters and the industry life cycle. *Review of Industrial Organization, 11(2)*, 253-73.

Audretsch, D. and Feldman, M. (1996b). R&D spillovers and the geography of innovation and production. *American Economic Review, 63(3)*, 630-40.

Audretsch, D. and Stephan, P. (1996). Company-Scientist locational links: The case of biotechnology. *American Economic Review, 86(3)*, 641-652.

Black, G. (forthcoming). *The geography of small firm innovation.* New York: Kluwer Academic Publishers.

Cohen, W. Nelson, R. and Walch, J. (2002). Links and impacts: The influence of public research on industrial R&D. *Management Science, 48(1)*, 1-23.

Deng, Z., Lev B. and Narin, F. (1999). Science and technology as predictors of stock performance. *Financial Analysts Journal, 55(3)*, 20-32.

Feldman, M. and Audretsch, D. (1999). Innovation in cities: Science-based diversity, specialization, and localized competition. *European Economic Review, 43*, 409-429.

Jaffe, A. (1989). Real effects of academic research. *American Economic Review, 79(5)*, 957-70.

Mowery, D. and Rosenberg, N. (1998). *Paths of innovation: technological change in 20th-century America.* Cambridge: Cambridge University Press.

Narin, F., Hamilton K. and Olivastro, D. (1997). The increasing linkage between U.S. technology and public science. *Research Policy, 26 (3)*, 317-30.

National Research Council (1995). *Research-Doctorate Programs in the United States: Continuity and Change.* Washington, DC: National Academy Press.

National Research Council (1999). *Measuring the science and engineering enterprise: Priorities for the division of science resources studies.* Washington, DC: National Academy Press.

National Science Board (2002). *Science and engineering indicators—2002.* Arlington, VA: National Science Foundation.

National Science Foundation/Science Resources Statistics (2001). *Academic research and development expenditures: Fiscal year 1999.* Arlington, VA: National Science Foundation.

Powell, W., Koput, K., Smith-Doerr, L. and Owen-Smith, J. (1999). Network position and firm performance: Organizational returns to collaboration in the biotechnology industry. *Research in the Sociology of Organizations, 16*, 129-159.

Sanderson, A., Dugoni, A., Hoffer, T. and Myers, S. (2000). *Doctorate recipients from United States universities: Summary report 1999.* Chicago, IL: National Opinion Research Center.

Stephan, P. (2002). Using human resource data to illuminate innovation and research utilization. In S. Merril and M. McGreary (Eds.). *Using human resource data to track innovation.* Washington, DC: National Academy Press.

Zucker, L. and Darby, M. (1997). The economists' case for biomedical research: Academic scientist-entrepreneurs and commercial success in biotechnology. In: C. Barfield and B. Smith, (Eds.). *The future of biomedical research.* Washington, D.C. American Enterprise Institute for Public Policy Research and The Brookings Institute.

Zucker, L., Darby, M. and Armstrong, J. (1998a). Intellectual capital and the firm: The technology of geographically localized knowledge spillovers. *Economic Inquiry, 36*, 65-86.

Zucker, L., Darby M. and Brewer, M. (1998b.) Intellectual capital and the birth of the U.S. biotechnology enterprise. *American Economic Review, 88(1),* 290-306.

CHAPTER 8

BASIC RESEARCH, LABOUR MOBILITY AND COMPETITIVENESS

Christian Zellner

Max Planck Institute for Research into Economic Systems, Jena

1. INTRODUCTION

Basic scientific research has long been recognised as an important factor determining national innovative capacity going back at least to Vannevar Bush's famous report (Bush 1945). More recently, it has received renewed attention in the literature on national systems of innovation (Edquist and McKelvey 2000). As many of the 20th century's technologies incorporate advances in previous basic science, great emphasis is usually placed on such theoretical insights – seen as the "results" of the research process – in assessing the socio-economic effects of basic research. The relationship between basic research and new products and technologies essentially provides the intellectual underpinning for innovation policy, particularly to the extent that the public funding of basic research as a policy measure is concerned. However, this dominant conceptualisation is unnecessarily restrictive. This chapter shall argue that approaching the link between basic research and the innovation process through the mobility of scientists potentially results in a much broader perception of its socio-economic benefits. The reason for this is that the focus on individuals as repositories of knowledge allows the adoption of a much broader notion of knowledge – and of the economic value of such knowledge – than has so far been the case.

In purely theoretical terms, the challenges in assessing the role of basic research in the innovation process result from its independence from utilitarian objectives, which is its main defining feature. According to the OECD's standard definition, "basic research is experimental or theoretical work undertaken primarily to acquire new knowledge of the underlying foundation of phenomena and observable facts, without any particular application or use in view" (OECD 1994, p. 13). From an empirical perspective, basic research has been shown to be associated with a number of economic effects, often resulting in positive social rates of return (for an overview, see Salter and Martin 2001). This raises the important issue of how and in what sense basic research can be seen as a component within the broader framework of innovation and technology policy. The conclusions that may be drawn in this respect are in important respects contingent on the design and scope of the investigation. These conceptual issues will briefly be commented on in section 2. Subsequently, it will be argued in section 3 that focusing the analysis on individual scientists who migrated from basic research organisations into the commercial sector leads to a more realistic account of the contribution of basic research to technological innovation. New insights from an individualistic approach to knowledge transfer can be gleaned in particular because it allows direct empirical assessments of the embodied knowledge transferred, as will be illustrated with reference to a specific case. The argument is developed in more detail by discussing in an exemplary fashion the case of the German chemical industry in section 4, underlining the fundamental role scientists' mobility plays in enabling technological advance. Some implications of the argument for innovation policy and the promotion of competitiveness are sketched in section 5. Section 6 concludes.

2. LABOUR MOBILITY: SCOPE AND CONCEPTS

The main motivation for studying the mobility of highly trained labour and scientists in particular is to gain a deeper understanding of the links among the various institutional actors in national innovation systems and their interplay in the innovation process. One possible approach is to link the public research sector to various industries by measuring total inward and outward migration (Graversen 2001), accounting for some of the personal and structural factors impacting upon mobility. Naturally, this approach depends on the availability of huge amounts of census data; and it is for that reason that much work in this area has focused on the Nordic countries, where such data is relatively more accessible. A second approach studies labour market prospects for science and engineering PhD graduates from survey data. Many of these studies have focused on the French innovation system (Martinelli 2001, Mangematin 2001, Beltramo *et al* 2001). A third line of research approaches scientists' mobility in the context of individual life-cycles (Audretsch and Stephan 1999), and emphasises the mobility of "star scientists" (Zucker *et al.* 1997). The common feature of these studies is that they consider as the relevant unit of analysis the individual, and that they relate the knowledge transfer to specific instances in individual careers. In other words, the link between two institutional actors is analysed in relation to individual career transitions.

This stands in some contrast with a different approach that essentially focuses on the innovating organisation, and sometimes even on a single innovation, seeking to determine the sources of the knowledge used. The most well-known example for this approach is the study by Gibbons and Johnston (1974), who identified the various pieces of "information" that enabled an innovation, and then tracked the source of that information. Taking as their starting point the insight that "technical change is, to a significant extent, based on the cumulative effect of small incremental innovations" (Gibbons and Johnston 1974, p. 224, and reference cited therein), they characterise industrial R&D as problem-solving. Gibbons and Johnston showed that in this context industrial scientists draw on a variety of sources internal and external to the firm. They found that out of all the information used by problem-solvers, 36 per cent was classified as personal: "developed principally in the course of the 'problem-solver's' experience and education" (*ibid.*, p. 225). Regarding the role of science in the innovations studied, they reported that approximately one-fifth of all information used had its origin in basic research (*ibid.*, p. 230). Finally, they suggested that people with an academic background were much more inclined to draw upon external sources of information, and hence gain access to a wider range of possible solutions (*ibid.*, p. 239).

A similar approach is taken by Faulkner and Senker (1995), who studied the contribution of public sector research to innovation in biotechnology, engineering ceramics and parallel computing, making the distinction into internal and external sources of knowledge and assessing their relative significance. In principle, the same strategy is adopted by a large literature on the evaluation of projects and programmes in the context of technology policy. Although an involvement of a research organisation in such a project raises questions on the extent to which its research can actually be classified as being "basic" in orientation, the conceptual issues are the same. For assessments of the contribution of basic research to innovative capacity, studies that are concerned with the role of public sector research more generally are interesting in so far as most – if not all – basic research is indeed publicly funded.

These points are important in several ways. First of all, an explicit focus on incremental innovation opens the way to a more general perspective of the role played by basic research in the innovation process. However, the result that personal knowledge that is, individuals' embodied knowledge, plays a central role in the innovation process raises the question *how* and *where* such knowledge was acquired. Addressing this question is difficult however within a framework that implies a relatively static perspective in comparison to mobility studies. Specifically, by seeking to determine whether a certain innovation involves "external" knowledge inputs, the personal history of the people involved is left implicit. As can be seen, the link among two institutional actors such as a research organisation and a commercial firm is conceptualised in an entirely different way. While the possibility that a career transition is initiated in the context of a specific innovative project exists, it is not central to the analysis.

Studies focusing on individual mobility and more direct investigations of innovative activities are generally complementary in illuminating the innovation process. With respect to the role of basic research, however, assessments may differ substantially, which is a direct consequence of the scope adopted and temporal perspective taken. The more one shifts emphasis to the processes of (individual) knowledge accumulation, hence taking a dynamic view, the less clear-cut the organisational boundaries tend to become. Especially in the context of sectoral competitiveness, one needs to be careful in drawing conclusions on the overall relevance of basic research. In a static context, potential contributions to a commercial innovation are effectively confined to the provision of solutions for a previously defined technological problem. Indirectly, this restricts the extent to which knowledge can become useful. Especially in the context of basic research, its agenda's independence from practical considerations implies that the scope for a direct transfer of theoretical results is by and large more limited than for applied research. This point is reinforced once one allows for the possibility that scientists originally trained in basic research pursue careers outside the immediate context of technological development in R&D, for example in production or management. For the formulation of policies relating to sectoral competitiveness, these issues are of central importance and deserve further clarification. The following section shall illustrate how studying mobility can give a more systematic assessment of the contribution of basic research to technological change, by allowing the adoption of a broader notion of knowledge. The inherent limits on the transferability of much of the knowledge to be discussed suggest that alternative transfer mechanisms would be rather imperfect substitutes.

3. EMBODIED KNOWLEDGE FROM BASIC RESEARCH

In order to obtain a more systematic account of how basic research contributes to innovation through the knowledge it confers on people, one may first consider the question of why firms may find it advantageous to hire people from basic research organisations. One important factor is of course that, for a variety of reasons, firms might find it advantageous to do basic research themselves (Rosenberg 1990, Cohen and Levinthal 1990, Pavitt 1991). Rosenberg has suggested that despite the serious problems faced by firms seeking to appropriate the returns on their basic research, factors such as potential first-mover advantages, the presence of complementary assets allowing the exploitation of unexpected results, and a variety of feedbacks between basic and applied research might increase the firms' willingness to privately fund basic research (Rosenberg 1990).

One special aspect of firms' motivation to engage in research that is not directly problem-oriented is highlighted by Cohen and Levinthal's (1990) famous argument that internal research activity plays a vital role in enhancing the "absorptive capacity" required to identify and incorporate relevant knowledge produced elsewhere in the innovation system. While it is somewhat self-evident that firms doing basic research will probably prefer hiring people with a scientific training in the relevant field, the contention here is that embodied knowledge from basic research is useful *beyond* that, extending to applied research, product and process development as well as activities outside R&D departments. In this sense, the concern here is much broader than establishing a correspondence between public sector and private sector research. Rather than the public-private distinction, what is relevant here is the epistemic relationship of basic research to other kinds of activity.

A study by Martin and Irvine (1981) investigates the benefits flowing from large -scale projects in the field of radioastronomy. Whereas they found it difficult to identify technological advances directly associated with the research projects, they pointed to the knowledge acquired in the process by the PhDs involved. They found that much of the knowledge acquired in radioastronomy research was relevant to subsequent jobs in industry, including knowledge specific to radioastronomy. Among the activities in the commercial sector, for example, were the construction of antennae and electronics equipment in the telecommunications industry, defense work, computing, the separation of weak signals from background noise in areas such as medical physics, satellite mapping and automatic fingerprint recognition (Martin and Irvine 1981, p. 210). Hence, the authors showed that an important part of the economic contribution lies in the knowledge and competencies acquired by those involved in basic research, as reflected in their subsequent career patterns.

The central implication of this result and other studies in a similar spirit is that it underscores the need for adopting a notion of basic research knowledge that systematically goes beyond the "results" of the research process. In particular, one must explicitly account for those aspects of knowledge that are instrumental in producing these results, and test them for their relevance in a commercial context. In a study among scientists who had formerly been employed by the Max Planck Society (Germany's main non-university organisation for basic research) and subsequently moved to the commercial sector, the various elements of the knowledge transferred were investigated (Zellner 2003). In this study, hypotheses on the relative significance of different knowledge elements for performance in a commercial environment were derived and statistically tested, based on the classification of knowledge presented in Table 8.1.

As can be seen, in the classification the actual "result" or product of the research process, namely specific propositional knowledge, represents but one aspect of basic research. Importantly, the different types of knowledge appear to lend themselves to differing degrees to codification, suggesting that their successful application in the research process in fact depends on their accumulation by individual scientists, who might later transfer them into other activities. The hypotheses sought to specify in more detail how basic research leads to economic effects in the commercial sector of the innovation system and were tested with the data obtained from 214 former scientists in different industries. They were asked to rate the importance of each one of the six elements of knowledge on a scale ranging from 1 (unimportant) to 6 (very important), judged from the perspective of their current job.

Table 8.1. A classification of the knowledge components of basic research

	NON-SPECIFIC KNOWLEDGE	SPECIFIC KNOWLEDGE
Scientific Skills	analytical skills for the recognition, formulation and solution of complex problems	methodological knowledge about experimental procedures and research techniques
Propositional Knowledge	broad, general knowledge of and familiarity with the discipline	propositional knowledge from current research
Technicalities	application of information technology and data processing, including data analysis, the design of simulations and programming	knowledge about and experience with physical instrumentation and laboratory equipment

The main result of the statistical analysis is that non-specific knowledge was rated more important than specific knowledge. This result holds for scientific skills and propositional knowledge as well as technicalities. In other words, the knowledge related specifically to the research questions the scientists worked on while employed by the Max Planck Society are not the most important elements transferred into the private sector. Rather, former scientists indicated that they primarily draw upon their acquired analytical skills and problem-solving capacity, informed by a broad familiarity with their respective discipline. Given the *a priori* isolation from utilitarian considerations under which basic research is conducted, this is indeed what one would expect.

A second important result of the study concerns the relative valuation of scientific skills and propositional knowledge. While theoretical arguments from the literature on science and innovation suggest that the set of skills scientists acquire during the research process may not only be important in the context of basic research, but beyond that, can also be an important input into other types of (search) activities, it was suggested above that the results of the research process have received by far the most attention in innovation studies. The results show that scientific skills are indeed rated more important than propositional knowledge both for the categories of knowledge classified as specific as well as for the non-specific knowledge categories. This indicates that methodological knowledge carries a higher potential for the creation of economic value in areas other than basic research.

Finally, the relative importance of the knowledge categories in Table 8.1 was analysed for different functions scientists take up in the destination sector. It turns out that a large share of the scientists moving into industry started their careers in the companies' research and development (R&D) departments. As discussed, employing scientists for R&D seems to have several motives. Most importantly, it brings people into a firm who have a background in structuring and solving a diverse range of problems. On the other hand, the continuous recruitment of scientists is a mechanism that allows the firm to systematically test and evaluate the potential of the latest extra-mural research with respect to its technological strategies. This potential arises from the fact that within a short time frame scientists are exposed to both "worlds" and therefore have a substantial advantage in assessing potential implications of the basic research currently conducted in public research organisations from a commercial point of view.

In the light of these considerations the study also showed that specific knowledge (i.e. the knowledge elements on the right-hand side of Table 8.1) is valued more highly by scientists in R&D, than by those in other functions. Therefore, it may be inferred that the employment of scientists from basic research organisations is an important way for firms to gain access to the latest methods, techniques and scientific insights. Naturally, it is of particular significance for firms in the so-called "science-based" industries.

If these insights are related to Gibbons and Johnston's observation that much innovative knowledge was personal, and "developed principally in the course of the 'problem-solver's' experience and education" (Gibbons and Johnston 1974, p. 225), the complementary relationship between the two approaches contrasted in section 2 is further underlined. Interestingly, once one explicitly accounts for the scientists' embodied knowledge, the contribution of basic research cannot anymore be exclusively classified as "external." In fact, to the extent the knowledge is embodied and used by the people employed by the innovating organisation, the effects of basic research – originally carried out elsewhere in the innovation system – are internalised through mobility. In this sense, a strong point can be made that scientists' mobility as a knowledge transfer mechanism operates on a more fundamental level than other types of mechanisms. From a dynamic perspective, a firm's ability to develop and maintain a highly qualified human capital base determines the extent to which it can identify and access other external sources of knowledge.

4. EMBODIED KNOWLEDGE TRANSFER IN THE GERMAN CHEMICAL INDUSTRY

After the preceding discussion of labour mobility from the perspective of the scientists involved, the argument can now be taken further by turning to the "demand" side – that is, to the users of the new knowledge. As the different implications of the conceptual approaches discussed above occur at the sectoral level, this section sketches in an exemplary fashion some of the relevant features of the German chemical industry, hence providing the some additional background to the discussion. The chemical industry's relationship to public science, and to basic research in particular, has a long history in Germany (Murmann 2003) and is unique in many respects in its present form. However, since it is not the objective of this section to conduct a comparative analysis, it should be noted that the structures and mechanisms analysed below could be quite different in other destination sectors.

Since the chemical industry is usually classified among science-based industries, it can be assumed to have close links to research institutions in the national innovation system, including those in which basic research is conducted. This section will show that from the point of view of industry, the most immediate benefit of basic research organisations is the provision of a continuous flow of highly trained scientists into industry, as this enables firms to maintain their innovative capacity. Beyond this, scientists constitute the most important mechanism for accessing new knowledge, including research findings and discoveries.

The migration of scientists and the significance of the effects associated with migration, must be viewed against the institutional background of the scientific labour market, since the set of career opportunities faced by scientists largely derives from the dynamics of the labour market, including the academic labour market. According to the OECD, in 1990 there were 16,000 researchers, scientists and engineers[1] active in the German chemical industry in chemical products R&D (OECD 1999). Since 1990, this number has declined steadily, falling to under 10,000 in 1997, according to the VCI, the association of the German chemical industry.

As regards the annual number of chemistry PhDs, the Society of German Chemists (GdCh) reports that from 1992 through 2000 the German innovation system produced more than 2,000 chemistry PhDs annually. This number has now started declining dramatically, and it is estimated that it will be about 700 in 2004.[2] This substantial time lag in the supply side's reaction to deteriorating employment conditions appears to be one of the main features of scientific labour markets (Freeman 1971, Ehrenberg 1992). In this sense, the cause of the decline in employment is partly related to the recession of the early 1990s. It may require significant adjustment periods for the number of graduates to stabilise after a drop in numbers resulting from temporary downturns. In other words, when demand for scientists picks up, the annual number of graduates may be very low. The time lag until the supply response has an impact could exceed eight years, if the time to acquire a PhD is added to the period spent on the first degree. This was exactly what happened after the recession of the early 1990s, and is currently felt in dramatically declining numbers of new chemistry PhDs.

As for the professional destinations of PhD -chemists, in 2001 about 40 per cent went to the chemical and pharmaceutical industry, approximately 16 per cent into other parts of the private sector, around 6 per cent went to (or stayed at) research institutes or universities, 14 per cent went abroad, and another 12 per cent took a post-doctoral position in Germany.[3] Thus, more than half of all PhDs move into the commercial sector, including some of the post-docs returning from abroad. Considering the sharp drop in annual numbers of PhD -chemists from 2,000 to 700, there will certainly be serious implications for the chemical industry and the "war for talents" in coming years.

These labour market developments are important to consider, in so far as they underlie the perceived scarcity of embodied scientific knowledge available in the innovation system. Moreover, they will have an impact on firms' overall knowledge -sourcing strategies and recruitment practices. The availability of highly trained labour therefore determines the extent, quality and success of R&D work in the commercial sector. In this sense, embodied knowledge transfer via migration is a precondition for other research-related activities – and this is why the broad trends sketched above could in future pose serious constraints on innovativeness in the chemical industry, and / or force firms to relocate their research activities. These constraints were summarised by Professor Marcinowski, of the BASF AG Executive Board, who said that, "researching and developing first of all means qualified heads and hands" (Max-Planck-Forum 1/99, p. 144, my translation). Other industry representatives at the Ringberg Symposium "Wirtschaft und Wissenschaft – Eine Allianz mit Zukunft in Deutschland?" ("Economy and Science – An Alliance for the Future in Germany?") strongly subscribed to this view.

Professor Offermanns, of the Degussa Hüls AG Executive Board, pointed to the "technologies" of basic research, arguing that "with increasingly sophisticated methods, basic research penetrates areas hidden from direct cognition" (Max-Planck-Forum 1/99, p. 105, my translation), with the knowledge thus gained providing the basis for future innovations. As regards industrial access to this knowledge, Offermanns noted that "knowledge transfer especially occurs through 'heads,' through the influx of well-trained and motivated young colleagues, for example" (*ibid.*, p. 107, my translation).

Professor Stetter at BAYER AG takes the argument further by relating the importance of migration to other forms of transfer. In a speech at the Wirtschaftstag Japan[4] (May 24th, 2002) he suggested that

> "While exact quantification is difficult, I am convinced that the lion's share of knowledge and know-how from basic research finds its way into industry via informal contacts and primarily through the acquisition of graduates and employees. Today, the route via patents and spin-offs is still secondary, notwithstanding public and political perceptions." (My translation)

As indicated before, migration not only affects innovativeness because of the transfer of the embodied knowledge associated with it, but also because migrating scientists transfer their contacts and professional networks into the firm. At the Ringberg Symposium Professor Quadbeck-Seeger, former member of the Executive Board of BASF AG, commented on the importance of networks spanning across institutional boundaries, suggesting that "cooperations are nearly always initiated on the level of the individual researcher" (Max-Planck-Forum 1/99, p. 329, my translation).[5] This supports the contention that scientists' mobility in many respects underlies other, more formalised ways of transferring knowledge (Zellner and Fornahl 2002).

Where previously identified external knowledge is deemed necessary for the success of a specific project, or where strategic decisions are made in the firm to move into newly emerging fields, directly approaching experts in the academic sphere and convincing them to migrate is of course an option. However, this mechanism appears to be much less widely used. Indeed, it may be speculated whether, after a certain age, the cultural differences between the academic and the industrial world become a real barrier to migration, and the risk associated with integration increases. At the same time, it can also be argued that in cases where expertise is sought in a very specific field, other mechanisms such as formal collaborations, common start-up activities or the co-financing of graduate students may simply be more viable.

Concerning one of the most central issues in the area of recruitment, namely how firms learn about where and whom to recruit, it is important to note the informal nature of many of the links (Granovetter 1974) with non-commercial spheres in the innovation system. While probably very difficult to test empirically on a large scale, it is likely that underlying firms' recruitment efforts are complex professional networks and informal contacts. A particular institution that deserves mention in the context of the German chemical industry is the Fonds der Chemischen Industrie (Chemical Industry Fund), through which members of the VCI (chemical industry association) support independent scientific research in chemistry and related areas. The chemical industry often holds up these financial contributions as proof of its commitment to basic research. In 2001, EUR 8 million were made available to scientists in public research institutions, with plans to spend the same amount in 2002 (VCI Annual Report 2001, p. 42). Contrary to what narrow utilitarian arguments may suggest, this budget is allocated primarily on the basis of quality assessments, rather than considerations of relevance. For example, in 2003 the fund will assess the research performance of more than 3,500 scientists in order to decide whom to support and to what extent (*ibid.*).

This industrial support for extra-mural basic research and the accompanying quality assessments also have a very practical dimension, however. Associated with these specific institutions is a range of informal communication channels that allow firms quite detailed insights into the research activities of working groups ("Arbeitskreise"). Presence on common platforms for professional exchange is virtually a precondition for establishing personal contacts and obtaining information about promising graduate students who might later move into industry.

To sum up, this institutional arrangement demonstrates a commitment to basic research as key determinant of sectoral competitiveness, in large parts because it ensures the identification of and access to scientific talent. This refers not only to the possibility of recruitment, but also to the identification of potential collaborations through personal contacts. In order to advance understanding of the structures and processes underlying knowledge transfer, it would be worthwhile pursuing this theme further, trying in particular to overcome the empirical obstacles one is likely to encounter in this kind of exercise. In particular, it would be interesting to study whether similar phenomena can be observed in other industries.

5. BASIC RESEARCH AND INNOVATION POLICY

The dynamic perspective on the individual accumulation of scientific knowledge and on the knowledge transfer associated with mobility results in the contention that basic research has substantial effects on commercial firms' innovative capacity. These effects go far beyond the provision of external expertise to innovating firms in certain instances of their R&D efforts, and are indeed of a more enabling and potential-creating nature. While the previous section discussed in some detail a specific case where this broader function is recognised and promoted by industry, the more general empirical evidence on commercial value of embodied knowledge discussed in section 3 strongly suggests that this phenomenon extends to other industries as well.

Implicitly, this questions the validity of not uncommon calls for making basic research more "relevant." Probably the most interesting aspect of this is that it is not always entirely clear whose interests are served by this search for greater usefulness. Obviously, the economic effects of applied collaborative research efforts are more immediately visible and thus may lend justification to policy initiatives. Heribert Offermanns, on the Board of Directors at Degussa and Director of the Fonds der chemischen Industrie (Chemical Industry Fund), noted, however, that while relevance is desirable, its promotion is dangerous as it can materialise only *ex post* (Max Planck Forum 1/99, p. 114). This cautious stance on the quest for greater relevance reflects the widespread awareness of the socio-economic function of basic research, and a general commitment to the institutional arrangement it represents. For the chemical industry more generally, the VCI takes a very clear position on this and considers the strengthening of high-quality basic research in public research institutions as one of the pillars of innovative success.[6]

While the question remains whether and in how far this can be extended to other industries, there are indications that industrialists appreciate the value of autonomous agenda setting in basic research (see, e.g., Casimir 1971/1972). As observed by Pavitt, it is generally not clear why private industry should want basic research to become more relevant, as "many of those managers in fact fully understand the benefits of publicly funded basic research activities complementary to their own applied research and development activities" (Pavitt 2001, p. 769). Given the great importance of this question to science and technology policy, it is surprising that it has received so little attention.

Behind the question of "relevance" are of course a number of issues that relate to the potential for promoting sectoral competitiveness by (publicly) supporting basic research. Due to the special role played by basic research in the systemic division of labour in generating new knowledge, the main question seems to be whether funding decisions should be contingent on research agendas, and the variety of research programmes that should be funded. With respect to the European Union's science and technology policy, Pavitt argued that "extensive attention to priority-setting amongst scientific and technological fields on the basis of predicted practical relevance should be avoided," in part because "our ability to understand the present and to predict successful future applications, is very limited" (Pavitt 1998, p. 565). He goes on to suggest that "in detail, prediction will often be wrong, and in broad scope it will be obvious" (*ibid.*). One alternative could be the more widespread use of quality assessments for the allocation of public research funding, as practised by the Chemical Industry Fund in the private sector. For both public and private decision makers, this entails the question of the relevant units to be supported, such as networks of individuals, departments or research organisations.

Generally, public funding can be allocated to research organisations ("institutional funding") or to individual projects and programmes. While this distinction does not coincide with the distinction between basic and applied research, project-based funding tends to figure more strongly in applied research and development. With respect to the complex interplay among European and national innovation policies, according to Pavitt "the budgetary and other pressures on national member-governments to increase the apparent (but not real) relevance of academic research" means that, "EU programmes could usefully play a countervailing role, similarly to many private foundations, in supporting more speculative basic research programmes and networks, especially at the boundaries amongst disciplines and institutions (including business firms)" (Pavitt 1998, p. 565).[7]

With respect to the balance of basic versus applied research funding, there is a further aspect to the finding that the public funding of basic research results in the individual accumulation of commercially valuable knowledge. If research support is entirely evaluated from the perspective of its effects on scientific human capital, policy makers are faced with the question of how individual knowledge accumulation can be encouraged most efficiently in terms of the resources required. Comparing what scientists are paid under a publicly supported applied R&D project in industry to PhD- students' and post-doctoral earnings in public basic research organisations, there is some reason to believe that the latter is the more cost-effective option. This is due to the fact that the reward system of "open science" (Dasgupta and David 1994) induces young scientists to do research and accumulate knowledge through a set of incentives among which the pecuniary ones may not be central. In the limit, one could even interpret the period that is spent working towards a PhD and post-doctoral employment as pure investment in one's human capital (Dasgupta and David 1994, p. 512), motivated by the prospect of future returns.

This argument could be assessed against the background of systematic calculations of the turnover rates from various research organisations into commercial and non-commercial destination sectors. Schmoch *et al.* (2000) show, for example, that while migration into the commercial sector is higher in universities and applied research institutions (p. 61), former Max Planck scientists have a higher probability of going into R&D (p. 63). Additional empirical work on embodied knowledge transfer along the lines laid out in section 3 could compare basic to applied research in terms of the knowledge created. Estimates of costs, turnover rates and the value of embodied knowledge should then be considered as important elements of the empirical foundation for innovation policy. Along with projections of the future supply of and demand for scientists, they should inform the design of policy measures that address the dynamic coordination failures on scientific labour markets.

One must not forget, however, that systemic mobility patterns are never exclusively driven by the knowledge people embody, but are socially and politically embedded, implying that the resulting patterns might be quite idiosyncratic across different innovation systems. In this context, effects of the social security system on the organisation of scientific careers and industrial careers are of particular interest, not only with respect to the timing of migration, but also to its direction. This chapter's argument suggests that comprehensive accounts of knowledge transfer in innovation systems should incorporate sequential regularities observed in individual careers, hence providing a more adequate basis for innovation policy.

6. CONCLUSIONS

Approaching basic research from the perspective of scientists' mobility sheds new light on its role in the innovation process and its wider socio-economic significance. Foremost, it draws attention to a type of beneficial effect that tends to be underemphasized in the innovation literature, where attention has been traditionally devoted primarily to those mechanisms of knowledge transfer that rely on some form of codification, and to the foundation of start-up companies. From a more dynamic perspective, the training and mobility of scientists was shown to be the most fundamental instance of knowledge transfer, in the sense that it directly contributes to creating the potential for technological problem -solving. It is crucial to note that the relevance in a commercial context of the knowledge embodied is not inconsistent with the relative isolation of basic research from utilitarian concerns. While historical studies suggest that theoretical advances often take a long time to become incorporated into new products and / or technological advance, the instrumental nature of much of the knowledge discussed leads to a more direct link between basic research organisations and firms.

ACKNOWLEDGEMENTS

I would like to thank Dirk Fornahl for helpful comments and discussions. The usual disclaimer applies.

NOTES

[1] Full-time equivalent.
[2] http://www.gdch.de/arbeitsv/gdch77.pdf ; accessed 25.11.02.
[3] http://www.gdch.de/arbeitsv/gdch55.pdf ; accessed 25.11.02.

⁴ At the NRW Forum Kultur und Wirtschaft (North-Rhine-Westfalia Forum for Culture and Economics).

⁵ This point is indirectly supported by studies suggesting that transfer-offices established at universities might by themselves not be sufficient to ensure effective knowledge transfer (Krücken 2003). Krücken finds that "personalised modes of interaction are a prerequisite for the effective pursuit of transfer between universities and industry" and that transfer offices "cannot substitute for direct contacts between transfer partners" (Krücken 2003, p. 31).

⁶ VCI-Positionen zur staatlichen Förderung von Forschung und Entwicklung (VCI-Positions on the Public Support of Research and Development) http://www.vci.de/start.asp?bhcp=1; accessed 25.11.02.

⁷ There are currently indications that the direct support for basic research will be given greater prominence under the EU's 7th Framework Programme (see, for example, Communication from the Commission: Europe and Basic Research, Brussels, 14.1.2004).

REFERENCES

Audretsch, D.B. and P.E. Stephan (1999). Knowledge Spillovers in Biotechnology: Sources and Incentives. *Journal of Evolutionary Economics, 9*, 97-107

Beltramo, J.P., J.J. Paul and C. Perret (2001). The Recruitment of Researchers and the Organization of Scientific Activity in Industry. *International Journal of Technology Management 22 (7/8)*, 811-834

Bush, V. (1945) (reprint 1960). *Science, The Endless Frontier. A Report to the President.* National Science Foundation: Washington, D.C.

Casimir, H.B.G. (1971/1972). Industries and Academic Freedom. *Research Policy, 1, 3-8.*

Cohen, W.M. and D.A. Levinthal (1990). Innovation and Learning: The Two Faces of R&D. *The Economic Journal 99*, 569-596.

Dasgupta, P. and P.A. David (1994). Toward a New Economics of Science. *Research Policy, 23*, 487-521.

Edquist, C. and M. McKelvey (eds.) (2000). *Systems of Innovation: Growth, Competitiveness and Employment.* Volume I. Edward Elgar Publishing: Cheltenham.

Ehrenberg, R.G. (1992). The Flow of New Doctorates. *Journal of Economic Literature, Vol. XXX*, 830-875.

Faulkner, W. and J. Senker (1995). *Knowledge Frontiers.* Clarendon Press: Oxford.

Freeman, R.B. (1971) *The Market for College-Trained Manpower. A Study in the Economics of Career Choice.* Harvard University Press: Cambridge, Massachusetts.

Gibbons, M. and R. Johnston (1974). The Roles of Science in Technological Innovation. *Research Policy, 3,* 220-242.

Granovetter, M. (1974). *Getting a Job.* Harvard University Press: Cambridge, M.A.

Graversen, E.K. (2001). Human Capital Mobility Into and Out of Sectors in the Nordic Countries. In: OECD (2001) *Innovative People – Mobility of Skilled Personnel in National Innovation Systems.* (OECD Science and Innovation) OECD Publications: Paris

Kruecken, G. (2003). Mission Impossible? Institutional Barriers to the Diffusion of the 'Third Academic Mission' at German Universities. *International Journal of Technology Management, 25 (1/2),* 18-33.

Mangematin, V. (2000). PhD Job Market: Professional Trajectories and Incentives During the PhD. *Research Policy, 29,* 741-756.

Martin, B.R. and J. Irvine (1981). Spin-Off From Basic Science: The Case of Radioastronomy. *Phys. Technology, 12.*

Martinelli, D. (2001). Labour Market Entry and Mobility of Young French PhDs. In: OECD (2001) *Innovative People – Mobility of Skilled Personnel in National Innovation Systems.* (OECD Science and Innovation) OECD Publications: Paris.

Max-Planck-Gesellschaft (1999). Wirtschaft und Wissenschaft – Eine Allianz mit Zukunft in Deutschland? *Max Planck Forum 1/1999,* Generalverwaltung der Max-Planck-Gesellschaft zur Förderung der Wissenschaften e.V., Referat Presse- und Öffentlichkeitsarbeit: München.

Murmann, J.P. (2003). *Knowledge and Competitive Advantage – The Coevolution of Firms, Technology, and National Institutions.* Cambridge University Press: Cambridge.

OECD (1994). *The Measurement of Scientific and Technological Activities: Standard Practice for Surveys of Research and Experimental Development.* Frascati Manual 1993. OECD Publications: Paris.

OECD (1999). Research and Development in Industry. Expenditure and Researchers, Scientists and Engineers 1976-1997. *OECD Statistics.* OECD Publications: Paris.

OECD (2001). *Innovative People – Mobility of Skilled Personnel in National Innovation Systems.* (OECD Science and Innovation) OECD Publications: Paris.

Pavitt, K. (1991). What Makes Basic Research Economically Useful? *Research Policy, 20,* 109-119.

Pavitt, K. (1998). The Inevitable Limits of EU R&D Funding. *Research Policy, 27,* 559-568.

Pavitt, K. (2001). Public Policies to Support Basic Research: What Can the Rest of the World Learn From US Theory and Practice? (And What They Should Not Learn). *Industrial and Corporate Change, 10 (3)*, 761-779.

Rosenberg, N. (1990). Why Do Firms Do Research (With Their Own Money)? *Research Policy, 19*, 165-174.

Salter, A.J. and B.R. Martin (2001). The Economic Benefits of Publicly Funded Basic Research: A Critical Review. *Research Policy, 30*, 509-532.

Schmoch, U., G. Licht and M. Reinhard (2000). *Wissens- und Technologietransfer in Deutschland*. Fraunhofer IRB Verlag: Stuttgart.

VCI (2002). *Annual Report 2001*. VCI: Frankfurt am Main.

Zellner, C. (2003). The Economic Effects of Basic Research: Evidence for Embodied Knowledge Transfer Via Scientists' Migration. *Research Policy, 32*, 1881-1895.

Zellner, C. and D. Fornahl (2002). Scientific Knowledge and Implications for its Diffusion. *Journal of Knowledge Management, 6*, 180-198.

Zucker, L.G., M.R. Darby and M. Torero (1997). Labour Mobility From Academe to Commerce. *NBER working paper series, No. 6050*.

CHAPTER 9

SCIENCE-INDUSTRY RELATIONSHIPS IN FRANCE: ENTREPRENEURSHIP AND INNOVATIVE INSTITUTIONS

Michel Quéré

CNRS-IDEFI, France

1. INTRODUCTION

With regard to science-industry relationships, France is a very specific context. For a long time, France has been characterized by a crude divide between academics and industry. There are a lot of historical reasons for explaining that divide. First, university training was centrally aimed at providing an elitist intellectual class (disconnected from industry); second, the unique French "grandes écoles" training system was either dedicated to the supply of a class of high-skilled civil servants, or to provide major large French firms with a class of relevant decision-makers; as a consequence, it was not centrally concerned with the working of French basic research infrastructure; third, until World-War Two, the research infrastructure has been organised along the existence of one large institution covering all disciplines (the CNRS-National Centre for Scientific Research) and complemented progressively by a set of thematically-dedicated smaller research institutions (like CEA, INRA, INRIA, INSERM[i], etc.). Both CNRS and thematic research institutions are much more connected to university research even if this should be mitigated by a significant increase of interest from the "grandes écoles" training system to improve its research infrastructure; fourth, the French industrial system has been characterized by a tradition of supporting national champions which R&D activity were mainly organised (and supported) by public-private relationships ensured by human resources issued from the "grandes écoles" training system (large technological programmes can be thought of as a good illustration of that interactive process). However, if these characteristics are among the main factors explaining a traditional divide between academics and industry, it appears that this is changing quite importantly. The economic pressure from the so-called globalisation process added to the fact that academic scientists are exploited by firms much more extensively than in the past are two basic reasons for significant changes in the characterization of science-industry relationships in France.

This contribution aims at discussing these major changes in science-industry relationships occurring within the French context within the last two decades. More precisely, section two portrays in more details some of the previous specific characters of the French academic and training systems in order to identify how and why the previous peculiarities of the French context have significantly evolved and influenced the characteristics of science-industry relationships. Section three provides an analytical framework aimed at fitting with those changes. That framework is essentially based on an Austrian approach of institutions, and of institutional devices. Section three also helps to revisit the French context by dividing the respective contributions of change in entrepreneurship's characteristics from change in larger French institutional patterns. The one is clearly related to evolution in the behaviours of the population of scientists (among which the mobility of human resources from public to private organisations is a central issue); the other is associated in the evolution of the French institutional infrastructure (mostly the legal and financial ones). We will finally argue that, despite the current effort from policy-making, a very weak mobility of human (academic) resources is still a dominant pattern for the French context and weaken the ability of French industry as a whole to fully benefit from the high quality of the national scientific infrastructure.

2. FRENCH SPECIFICITIES IN THE REALM OF SCIENCE-INDUSTRY RELATIONSHIPS

2.1 Context and French Historical Background

France is a very specific context when discussing science-industry relationships for at least four complementary reasons. First, a major aim of the educational system has traditionally been to provide French state with a class of highly-educated civil servants. The "grandes écoles" training system is an inheritance of that need to produce human resources for managing public authorities (that system originates even before the French revolution in the eighteen century). Because of that central purpose, the "grandes écoles" system has for a long time been largely isolated from public research infrastructure. Even if, with regards to that matter, there has been an important evolution since the second half of the last century, it is not a tradition for that system to provide entrepreneurial resources. One has here to make that point more precise. The "grandes écoles" system provides numerous human resources to firms, specially to large public-owned firms. Main executives of large French firms are issued from that training system and form the majority of management and decision-making resources. The usual profile for those executives is to spend a couple of years in the public system and to move toward the private sector (the so-called "pantouflage" process). Actually, this peculiarity has been more challenged by sociologists and political scientists than by economists (see, among others, Grelon, 1998 for general considerations, and Latour 1989, Callon 1993, and Cassier 1995 for science implications). This peculiarity, with regards to the mobility of human resources, is quite unique to France and that mobility system influences quite importantly the regulation of large domestic firms. But this is not exactly what is usually expected to favour an entrepreneurial system as that peculiarity expresses more a specific regulation between French public and private systems than the fundamentals of an actual entrepreneurial context. However, this is more or less a basic characteristic for the French entrepreneurial system, as those individuals form quite exclusively the population of decision-makers in large French firms.

This French engineers' training system has recently increased tremendously in quantitative terms. There are now numerous individuals that directly start their carrier in the private sector. Table 9.1 shows the distribution of initial industrial employment by cohorts of French engineers students (including "grandes écoles", other engineering schools, and business schools, that is a sample of more than 18,000 individuals).

Table 9.1. Distribution of engineers among firms; (source: CGE, enquête 2002, Table IX-adapted)

Firm size	Less than 100 employees	From 100 to 500 employees	More than 500 employees
1998 Survey	23%	19%	58%
1999 Survey	23%	22%	55%
2000 Survey	23%	22%	55%
2001 Survey	22%	20%	58%
2002 Survey	21%	17%	62%

A major characteristic of France lies in the higher attractiveness of large firms than that of SMEs. For engineers' selfishness, there is a tradition of considering that large firms will allow them to make a better carrier. Underlying that purpose, what has characterised the French entrepreneurial system is the ability to participate in the management of large technological projects which mix quite effectively State resources and resources from a few large firms. Indeed, the French tradition of large technological programmes (nuclear energy, transportation systems, etc.) appears as a derivative of this somewhat unique type of coordination between public and private resources and in the carrier's vision of engineers, large French firms looked to offer higher prospects.

Second, in this context, it is no doubt that the interaction between the university system and large French firms is really weak, and this leads to an industrial structure dominated by a national champion philosophy where large (public) firms were part of a political aim which was to ensure French autonomy and independency. Here, the previous interaction between the management of public central authorities and the headquarters of major large French firms has played an important role. As a consequence, the science system has been interacting very few with large firms and, for a long time, PhD-students were not thought of as operational resources for firms.

Third, and as a consequence of that previous national peculiarity, university training has assumed the leadership in providing the country with an intellectual class devoted to fundamental research and high-educational training. Thus, universities trained individuals that, for a long time, have not been connected to the private sector, as their main target was purely the progress of science and the accumulation of scientific knowledge. More, the private sector was perceived as a kind of "devil" because firms' search for profitability was thought of as incompatible with the progress of intellectual knowledge. After world-war II, the university system has been complemented by specific institutions dedicated to basic research. The so-called "research organisms" like CNRS, CEA, INRA, INRIA, INSERM, etc… are institutions that concentrate public funds for fundamental research activity. As people involved in those research institutions are for a large majority issued from academic resources, there is no huge difference with the university system, with regards to the weak importance of science-industry relationships. French historical inheritance has produced an important divide between the world of science (and the population of scientists) and the world of industry (and the engineers' population) that is still present. Here lies a major explanation for the low level of entrepreneurial attempts from academic resources in France.

Fourth, this system knew a double shock in the 1980s that results in significant change for previous structural patterns. First, at that time, the left party succeeds to come into power after a long time, and second, the philosophy of French champions has significantly been challenged by the increasing importance of the globalisation process. The first shock induces a change in the national representation of entrepreneurship and the left government establishes new incentives to promote individual entrepreneurship. At that time, a large increase in the amount of the so-called incentives funds ("financements incitatifs") has gone hand in hand with a similarly significant decrease in public support allocated to "large technological programmes" (see Bernard, Quéré, 1994). As a consequence, a huge amount of individual initiatives occur and a lot of small and very small enterprises started, part of them contributing to the adaptation and the competitiveness of the French productive system. This transition towards an increasing importance of services activities has also been supported by opportunities derived from the growth of ICT sectors. But that evolution also induces a relative decrease in the political role of large French firms. Because of the obvious internationalisation of economic activity (the globalisation process), it becomes very clear to policy-makers that French national champions were no more appropriate to the international context. Therefore, public effort to promote entrepreneurship has been made at the expense of a deficit of the national champions' policy.

A very recent debate in France is now to discuss the conditions of public support to R&D activities. Using the US context as a benchmark, public policy-makers are aware of the significant difference in the ratio public R&D to private R&D (around one third in the US context against two thirds in France). Consequently, there is a current political debate considering that France suffers from a deficit in industrial research and that a major target for policy-making should be to encourage firms in increasing R&D expenditures. As a consequence, the effort towards public and fundamental research is expected to be decreasing in the short run whereas the effort to promote academic entrepreneurship should increase. Incentives are then targeted to increase the number of firms created from the academic milieu and sustaining academic entrepreneurship is becoming a new powerful philosophy for public intervention, even if our knowledge of this kind of very specific entrepreneurship is, at least according to me, very preliminary.

One of the most recent public policy supporting academic entrepreneurship is the so-called "law on innovation" approved in July 1999. The latter offers a new legal regime for academic researchers in their ability to become entrepreneurs. A derivative of that law has been the creation by the French Research Ministry of a series of incentives that result in the establishing of 31 academic incubators all around the country. The latter are considered as institutional devices aimed at expressing the new philosophy of public intervention, with regards to establishing incentives dedicated to academic entrepreneurship. More recently, in order to complement that law on innovation, a new legal framework for the young innovative firm is under discussion currently, where important advantages in terms of fiscal regimes (for investors as well as for the entrepreneurs) should be available. In short, a new series of public measures are clearly under discussion with the aim of encouraging the mobility of individuals (academic people) from public research institutions towards industry.

2.2 Science-industry relationships in France: empirical characteristics

With regard to the characteristics of science-industry relationships, the French context does not seem very specific. One can identify different types of science-industry relationships with regards to the degree of implications of academic resources. In that respect, academic start-ups are at one extreme of these characteristics whereas patents and/or licenses are at the other. Consequently, all kinds of contractual agreements and of individual mobility from scientists to industry are part of "intermediate" types of science-industry relationships. These are usual characteristics but a main change lies in the trend of evolution of those modalities. It is not so easy to have an overall picture of the French context because of problems in data collection. In what follows, I just emphasise the case of CNRS to give an empirical illustration of change in those characteristics during the recent years.

Starting with academic entrepreneurship, information is not systematic and people working on that issue are not using exhaustive data. Mustar (1995) collects information from a sample of more than 200 academic start-ups and establishes interesting empirical features from that set of firms (see Tables 9.2 and 9.3). He considers that the flow of academic start-ups was around 40 a year in the mid-nineties; an immediate comment is that these are not highly significant numbers for France as a whole.

Table 9.2. Origin of French academic start-ups from a sample analysis (source: Mustar, 1995)

Origin of academic entrepreneurs	Percentage
Universities	36%
Other public institutions	36%
Industrial labs	16%
Engineers schools	12%

Table 9.3. Sectoral distribution of academic start-ups (source: Mustar, 1995)

Sectoral distribution	(From a total of 202 firms)
Biotech and Medicine	28%
Computer science, including software	27%
Electronics	15%
Opto-electronics	10%
Environment	6%
Telecom	6%
Robotics	5%
Materials	3%

Beyond those basic characteristics, the most significant learning lies in the relatively good performance of that sample. Five years after their emergence, they perform quite well either in survival rates (75% against 50% for the overall population of newly-established firms), or in creating employment (12 on average, against 3,8 for the overall population). However, those enterprises are not really experiencing high growth rates. After six years of existence, only 10% of them are more than 50 employees and 3% more than 100. Among those who succeed the best, the ties developed with the academic milieu are perceived as a critical factor, be connections with their initial public research labs, but also and more largely, connections with international academic resources (see Mustar, 1995).

Focussing more especially on the case of CNRS, and looking to other types of science-industry relationships, Figures 9.1 to 9.4 and the Table 9.4 represent respectively the current evolution of contractual agreements taken by CNRS labs, the distribution of related financial resources, the distribution of active patents (flow and stock), the distribution of licenses and their financial importance. First of all, until 1999, the CNRS itself contributes to the creation of 100 academic start-ups, half of them related to medicine and biotechnology. When ICTs activities (25 %), Materials (7%), and Environment (7%) are excluded, the rest is widely spread among the overall disciplines covered by CNRS, but becomes negligible. Indeed, the most important aspect of academic entrepreneurship is the fact that 75% of it result from two main domains (life sciences and information technologies).

Second, Figure 9.1 is interesting as it shows how the recent increase in contractual agreements is more due to relationships with public organisms than to relationships with industry. Industrial contracts are only increasing slightly in the short run.

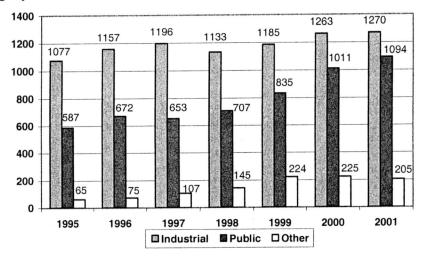

Figure 9.1. Contractual agreements from CNRS Labs (source: CNRS-DAE)

This stability is further confirmed by the financial distribution of those contracts where the relative importance of private and public resources is quite re-equilibrating over time (Figure 9.2). Those agreements are contracted with around 1,700 partners, among which 1,100 firms.

There is an obvious correlation between contractual agreements and patent distribution, be flow or stock of "active" patents (Table 9.4), that are patents effectively used by firms. Again, Medicine and Biotechnology on the one hand, Information technologies on the other hand, represent a large amount of active patents granted by CNRS. The only significant difference lies in the contrasted patterns of chemistry which represent 30% of the stock of active patents of CNRS whereas academic start-ups are negligible in those areas. Indeed, one explanation is that traditional process-oriented industries experience high sunk costs that are associated in high entry barriers limiting opportunities for academic entrepreneurship in those areas.

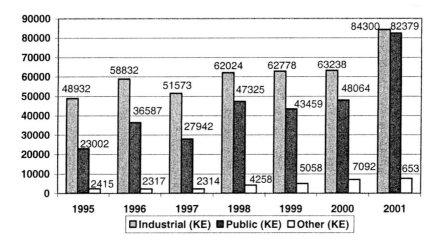

Figure 9.2. Financial distribution of Contractual agreements (source: CNRS-DAE)

Interesting differences are also sensitive between the flow and the stock of patents. Even if chemistry represents even today 30% of the active patents' stock, obviously the 2001 population shows a displacement effect as the majority of new active patents are now to be found in life sciences and no more in chemistry or even information technologies.

A similar trend emerges from data on licenses. Here, the relative importance of life sciences and of information technologies is obvious but a significant difference also appears (Figure 9.2).

Table 9.4. Distribution of the flow and stock of active patents (total = 187 and 1155; ref. year = 2001); (source: CNRS-DAE)

Scientific Domains	Flow of active patents (% of total)	Stock of active patents (% of total)
Life Sciences (Medicine, Agrotech, Biotech, Cosmetics and Pharmaceuticals)	48	38
Information Technologies (Electronics, Optics, Telecom, Instrumentation)	23	18
Physics, Mecanics, Materials, and Energy	15	8
Chemistry	9	32
Environment	4	1
Others	1	3
Total	100	100

Whereas licensing patents is the dominant source of funding in life sciences, it is much less the case for information technologies where licensing essentially occurs from software packaging. Now, when looking to Figure 9.4, one can see how software licenses are marginal in the earnings stemming from licenses. In financial terms, licenses revenues from life sciences are becoming much more strategically important for CNRS than those from software activities.

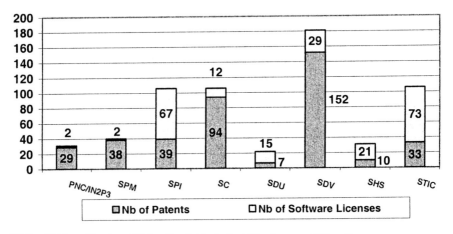

PNC = Nuclear Physics   SPM = Fund. Math. And Physics   SPI = Computer
SciencesSC =Chemistry   SDU = Earth and Env. Sciences   SDV = Life Sciences
SHS = Human Sciences   STIC = Information Technologies

Figure 9.3. Distribution of licenses (total = 522; reference year = 2001); (source: CNRS-DAE)

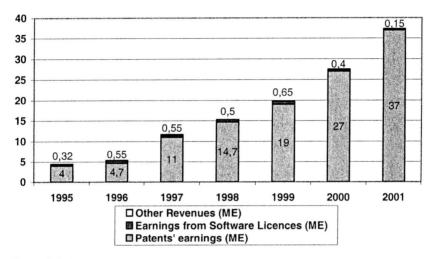

Figure 9.4. Cumulative earnings from active licenses (Total = 37,6 M€; ref. year = 2001); (source: CNRS-DAE)

These recent trends faced by CNRS are helpful to point out a few relevant questions from an economic viewpoint. Why such diversity in science-industry relationships is certainly at the top of the list. One can also wonder why some disciplines are more accurate to concentrate those relationships whereas others are still marginal in their connections to industry. In order to highlight those questions more than to provide definite answers, one can insist on the need for a process analysis to deal with those relationships. As already pointed out by empirical observation from academic start-ups, Mustar (1991, 1995) insists on the fact that successful academic start-ups are those which are able to be embedded in networks implying cooperation and partnerships resulting in sustainable connections with the academic milieu but also with premium customers, other firms, venture capitalists, and other types of public institutions. This ability to connect with other partners and resources is thought of as conditional to the survival of those firms. In other words, the importance of the institutional infrastructure that those firms are setting-up, and implementing as well, is really crucial. This is why institutions matter for science-industry relationships as creating an academic start-up is, in some sense, determined by the construction of an appropriate institutional device. This is also why a process analysis matters as an academic start-up cannot be but the result of a process, which is highly uncertain and even not at all imaginable at the start.

Looking to the institutional embeddedness is an original way to deal with the diversity of science-industry relationships. At least, a central hypothesis is that patents, licenses, contractual agreements, individual mobility, academic start-ups are, *ex post,* alternative results of a process analysis, an entrepreneurial institutional improvisation (Cole, 1968) which has to be more deeply investigated and depicted. This is where an Austrian approach of institutions can reveal helpful.

3. ANALYTICAL INSIGHTS TO CHARACTERIZE ENTREPRENEURIAL BEHAVIOURS IN SCIENCE-INDUSTRY RELATIONSHIPS

3.1 The framework

Referring to an Austrian view of institutions in order to deal with science-industry relationships can be firstly thought of an old-fashioned perspective. However, the focus put by Austrian analysis on the fundamental problem of the coordination of economic activity is helpful to deal with my topic. The core of modern Austrian economics can be exemplify by the spontaneous order principle (O'Driscoll, 1977). But I feel excessive to organise the profession in terms of *cons* and *pros* the spontaneous order principle and I simply consider here that the spontaneous order principle allows for important learning about the regulation of market processes. Consequently, it is fundamentally helpful for contemporary puzzles, and especially in the realm of science-industry relationships.

In particular, in a context of rapid change, (be the renewal of consumers' preferences, the creation of new markets and/or an increase of technological opportunities), context which is precisely that of science-industry relationships, managing the coordination problems faced by economic agents becomes the cornerstone of any successful innovation process. Basically, the reason why an Austrian framework is helpful lies in its capability to highlight situations where imperfect knowledge prevails and consequently, where prices mechanisms are not sufficient to ensure a suited economic coordination. Instability, disturbances, reactions to shocks are central problems to be dealt with, when considering the actual working of a market economy. Therefore, the price system is a necessary but non-sufficient condition to that working in that "pricing, in short, is seen as a continuous information-collecting and disseminating process, but it is the institutional framework that determines both the extent to which and the degree of success with which prices are enabled to perform this potential signalling or allocative function" (Shenoy, 1972, cited by O'Driscoll, 1977, p.143). Underlying the relative importance of price mechanisms is the respective role of *ex ante* and *ex post* coordination mechanisms. The belief that there is a room for considering the importance of *ex ante* coordination among economic agents is certainly part of the distinctive feature of Austrian economics. That distinction is also central to a proper understanding of science-industry relationships as the central characteristic of science-industry relationships, i.e. innovation process, tends to continuously place economic activity in a disequilibrium situation which requires economic systems to adjust continuously. This doesn't mean that any tendency toward equilibrium does not exist but simply that the proper nature of science-industry relationships is to displace any stable coordinating device for economic activity and create successive stages of economic environment marked by strong and renewed economic (productive and market) opportunities. This is actually what is highly puzzling when attempting to characterize science-industry relationships and, conversely, why the emphasis put by Austrian analysis on institutions appears particularly fruitful.

In the economic profession, we are used to limit an Austrian approach to its modern characterisation as developed by Mises and Hayek analyses until the thirties (see Kirzner, 1997). However, my ambition here is simply to focus on a limited part of that Austrian tradition, namely considerations about the entrepreuneurial discovery process and about the role of institutions for the coordination of economic activity. As such, that contribution elaborates from the work of Langlois (1986) and Loasby (1991) who pinpoint how Hayek imports in modern Austrian economics the Mengerian theory of social institutions. That proximity between the Mengerian and Hayekian conceptions of institutions can be thought of as the starting point for an analytical discussion about science-industry relationships (see Quéré, Ravix, 1997, 2002).

Menger conception of institutions is basically dedicated to find an answer to the following question: "how can it be that institutions which serve the common welfare and are extremely significant for its development come into being without a *common will* directed toward establishing them ?" (Menger, 1883/1963, p. 146). Penetrating that mystery was obviously his purpose and leads him to considerations centred on the emergence of institutions. His basic observation of social structures is that some "are the results of a *common will* directed toward their establishment (agreement, positive legislation, etc.) while others are the unintended result of human efforts aimed at attaining essentially individual goals (the unintended results of these)." (ibid., p. 133). Two remarks are here important for my purpose. The one is that, as already pointed out by Langlois (1986), the most important contribution of Menger to economics lies in that emphasis on the importance of the origin of institutions. The other is the importance of the distinction Menger stresses about the origin of institutions. Exploring the analogy with natural organisms as a means of presentation, Menger emphasises the organic character of institutions that comes about as the unintended result of individual actions; however, in contrast to that organic origin of institutions, some others are the intended result of human action as they are appearing purposefully. There is a strong contrast between those two types of institutions (organic vs pragmatic origins) to which I will come back later on.

By contrast, the strength of Menger analysis of institutions is more or less the weakness of Hayek analysis: there is no clear analytical evidence about the emergence of institutions in Hayek analysis. Hayek is first concerned with the economics of (imperfect) knowledge. The conditions by which people are likely to acquire the necessary knowledge for sustaining an equilibrium analysis are at central stake in the initial Hayek research program. More, it is not only the question of the conditions under which knowledge is acquired but mainly that of how much and what sort of knowledge is it desirable to acquire. The answer to that phase of his research program (Witt, 1997) refers centrally to the analysis of spontaneous actions of individuals which will "under conditions which we can define bring about a distribution of resources which can be understood as if it were made according to a single plan, although nobody has planned it" (Hayek, 1936, p.52). This is where a central place for institutions occurs as the latter, despite "the fact that pure analysis seems to have so extraordinarily little to say about" (ibid., p. 53). The role to be given to institutions in Hayek framework has to do with designing an appropriate space between "laissez-faire" and planning. Even if the market is thought of as the best mechanism to ensure the most suited coordination among individual plans, the way by which market regulation occurs implies something more than the collection of individual plans to ensure a viable regulation for economic systems. Rules, laws, but also media, advertising, informal relations are means of reconciling expectations with real facts and, as such, provide the most reasonable explanation to excessive disruptions in the regulation of economics systems. Therefore, with regards to institutions, the main issue in Hayek analysis is to consider the reasons why institutions are designed for or, in other words, what goals are they achieving. Contrary to Menger who centrally focuses on the emergence of institutions, Hayek's main concern is that of its purpose and evolution. To Menger, institutions result from the need of individuals to acquire knowledge whereas in Hayek analysis, institutions transcend individual actions; institutions favour the coordination of individual subjective perception and knowledge, at the same time that they also contribute to enforce knowledge; spontaneous orders are facing continuous adjustments and continuous learning, and adaptation of individual actions and plans justifies that central emphasis on the purpose and evolution of institutions (Garrouste, 1994, p.868).

That distinctive mark of analysing the role of institutions as pointed out respectively by Langlois (1986) and Garrouste (1994) can be further explored (Quéré, Ravix, 1997, 2002). More particularly, the role of institutions, both with regards to their emergence and their evolution, is useful to be revisited when dealing with the organisation of science-industry relationships. Loasby's specific characterization of the organisation of science (Loasby, 1991, pp. 36-38) provides a good illustration. He identifies five major aspects in the working of science synthesized as followed:

- Science is unmistakably a highly competitive activity;

- Competition is not anonymous and does not preclude collaboration;
- Science framework should not be refrained to novelty;
- Discontinuity never fully exists;
- The quality of science results largely depends on the process that produces it.

Loasby's characterisation of science is somewhat differentiated from the usual way to deal with the economics of science, at least as it recently developed (see Dasgupta, David, 1994; Stephan, 1996; Diamond, 1996). Indeed, Loasby's descriptive set of propositions regarding science organisation centrally emphasised the institutional embeddedness of scientific activity. To a large extent, science discovery has to be thought of as an organised activity, the understanding of which requires adaptive institutional devices and, therefore, a process analysis. The previous Austrian roots fully apply to those characteristics. More, the adaptation from science organisation to the current working of science-industry relationships is obviously relevant and the usefulness of a process analysis based on an institutional approach is then useful to perform their understanding.

To develop that adaptation, I suggest to consider science-industry relationships as an entrepreneurial discovery process that requires to qualify both the setting-up and the evolution of institutional devices. Those institutional devices are usually defined only in an *ex post* perspective as the results of entrepreneurial behaviours. Academic start-ups, patents, licenses, research contracts are among those institutional devices that are taken as granted in an ex post perspective. The ambition now is to discuss the process by which those devices appear and are selected in an *ex ante* perspective. In other words, I want to address the issue of what determines the selection process by which science-industry relationships result in a variety of economic results. To solve for that problem, the previous distinctive features between the Menger and Hayek research programmes are of a clear cut help.

The following Figure 9.5 offers a framework to discuss the complementary perspective issued from the distinction between the origin and the evolution of institutions:

In that figure, the distinctive characteristics of Menger and Hayek research programs (origin versus evolution of institutions) are opposed along the vertical and the horizontal axes of the figure. The vertical one distinguishes institutions emerging deliberately from common will (pragmatic ones), from those resulting from the unintended consequences of human actions (organic ones). The horizontal line focuses on the evolution of institutions by distinguishing non purposive from purposive evolution. Now, a few comments can be addressed from the figure.

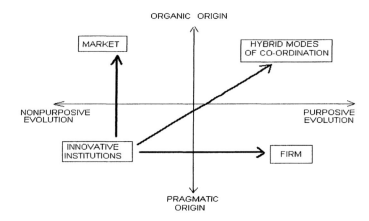

Figure 9.5. Institution framework for science-industry relationship based on Menger-Hayek research programmes (adapted from Quéré and Ravix, 1997)

First, that distinction allows to consider the usual way of thinking about business institutions (Langlois, Robertson, 1995) or, more precisely, to identify the three dominant and traditional modes of coordinating economic activity: direction, market and cooperation. The left-upstream part of the figure includes Mengerian organic institutions and Hayekian spontaneous orders. Traditional examples are market or money as institutions emerging "organically" and regulating economic activity spontaneously, i.e. without any definite and purposeful vision of their evolution. To the contrary, the right-downstream part of the figure refers to pragmatic institutions resulting from a deliberate common will; organisations such as firms are an obvious example. Finally, the right-upstream part of the figure includes the so-called "hybrid" modes of governance belonging to the *continuum* between firm and market as defined by Williamson (1985); these institutions are concerned with a purposive evolution but their origin is organic rather than pragmatic, in the sense that they result from the pursuit of individual interests rather than from a collective common will.

Now, the heuristics of that figure lies in the fact that a fourth type of institutions clearly appears from that basic distinction among the Menger and Hayek conception of institutions.

The left-downstream part of the figure includes institutions which are at the same time pragmatic at their origin and *ex ante* nonpurposive in their evolution. These institutions are dedicated to face process uncertainty (Langlois, 1986) in that they exist and develop even if their future outcome is not known initially. That category of institutions, named "innovative institutions", are suited to the characterization of science-industry relationships. They appear fundamentally different from other business institutions as they are producing knowledge which should progressively be transformed into a more traditional business institution. In other words, innovative institutions have a basic peculiarity which oppose them to other types of coordinating devices: they are structurally unstable. Innovative institutions are business institutions suited to innovation: they aim at organising discovery procedures and are a means of progressively facing process uncertainty. Consequently, as time is going on, innovative institutions are condemned to transform themselves into a more stable pattern of business institutions, be market, firm or cooperation.

3.2 Framework's Implementation

The translation of those analytical considerations about business institutions into a more operational learning related to science industry relationships can be made through two main complementary remarks.

The one is related to process analysis and its incidence on the understanding of science-industry relationships. Innovative institutions have been defined as institutional arrangements for which the origin is pragmatic but the evolution is not established *ex ante*. Then, the main issue becomes that of the determinants which influence the future of innovative institutions, i.e. of the mechanisms orienting their transformation from an unstable toward a more stable type of institution.

The other is policy implications. This analysis questions policy-making in the realm of science-industry relationships because of the shift in strategic concern. If this process analysis is followed, policy-making should not only target points of arrivals as the main issue but should also take into better consideration the incentives' aspects that structure the transformation of innovative institutions into more stable institutional devices, whatever they finally are.

3.2.1 Process analysis and the understanding of entrepreneurship with regards to science-industry relationships

With regards to process analysis, three different sets of determinants characterize the structuring of innovative institutions: individual capabilities, networking capabilities, and environmental factors. Individual capabilities not only include research ability and expertise, but also all other capabilities necessary to develop the implementation of innovative institutions (including economic, financial, and managerial competencies). Individual capabilities appear as a necessary but not a sufficient condition to guarantee the sustainability of science-industry relationships. They are a necessary condition because scientific expertise, development, and progress are important to start with innovative institutions as well as to influence the institutional device finally chosen at the end of their implementation. Then, the ability of individuals to anticipate on the direction and rate of scientific change, to establish forecasting conjectures on productive opportunities to be derived from scientific progress is a significant aspect of the evolution of innovative institutions in time. However, this is not sufficient for at least two reasons. The one is the need to complement scientific expertise by other types of knowledge derived from business, accounting, and/or finance information. The latter also appear very influential to determine the design of the final point of arrival. The other is the existence of discontinuities in scientific progress that can force innovative institutions to drastic change and even disruptions in their initial organisation and evolution.

The second factor determining the evolution of innovative institutions is strongly related to individual expertise. It is that ability of scientists to combine the overall knowledge necessary for the development of an innovative process and to establish useful connections among different types of organisations in order to solve for process uncertainty. This is not only access to relevant information but includes the coordination of the overall knowledge (economic, finance, competition, market analysis, legal affairs, etc.) necessary to the implementation of innovative institutions. The way by which that knowledge is progressively collected and aggregated in innovative institutions largely influences the point of arrival that will be chosen by entrepreneurs as well as modifies the frontiers of innovative institutions in the course of action. This networking capability can result in an internal improvement of individual (entrepreneurial) capabilities that expand his (her) knowledge beyond the frontiers of academic expertise. But it mainly results in the use of external resources by interacting with other individuals or firms in order to answer to that need for further knowledge to be encapsulated. In that respect, the aggregation of complementary resources is part of the evolution of innovative institutions and of the way they proceed to solve for process uncertainty. This networking capability also includes the ability to associate industrial partners in the working of innovative institutions and, consequently, reshuffle the organisational design in the process of implementing innovative institutions. Both aspects appear complementary and influential for understanding how a specific point of arrival is progressively designed over time.

Lastly, the third category of determinants is the environmental influence that academic people are facing. This environment also contributes to establish collective learning and practices influencing the process of choosing among potential points of arrival; therefore, the environment helps to design progressively the business vision of the entrepreneurial process. For instance, the legal system to which academics are confronted contribute to favour specific options for academic entrepreneurship. According to France, the law on innovation that has recently been adopted induces important consequences on the ability of public researchers to take part in industrial firms as well as to develop academic start-ups by themselves. More generally, the importance of public infrastructures depends from one national context to another and their characteristics contribute to influence options and to secure innovative institutions in more stable forms of institutional arrangements. It is rather difficult to identify quite exhaustively factors that characterise this environmental influence. However, public authorities play a central role through direct or indirect actions. Financial facilities for academic entrepreneurship (be direct support or advantageous fiscal regime), simplifying patenting procedures, supporting doctoral students, encouraging technology transfers in industrial firms, all these measures are only examples of the huge range of public intervention that contribute to the evolution of innovative institutions towards one or the other specific points of arrival.

Based on such understanding of that process, it appears that current change in French science-industry relationships is essentially change in environmental conditions. The latter appear as a major explanation for that renewed emphasis on academic entrepreneurship. Qualitative interviews with academic entrepreneurs show that no highly significant distinction occurs in the way by which scientists are tackling that science-industry issue. More precisely, the individual, as a basic component for science-industry relationships, has not drastically changed: good scientists are not making good entrepreneurs, yesterday no more than today. Candidates for academic entrepreneurship can be mainly divided into two different populations: that of doctoral and post-doctoral students which are facing the impossibility to benefit from a position in the academic system and who found firms in order to solve for employment issue; that of already established-academic individuals that decide to move from science to industry. However, in the latter case, the majority of them are not top-ranked scientists but good technicians located in performing scientific environments. Change in individual mentality for entrepreneurship is rather slow, and the identification of business opportunities mainly results from change in environmental conditions, or, more precisely, from change in French policy-making.

3.2.2 Policy implications

Therefore, with regard to policy-making implications, one has first to address the existence of important changes in French incentives' structures. Policy-makers are progressively modifying their representation of the importance of scientists for economic purpose. The collective vision of what public intervention should currently be is centred on encouraging scientists to move from the public sector towards the private one. The way to do so is to identify targets and to establish incentives' structures that seem suited to those targets. For instance, the French government is currently identifying three central objectives: increase in innovative start-ups (through the public incubator policy), increase in R&D expenditures of existing firms (through fiscal incentives), and establishing a new favourable legal and fiscal status for specific (high R&D-consuming) start-ups mainly to be found in biotech, information technologies and nano-technologies activities.

Science-industry relationships are directly concerned with the first and third targets. This is obviously related to the change in the legal framework that occurs with the so-called law on innovation in July 1999. As already mentioned, that law introduces three new options for scientists: to create academic start-ups in order to implement their research results; to participate in the capital and/or in the board of start-ups; to provide expertise to existing firms. However, this novelty (some of those options were not allowed before July 1999) nevertheless induces the continuity for a strict divide between public research and private activities. In the case of establishing a start-up, this implies for the entrepreneur to abandon (at least temporary) his (her) position in the public system. In order to take any active role in entrepreneurship, individual scientists cannot anymore be involved in public research infrastructure; that is any attempt to create your own business has still to be thought of as a sort of disruption from public research institutions. The reverse is also true. Any comeback to the public system is for an entrepreneurial scientist conditional to a complete dissociation from his (her) previous private business. In case of participating to the capital structure (or to the board) of a start-up, this is only possible if you had no previous link with that enterprise; in case of providing expertise to existing firms, this is thought only with the aim of favouring technology transfers from scientists to firms. No research contract can be established in that respect, as expertise should only be concerned with the use of already existing (public) research results or capabilities. Research contracts are still strictly limited to public institutions and individual scientists cannot contract on their own.

Then, it is quite clear that underlying the law on innovation is the continuation of that divided view between public and private interest, and the lack of porosity that is, according to me, inconsistent with any science-industry relation understood as a process analysis. To some extent, current French policy-making can be thought of as not really appropriate to challenge the issue of encouraging science-industry relationships as it odes not allow to establish appropriate incentives to bridge effectively science to industry.

Looking back to the analytical framework developed in the previous section, the argument here is that French policy effort is somewhat condemned to a weak effectiveness. Not only it is misleading to consider an expected number of academic start-ups as a benchmark of success, or to establish public infrastructure like public incubators to reach those expected numbers, but it is also misleading in the aim. That is: policy effort does not take care of the process analysis already stressed in the previous section but only of some of the "points of arrivals" identified in the characterisation of science-industry relationships.

In other words, a process analysis is required to discuss the relevance of policy support. With regard to my framework, what is effective is a policy designed for encouraging the transformation of public knowledge and resources into private business. This is not reducible to a discussion about the adequacy (and inadequacy respectively) of some infrastructures; it is a wider issue related to the efficacy of any entrepreneurial effort, i.e. to the support and development of innovative institutions. And, precisely, the sustainability of the current policy effort seems weakly compatible with the existence of innovative institutions (and their unstable character more especially).

To contrast the current policy effort to some other (previous) policy experiments in France, it is interesting to learn from the example of the CIFRE incentives (Convention Industrielle de Formation par la Recherche). The latter are specific employment contracts from firms for Ph-d students which stipulate that half of the time of the individuals has to be spend in a public research lab in order to make a PhD thesis dedicated to solve an industrial problem faced by firms; conversely, half of employment cost is subsidised by public funds. Besides that cost effect, those contracts have been successful in terms of economic relevance for French firms (see Quéré, 1998); more, those CIFRE are also indirectly helpful to structure paths for innovative institutions. CIFRE are vectors of knowledge generation in the sense they allow scientists to identify industrial problems and, consequently, related market opportunities. In that way, they indirectly orient the direction of innovative institutions in the course of their evolution and path the way by which potential entrepreneurs are progressively figuring out their initial attempts or projects. Such incentives have created pervasiveness among public and private science as well as flexible and temporary percolation through the development of common research projects. This is the reason why even if they were not initially designed for encouraging science-industry relationships (but to promote employment of PhD-students in industry), those incentives reveal, at least, as far important as all the new opportunities introduced by the 1999 law on innovation for supporting academic entrepreneurship. Learning from that contrasting policy support is: what appears crucial is the way by which efforts to transform scientific resources into private opportunities can be sustained, and this cannot be fully obtained by establishing policy-making dedicated to supporting the "points of arrivals" of that transformation process.

4. CONCLUSIVE REMARKS

This contribution is basically a plea for considering the usefulness of an Austrian approach of institutions for the understanding of science-industry relationships. The heuristic content of such an approach is established by pointing out the importance of a peculiar type of institutions, named innovative institutions. The latter appear as unstable forms of institutions playing an important role for the understanding of science-industry relationships. The way by which innovative institutions develop and evolve contributes progressively to organise a reasonable innovative path for entrepreneurs and to design a more stable economic point of arrival for their innovative activities. The use of an Austrian approach of institutions reveals appropriate for understanding how entrepreneurial activity is facing a context of process uncertainty that cannot be designed *ex ante* by a defined institutional device. Therefore, the process analysis characterising the Austrian approach of institutions appears particularly interesting to cope with the conjectural rather than normative dimension of empirical observation in science-industry relationships. Consequently, it looks convincing for shifting the focus of policy-making from policies devoted to encourage established forms of science-industry relationships to policies aimed at encouraging entrepreneurial behaviours, i.e. at making sustainable the efforts of scientists in their evolvement from public to private environments. Looking back to the French context, it appears very much that current expectations about increase in academic entrepreneurship are much more due to opportunistic responses of scientists to change in environmental conditions (due to policy measures) than to a real change in individual mentality of academic people, with regards to entrepreneurship and business visions.

NOTE

[1] CEA (Commissariat à l'énergie atomique) is mainly dedicated to nuclear power energy research, INRA (Institut National de Recherche en Agronomie) to agriculture and agro-business research, INRIA (Institut National de Recherche en Informatique et Automatique) to computer science research, INSERM (Institut National de la Santé et de la Recherche Médicale) to health research. This is not exhaustive and other thematically-oriented research institutions exist in France.

REFERENCES

Bernard J, Quéré M. (1994). L'évolution du financement public sur l'activité de recherche des PME/PMI, *Revue d'Economie Industrielle, 67*, 211-224.

Callon M. (1993). *Is Science (Still) a Public Good?*, Contribution to the Fifth Mullins Lecture, Virginia Polytechnic Institute, March.

Cassier M. (1995). *Les contrats de recherche entre l'université et l'industrie: l'émergence d'un nouvelle forme d'organisation industrielle*, Thesis, Ecole des Mines de Paris, Paris.

Cole A. (1968). The entrepreneur, Introductory remarks, *American Economic Review Paper and Proceedings, 58(2)*, 60-63.

Dasgupta P., David P (1994). Toward a new economics of science, *Research Policy, 23*, 487-521.

Garrouste P., (1994). Carl Menger and Friedrich A. Hayek à propos des institutions: continuité et ruptures, *Revue d'Economie Politique, 104(6)*, 851-872.

Grelon A., (1998). Le poids de l'histoire: l'héritage de l'ingénieur contemporain, in: Lanciano, C., Maurice, M., Silvestre, J.J., Nohara, H. (eds.), *Les acteurs de l'innovation et l'entreprise*, Paris: L'Harmattan.

Hayek F. (1937). Economics and Knowledge, in F. Hayek *Individualism and Economic Order*, Chicago: University of Chicago Press, 1948.

Hayek F. (1945). The use of knowledge in society, in F. Hayek *Individualism and Economic Order*, Chicago: University of Chicago Press, 1948.

Hayek F. (1967). *Studies in Philosophy, Politics, and Economics*, London: Routledge & Kegan Paul.

Hayek F. (1978). Competition as a discovery procedure, in F. Hayek, *New studies in philosophy, politics, economics and the history of ideas*, Chicago: University of Chicago Press.

Kirzner I. (1973). *Competition and Entrepreneurship*, Chicago: University of Chicago Press.

Kirzner I. (1997). Entrepreneurial Discovery and the Competitive Market Process: An Austrian Approach, *Journal of Economic Literature, 1*, 60-85.

Langlois R. (1986). Rationality, institutions and explanations, in R. Langlois (ed.), *Economics as a Process, Essays in the New Institutional Economics*, Cambridge: Cambridge University Press.

Langlois R., Robertson P. (1995). *Firms, Markets and Economic Change, a dynamic theory of business institutions*, London: Routledge.

Latour B. (1989). *La science en action*, Paris: La découverte.

Loasby B. (1991). *Equilibrium and Evolution*, Manchester: Manchester University Press.

Menger C. (1883). *Problems of Economics and Sociology*, Urbana: University of Illinois Press, 1963.

Mustar P. (1991). Processes of Integration Science with the Market: the Creation of Technology-based Businesses, Contribution to the Conference "Management de la Technologie", Paris, May.

Mustar P., (1995). *Science & innovation 1995. Annuaire raisonné de la création d'entreprises par les chercheurs*. Paris: Economica.

O'Driscoll G. P. (1977). Spontaneous orders and the coordination of economic activities, *Journal of Libertarian Studies, 1(2)*, 137-151.

Quéré M. (1998). La convention CIFRE comme indicateur de caractéristiques des processus d'innvation au sein du système productif français, in: C. Lanciano, Maurice M., Silvestre J.J., Nohara H. (eds.). *Les acteurs de l'innovation et l'entreprise*, Paris: L'Harmattan.

Quéré M., Ravix J.L. (1997). Relations science-industrie et institutions innovatrices, *Revue d'Economie industrielle, 79*, 213-232.

Quéré M., Ravix J.L. (2002). The Austrian Theory of Institutions Applied to Science-Industry Relationships: the Relevance of Innovative Institutions, *Review of Austrian Economics, 16*, (2-3), 271-284.

Schumpeter J. (1934). *The Theory of Economic Development*, Oxford: Oxford University Press (1974).
Schumpeter J. (1942). *Capitalism, Socialism and Democracy,* French trad., Paris, Payot (1951).
Stephan P. (1996). The Economics of Science, *Journal of Economic Literature, 34,* 1199-1235
Williamson O. (1975). *Markets and Hierarchy*, New-York: The Free Press.
Williamson O. (1985). *The Economic Institutions of Capitalism: Firms, Markets, Relational Contracting*, New York, The Free Press.
Witt U. (1997). The Hayekian Puzzle: Spontaneous Order and the Business Cycle, *Scottish Journal of Political Economy, 44 (1),* 44-58.

CHAPTER 10

KNOWLEDGE CREATION AND FLOWS IN SCIENCE

Robin Cowan

University of Maastricht, Netherlands

Nicolas Jonard

CNRS, CREA Paris, France

1. INTRODUCTION

This paper is concerned with creation and diffusion of knowledge within the scientific community. We invoke the distinction between open and closed science to focus attention solely on those agents for whom knowledge is an end in itself.[1] Our concern here is the flow of knowledge within a discipline, such as economics for example, in which the discipline is defined broadly enough that it contains several well-defined sub-disciplines (micro-theory, applied micro, econometrics, labour economics, industrial organization, macro-economics and so on). Within a discipline individual scientists interact directly with other scientists in a variety of ways — they collaborate; they read each other's working papers; they talk in the corridors; they attend each others' seminars and conference presentations and so on. If these are considered direct interactions, it is clear that all economists do not interact directly with all others. Indeed, any economist will interact directly only with a small number of other economists. The types of interactions listed above are all largely concerned with the diffusion of knowledge. These are important communication channels in the scientific community, so a knowledge diffusion model will have to treat a population of agents, each of whom interacts only with a very small subset of the rest of the population. Each agent interacts with his or her own subset, so we have essentially a network, or graph structure over which knowledge diffuses.

Part of the motivation for this approach is that it resonates well with recent science and innovation policy, especially at the European level. A policy view that was very common historically was that the geographical agglomeration of "knowledge workers" was, if not necessary, at least very highly beneficial to the production of knowledge and innovation. Many policies were implemented, from "big science" such as the CERN accelerator, to industrial-science parks, such as Sophia-Antipolis. With some exceptions (often in the realm of big science) these moves were limited by national boundaries. It was relatively easy to create an agglomeration within a country of nationals from that country, but difficulties of cross-border mobility remained a "cost of non-Europe". One response of the Commission to this "non-Europe" problem was to introduce policies to encourage networking. This is clear in the fifth framework programmes, and seems to be becoming even more so in the sixth framework.

The rationale for this networking policy is clear. It can be an important channel for the global distribution of knowledge. Economists remain attached to departments of economists, and this provides local agglomerations and critical masses for certain types of knowledge creation. But relative to a world of isolated departments, a networked structure will provide inter-department knowledge flows which will directly improve diffusion, and indirectly improve knowledge creation. The latter point, improving knowledge creation, arises from two considerations. First, it permits a more global "standing on the shoulders of giants—when an agent innovates, he is not re-inventing the wheel, and is, in fact starting from a higher level if he has had access to innovations from other parts of the world. Second, most innovation is the recombination of existing ideas.[2] Thus increasing the general level of access to ideas, particularly if it increases as well the range of types of ideas that are easily assimilated, should facilitate knowledge creation.

But from the policy perspective, there is already networking, and there has been networking of one sort or another for centuries. Thus the policy rationale must be something like "More networking will lead to more rapid knowledge growth in aggregate." This immediately raises the issue of what, exactly, is meant by "more networking". It could mean more networking on average— everyone who goes to conferences goes to more each year. Or it could mean that more people go to conferences. It could be an issue of the amount of network activity, or it could be an issue of its distribution among the population. This is one of the issues we address in this paper—is it the mean or the variance (or more likely the skewness) of the distribution of networking activity that matters?

There are, in addition to those mentioned above, two other distribution channels. First is global diffusion through journal (and to a lesser extent working paper) publication of results. Second is the academic job market. The first issue we put aside in this paper. Recent work on knowledge emphasizes its sticky aspect: even codified knowledge is difficult to transmit, and tacit knowledge extremely so.[3] The parts of knowledge that are hard to transmit as codified knowledge are typically transmitted in close, (often face-to-face), interactions. It is this aspect of knowledge transmission that is addressed by network policies, and thus we focus exclusively on it, leaving aside the more global transmission through activities such as publication. The second form of knowledge transmission that does deal very effectively with tacit knowledge is labour mobility. If a scientist moves from one department to another, he takes with him all of his tacit knowledge. This is far and away the most effective (at least in the medium run) means of diffusing tacit knowledge. This we include in our model, as we are interested in the interaction the job market and networking as modes of knowledge diffusion.

In what follows we develop a model of knowledge creation and diffusion. It is a network model of sufficient complexity that analytic solutions for the types of effects we examine are not possible, so we perform numerical experiments aimed at understanding how knowledge levels, inter-agent and inter-group variance, and agent and group specialization respond to changes in various parameters. The goal is to shed light on possible and recent actual policy actions in the field of science and technology.

2. THE MODEL

In Open Science individuals have no incentive to keep their discoveries secret. Rather they have every incentive to diffuse them as largely as possible.[4] Do they perform this task naively, by simply giving away for free a knowledge that has been costly to produce? Engineers or scientists in departments have colleagues with whom they interact as members of this particular department, but they are also embedded in a more persistent set of interpersonal relationships that we will refer to as their permanent networks. In the latter, probably the rule for transmitting knowledge is a unilateral broadcast. Individuals transmit what they know to their neighbors in the network at every opportunity, and expect them to do the same when their turn comes. Alternatively, we can think of a network like this as creating a common knowledge pool, to which everyone contributes, (by giving seminars, attending conferences, mailing working papers to friends) and from which everyone draws (by being on the receiving end of all those activities). In addition, scientists also belong to a contrasting network whose lifetime is often shorter (the length of the stay within a department), which is under stronger competitive pressures and through which knowledge circulation is rather organized as a quid pro quo.[5] Knowledge is exchanged, but in a barter arrangement.[6] Hence knowledge is traded rather than broadcast, and a double coincidence of wants (over the relevant time scale) is necessary for the exchange to take place.

Schematically, the dynamics of the model are as follows. Each period one individual is chosen. Consider him to be working on a problem. He discusses the problem with each of the members of his department with whom he has direct connections, making trades to acquire knowledge that will be helpful in solving the problem.[7] He then uses the accumulated knowledge to innovate. This innovation is then broadcast to the members of his permanent network. Every M periods there is a job market in which agents can change departments. The mechanisms of the market are discussed below.

In the world we consider, there is a large set S of n individuals, each having direct connections with d-$1 << n$ other individuals. This can be represented as an undirected graph $G(S, V)$ where V is the list of edges connecting people. The set of neighbors of individual $i \in S$ is denoted V_i, with $V_i = \{j \in V - \{i\} | (i,j) \in V\}$. The size of neighborhoods is held constant to maintain a constant density of the graph as we vary the nature of the individuals' neighborhoods. Individual i is located within department $\delta_i \in \Delta$ (Δ is the set of academic or intra-firm departments), and departments are modeled as very dense, almost complete sub graphs. There are n/d departments, each department having exactly d members. Individuals have connections inside (with colleagues) but also outside the department (the kinship network, though a permanent connection of i can be in his department). These links are fixed, and maintained, unchanging, forever. Assuming a constant number of neighbors can be seen as arising from a constraint — any individual has only a certain amount of time and energy to devote to "networking activity" — if extra-department networking increases, intra-department networking must decrease.[8]

Each individual $i \in S$ has a knowledge endowment in the form of a real-valued vector $\upsilon_i = (\upsilon_{i,c})$, with $c \in C = \{1, ..., \ell\}$ the knowledge categories. This vector evolves over time as the individual receives broadcasts from his colleagues, trades knowledge and produces new knowledge (innovates). We can think that each element $v_{i,c}$ corresponds to a particular academic or technological sub-field. As we are interested in innovation as recombination, we model knowledge complementarity explicitly. We assume a one-dimensional, circular knowledge space in which types of knowledge near to each other combine readily to create innovations. Learning a little more econometrics is more likely to be useful to a labour-economist than it is to a game theorist. In the set of disciplines the fields related to c^* are therefore fields $c^* \pm 1$.

Utility is measured in knowledge, and used to increase individual knowledge endowments. Each individual is a production unit that uses his or her knowledge endowments as inputs and returns knowledge as an output. Individuals seek to maximize outputs, where the output for individual i in category c is Cobb-Douglas according to

f $(i,c)=A\upsilon_{i,c-1}^{\alpha/2}\upsilon_{i,c+1}^{\alpha/2}\upsilon_{i,c}^{1-\alpha}$, with $\alpha=1/2$. Most often the category maximizing output will be the expertise of individual i, denoted c^* $(i)=\mathrm{argmax}_c\,\upsilon_{i,c}$.

At random times, one person is selected and engages in knowledge production. First there is knowledge trading within the department. Maximizing knowledge output implies trading within the department in the domain of expertise and the adjacent categories. (If the agent's expertise is in type c^* then he looks to increase his knowledge of type c^* and $c^*\pm1$. After that has taken place the individual innovates in category c^* (i) and his endowment in that category becomes $\upsilon_{i,c}{}^*{}_{(i)}+f$ $(i,c^*$ $(i))$ He then broadcasts knowledge in his area of expertise to the individuals in his permanent network (by presenting a paper at a conference for example).

Intermittently, at fixed intervals, there is a job market. An individual enters the job market either if he is unhappy with his department, or if his department is unhappy with him. The purpose of the job market is to re-allocate individuals among departments. This implies that while the permanent links of an individual never change, his or her department links will change if he or she moves from one department to another. Thus with every job market, the global network structure can change as individuals move.

2.1 Individuals and departments

Out of a total of d-1 neighbors, individuals have both intra-departmental connections and permanent connections. In the complete absence of long distance networking, each department would be a complete sub graph of size d, and the entire graph would be a caveman graph. But if there are permanent links, this graph changes: the caves become connected and, due to the "networking time budget constraint", the caves become less densely connected internally. In general, the global graph can be described by a parameter p, where $p\in[0.1,1]$ is the share of permanent links in the economy. Here we describe the algorithm used to create the global graph.

Key is the idea that the distribution of permanent links of scientists is likely to be very skewed. Most scientists have very few, if any, and a small number of scientists have very many extra-department contacts.[9] The skew ness of this distribution is something we control. Suppose the frequency distribution of permanent links is $f(x)$ where x is the number of links. To create the graph on which the simulation is run, begin with a caveman graph.[10] Then for each value of $x\in\{0,...,n\}$ select $g(x)/2$ pairs of agents and create a permanent link between the 2 members of each of those pairs.

Simply adding these permanent links will clearly increase the density of the graph, so to maintain a constant density, and to account for an agent's time budget, for each agent, remove department links equal in number to half of his permanent links.[11] Thus at the end, every agent retains close to d-1 links total, and on average exactly d-1 links, some of which are permanent and some of which are intra-departmental. By manipulating $g(x)$, we can control the mean number of permanent links and the distribution of them over agents. To illustrate, Figure 10.1 displays two illustrative configurations where at one extreme the graph is a set of $n/d=16/4=4$ complete, disconnected sub graphs — the Caveman graph, each cave representing a department. Each vertex has d-1=3 edges emanating from it, hence a total of $16 \cdot 3/2=24$ edges, and no long-distance links exist. The right part of Figure 10.1 is a randomly rewired Caveman graph still having d-1=3 edges emanating from each vertex, but now globally connected through a small number of inter-department links. The graph is still locally dense, though no longer locally complete. Some individuals now have more than 3 edges connecting them, though on average everyone still has 3 as the total number of links has not changed.

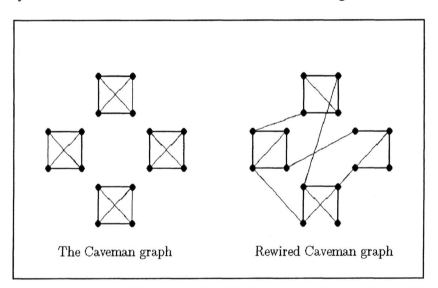

The Caveman graph   Rewired Caveman graph

Figure 10.1. The original Caveman graph and the Caveman graph after random rewiring: illustrative case with 4 departments and 16 individuals.

Regarding the distribution of links, it is assumed that if n_i is the number of edges connected to individual i, then for all $i \in S$ one has $\Pr\{n_i=m\} \sim \lambda^{m+1}$, with $\lambda \in (0,1)$.

Figure 10.2 represents the distribution of links in two polar cases: $\lambda=0.1$ and $\lambda=0.9$. The case $\lambda=0.1$ corresponds to a situation in which most people have very few links and only a few have a large number of relationships; by contrast when $\lambda=0.9$ people can have almost any number of links (which does not imply that they all have the same number).

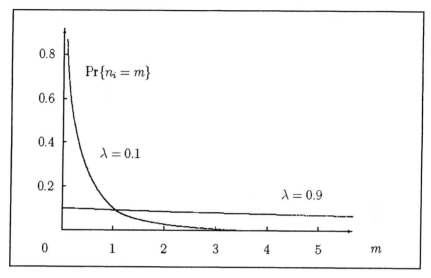

Figure 10.2. The frequency distribution of links for $\lambda=0.1$ and $\lambda=0.9$.

If a job market moves an individual, he takes with him his permanent connections but forms new connections in the department where he gets hired so his total number does not change. If he had permanent links in his old department, he retains them even after the move. We can interpret the kinship network, in this stylized model, as the source of long distance networking. The corresponding links are created through means other than the convenience of location or departmental interactions. They can thus be the links that connect distant parts of the knowledge production structure or economy. Focusing on this variable can be interpreted as focusing on the networking aspect of current science and technology policy.

2.2 Knowledge

In a barter episode, agents i and $j \in \delta_i \cap V_i$ trade if trading is mutually advantageous, that is if $v_{j,c*(i)-1} > v_{i,c*(i)-1}$ or $v_{j,c*(i)-1} > v_{i,c*(i)-1}$, and at the same time $v_{i,c*(i)} > v_{j,c*(i)}$. This condition states that there must be a double coincidence of wants for barter to take place. In keeping with much recent work on the economics of knowledge, we have assumed that knowledge is only partly assimilable,[12] hence trading, when it occurs, results in a gain equal to a share α of the knowledge differential. Suppose agent j dominates agent i in category c. After the exchange, j's knowledge of type c has not changed, but i's has: $v_{i,c}$ has become $v_{i,c} + \alpha(v_{j,c} - v_{i,c})$. Note that 'trade' here is a barter — one agent 'transfers' part of his knowledge to another one and is paid back with knowledge of a different category. But the mechanism also captures the non-rivalry property of knowledge: when j gives knowledge to i, there is no loss to j.

For individual i, the addition of knowledge creates opportunity for recombination with his existing knowledge of different types. As we said previously, for simplicity we restrict this recombination to adjacent knowledge types according to $f(i,c) = v_{i,c-1}^{1/4} v_{i,c+1}^{1/4} v_{i,c}^{1/2}$.

Agent i then broadcast his knowledge. This broadcast is "heard" by every $j \in V_i$-δ_i. Individuals do not broadcast everything they know, however, they only broadcast in the subject of their expertise. The receiving individual, j, is able to use the information if he does not already possess it. Thus if $v_{j,c^*(i)} < v_{i,c^*(i)}$, individual j's knowledge increases by $\alpha(v_{i,c^*(i)} - v_{j,c^*(i)})$.

This describes the first, direct, mechanism of knowledge distribution and creation. The second distribution mechanism is the job market.

2.3 The job market

Every M periods there is a job market. Individuals who are unhappy with their departments, or whose departments are unhappy with them, enter the job market. Intuitively, when an individual evaluates a department (his own or any other) he considers whether he will learn or teach if he is located in that department. A synthetic (though imperfect) way of measuring that is to aggregate all the knowledge of a department into a number: the aggregate knowledge they represent, which is simply the sum over members and categories $\sum_{j \in \delta, c \in C} v_{j,c}$. From the individual's point of view, learning is preferred, and he will learn if in general the members of the department know more than he does. The department asks the same question, namely "Will the candidate bring a lot of knowledge with him?". Departments rank people by their total knowledge $\sum_{c \in C} v_{i,c}$. Individuals want to join knowledgeable departments, departments want to attract knowledgeable individuals. This means individuals all have the same ranking of departments, and individuals all have the same ranking of people. The mechanics of the job market are stylized, but do represent features that we see in parts of the academic world.[13] Individual i will enter the job market if he is smarter than the average individual in his department by a percentage $\theta \in (0,1)$. On the other hand, i will be "asked" to enter the job market by his department if he is less knowledgeable than the average department member by a percentage θ. (The symmetry here is unimportant; it is simply a way of keeping the number of parameters manageable.) This creates a set of job openings (within departments) and job seekers. To match seekers with openings we use the stable marriage matching algorithm of Shapley and Gale (1962). This algorithm ensures that in the resultant matching no agent-department pair prefers each other to their current matches. The equilibrium in the job market is a stable matching in the sense that we just gave: no move performed jointly by an individual and a department is able to improve the outcome.

3. NUMERICAL ANALYSIS

Network models of any degree of complexity are notoriously difficult to deal with analytically, so the analysis here is numerical. We are primarily interested in knowledge creation and diffusion, and whether there are conditions under which these processes thrive, or the reverse. We also examine issues having to do with expertise and specialization, namely whether departments and/or individuals become specialists in certain types of knowledge, or whether they retain a diversity.

3.1 Statistics

First the average level of knowledge in the economy is defined as

$$\bar{\mu} = \frac{1}{n} \sum_{i \in S} \mu_i \,,$$

where

$$\mu_i = \frac{1}{\ell} \sum_{c \in C} \upsilon_{i,c}$$

is individual i's average knowledge level. This is a straightforward measure of the system's efficiency when we assume that more knowledge is unambiguously better. Also of interest is the equity of knowledge allocation, for which an absolute measure is the variance in knowledge allocation across agents

$$\sigma^2 = \frac{1}{n} \sum_{i \in S} \mu_i^2 - \bar{\mu}^2 \,,$$

and a measure in relative terms is the coefficient of variation $cv = \sigma / \bar{\mu}$. The coefficient of variation corrects for increases in variance that would arise from a simple global increase in the knowledge level of the individuals, so it is more relevant for our purposes than is the variance. The same calculation can be performed at the department level, with the knowledge endowment of department δ being the sum of its members' endowments

$$\mu_\delta = \sum_{j \in \delta} \mu_j .$$

We are also concerned with the emergence of expertise, both at the individual level (are people becoming experts or generalists?) and at the department level (do we see departments with a single expertise, or are there experts of different sorts in the departments?). To get further insights into the process of specialization, Herfindahl indexes of concentration can be computed. At the individual level the concentration index for individual i is written as

$$h_i = \sum_{c \in C} \left(\frac{\upsilon_{i,c}}{\sum_{l \in C} \upsilon_{i,l}} \right)^2 .$$

An individual is specialized if h_i is high. More precisely, index h_i lies in $[1/\ell, 1]$ and measures how evenly knowledge is allocated across all the categories. When expertise is concentrated in a single knowledge category $h_i = 1$, whereas a homogeneous knowledge profile yields $h_i = 1/\ell$. Averaging over individuals $\bar{h} = 1/n \sum_{j \in \delta} h_i$. The same indicator can be computed at the department level, where again the knowledge endowment of department δ in category c simply consists of the sum of individual endowments $\upsilon_{\delta,c} = \sum_{j \in \delta} \upsilon_{j,c}$, so that

$$h_\delta = \sum_{c \in C} \left(\frac{\upsilon_{\delta,c}}{\sum_{l \in C} \upsilon_{\delta,l}} \right)^2 .$$

Finally we are interested in knowing whether there is a shared expertise at the economy level: do individuals and departments tend to specialize all on the same few disciplines, or is there persistent diversification across disciplines when things are examined from the macro level? Pooling all knowledge endowments together and computing again a concentration index, this time for the economy as a whole, measure this:

$$H = \sum_{c \in C} \left(\frac{\sum_{j \in S} v_{j,c}}{\sum_{j \in S, l \in C} v_{j,l}} \right)^2 .$$

3.2 Settings

The basic structure of the simulation is as follows. We have $N=210$ individuals, and the department size is $d=15$ (equally, each individual has $d-1=14$ undirected connections). This is a relatively sparse graph as it contains $210 \times 14/2 = 1,470$ distinct edges while the number of possible edges in the complete graph is $210 \times 209/2 = 21,945$ (so roughly 7% of the possible connections are active). There are $\ell=10$ types of knowledge, and each individual's knowledge vector has initial values drawn from a uniform distribution $U[0,1]$. We run the dynamic process for 15,000 periods, by which time stable patterns have emerged. All the results reported here concern the state of the world after these 15,000 periods. For each set of parameter values, we run 10 replications, and present average results for the statistics.

The parameters we vary are two.

• Individuals enter the job market if they are dissatisfied with their current departments, or *vice versa*. We vary the degree of dissatisfaction θ required before an individual is willing to bear the costs of job search and re-location. With this parameter we can examine the effect of job market frictions. Three values for this parameter are examined: $\theta=0.55$ corresponds to an active job-market (a market with low frictions), whereas $\theta=0.65$ corresponds to a much less active job-market (a market with high frictions). The intermediate value of $\theta=0.6$ is also examined. What would be the effect of a policy aimed at reducing (or increasing) the costs of changing jobs in terms of an economy's ability to produce knowledge?

• The presence of permanent links represents extra-departmental, long-distance (pan-European?) networking. Increasing the quantity of networking as a policy goal can affect both the mean number of links and/or the distribution of them. This issue we address by changing the frequency distribution of the links. We control the mean number of links directly with the parameter $p \in [0.1, 1]$.

We do not control the concentration of the links directly, but this emerges from the frequency distribution.[14]

While we vary two parameters, θ and p, we present results on the effects of the job market, and on the effects both of changing the mean number of links and of the concentration of them. To measure concentration, after assigning links to agents at the beginning of each simulation run we calculate the Herfindahl index to measure how concentrated the links are among individuals.

4. RESULTS

The ability of the economy to produce and distribute knowledge is appraised by observing the average knowledge level in the economy, and examining how it responds to changes in parameter values. Heterogeneity at the individual and the department level (allocative efficiency) is discussed in the second section. Expertise is also of interest, and this is examined in the last section.

In all of the graphs that follow we are showing a three dimensional relationship between number of permanent links, the distribution of them, and various variables of interest.[15] We use contour plots to show these relationships. These should be read like maps in an atlas: the dark regions show peaks, and the light regions show valleys. So this is a landscape shading from black at the highest altitude, to white at the lowest. To measure distribution we use the Herfindahl index of links over agents. Thus an index of 1 implies that only one person has permanent links, an index of $1/n$ indicates that the each agent has the same number of permanent links. We should remark that this creates a rather peculiarly shaped state space. This arises from the constraints of having a finite number of agents. It is easiest to see in the extreme. To see a Herfindahl index of 1, a single agent has all the links. If the average number of permanent links is 2, say, then the agent has $2n$ permanent links. But there are only n agents to whom he can be linked, so this combination (Herfindahl equal to 1, and an average number of 2 permanent links) is not possible. This creates, in general, a triangular shape for the state space, and this is apparent in every graph.

4.1 Knowledge growth

Figure 10.3 shows the way average knowledge levels in the economy are affected by the number of permanent links, and how they are distributed.

We observe two patterns. First, as the number of permanent links increases, knowledge levels increase and then decrease. This is true for every distribution, so we can safely conclude that there is an interior optimum number of links.

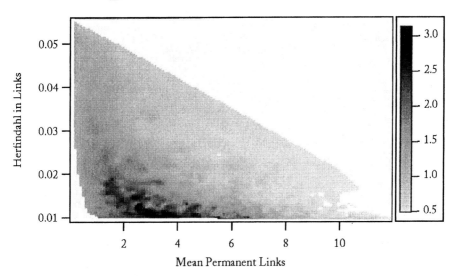

Figure 10.3. Average knowledge levels as a function of the number and concentration of permanent links.

It is possible to have too much networking. The explanation is that there are two sources of knowledge accumulation and distribution, and that increasing one of them (through increasing networking) must decrease the other (intradepartmental trading). Eventually the latter effect outweighs the former. The second observation from Figure 10.3 is that distribution matters. In general, knowledge levels increase as the distribution of networking is more uniform over the agents, that is to say more agents can have a significant number of outside links. So a few stars in a sea of almost isolated people is not preferable to the absence of stars and a more dispersed allocation of links. These results suggest that policy must focus both on the amount of networking, and on who is doing it. Almost always, bringing more people into the set of those who have long distance, a permanent connection is a valuable policy goal.

4.2 Knowledge distribution

We examine the distribution of knowledge both at the agent level, and at the department level. The question is whether the modes of knowledge creation and diffusion we model here have in them forces tending to create good and bad departments, or whether there is a tendency for departments to maintain a roughly equal level of knowledge, growing together. The same questions are asked of agents.

Figure 10.4 shows the effects of networking on the dispersion of knowledge among agents. The measure of dispersion we use is the coefficient of variation, in order to correct for the scaling effects from which the variance suffers. As an agent is carrying a knowledge endowment in the form of a vector, we just sum the numbers in each category and compute a coefficient of variation on the set of these sums.

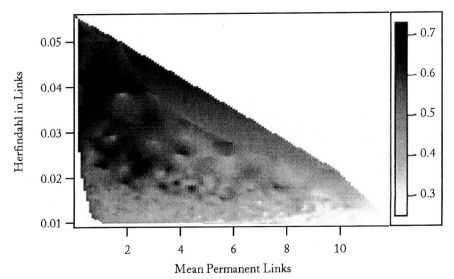

Figure 10.4. Dispersion (as measured by the coefficient of variation) as a function of the number and concentration of permanent links.

The results are intuitively appealing: as the number of permanent links increases, agents' knowledge levels are more homogeneous. Permanent links are a channel for global knowledge distribution, increasing the rate of diffusion. Agents in distant parts of the economy can rapidly acquire the same information, and this has a clear convergent effect on their knowledge levels. Similarly, as the links are distributed more evenly among the agents, knowledge levels converge. So "social" stars again are rather a negative factor and a more scattered allocation of links is better.

The coefficient of variation for departments shows the same pattern to that just discussed, but slightly more pronounced. The mechanisms at work are the same.

4.3 Specialization in knowledge

Do agents or departments become specialists, each agent or department focusing accumulation on a small number of categories; or does their knowledge remain general, i.e. spread over all knowledge types? We use again a Herfindahl index to address this question.

An agent's knowledge is distributed over the ℓ categories. Using his knowledge vector, we can calculate the share of his knowledge represented by each type, and from this a Herfindahl showing the degree to which he is a generalist or a specialist (1 means total specialization, $1/\ell$ means a generalist's profile). We report the mean of this Herfindahl over all agents. At the department level we can create a department knowledge vector by summing element-wise the vectors of the agents in the department. Patterns at the agent and department levels are the same.

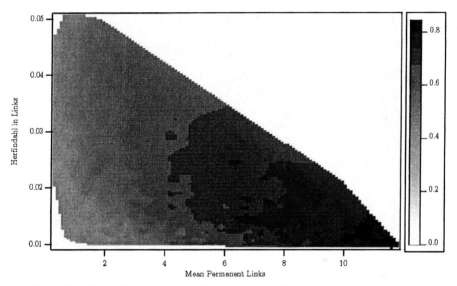

Figure 10.5. Expertise (as measured by the Herfindahl index) as a function of the number and concentration of permanent links.

Figure 10.5 shows the evolution of expertise with the number and concentration of permanent links. The two effects that we observe are that as the number of permanent links increases agents and departments become more specialized. As the distribution of links becomes more uniform, agents and departments become less specialized.

4.4 The value of links

At the heart of this discussion has been the assumption that networking is a good thing, and that increasing the amount of networking somehow will increase knowledge production. Is it the case that this effect is direct, in the sense that the more networking an agent does the more knowledge he accumulates? Figure 10.6 responds to this question.

The general answer seems to be yes, the correlation coefficient between an agent's knowledge and the number of permanent links he has is very high, in the range of 0.5-0.7 in general. There seems to be little effect here of either the number of links or their distribution. It is possible that the correlation falls as the number of links increases, but whether this is statistically real or simply an artefact is something yet to be uncovered.

Curiously, the same effect is not true at the department level. Figure 10.7 shows that the correlation coefficient between the number of permanent links held by members of a department and the aggregate knowledge held in that department has a value close to 0.

This suggests that there is always a relatively large amount of intra-department heterogeneity in the knowledge levels of agents.

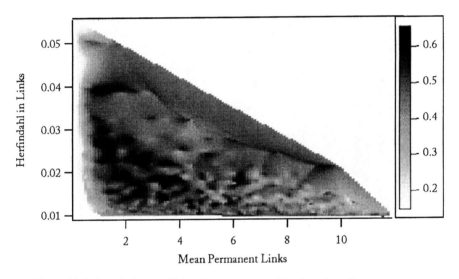

Figure 10.6. Correlation coefficient between networking (number of permanent connections) and knowledge for individuals.

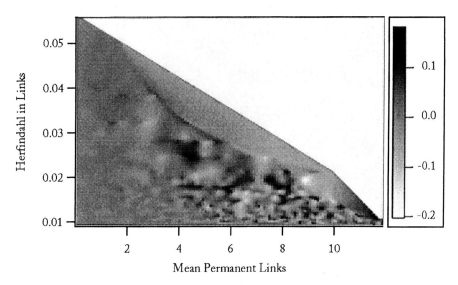

Figure 10.7. Correlation coefficient between networking (number of permanent connections) and knowledge for departments.

4.5 Job market activity

As part of the model we have included a job market every 50 periods. Figure 10.8 shows the average number of moves per job market under different parameters.[16]

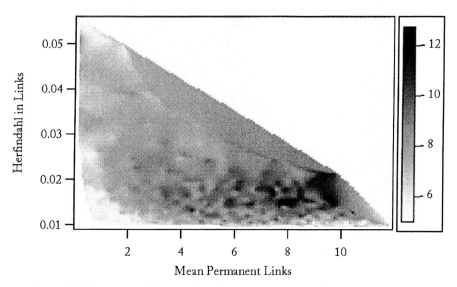

Figure 10.8. Labour mobility: number of agents moving per job market

The result we observe in Figure 10.8 is that for given number of permanent links, some concentration promotes mobility, and for given concentration more links increases mobility. It is important here to recall that more permanent links for an individual means easier access to distant knowledge, and in general (as shown by the previous paragraph) more knowledge. Skewness in the distribution of links is therefore equivalent to skewness in the distribution of knowledge, which means that generally speaking more people tend to be away (either above or below) from the department average. Why then isn't it that the largest possible number of links and the highest possible concentration don't produce the largest number of moves? The willingness to move (willingness to go for an individual, and willingness to get rid of a person for a department) and the actual mobility are two different things. With high concentration and high number of links, good people quickly tend to gather in what become good departments, and the opposite is true for poorly knowledgeable individuals. Then actual mobility becomes much lower: there is no other place to go for the best people than the best department, and no other place to go for the worst people than the worst department. Action remains limited to intermediate departments. The significant effects of changing the level of job market activity, by reducing job market frictions, for example, tend to be confined to its effects on average knowledge levels. Increases in job market activity generally increase knowledge levels for all networking parameters. However, a more active job market implies a slight decrease in the optimal number of links in the economy. There is some tradeoff—both the job market and networking transfer useful knowledge, and they can to some extent substitute for each other. The substitution is not linear, though, with the biggest effect of job markets existing when the effects of networking are relatively weak. The other observation regarding increasing job market activity is that it has little effect on the pattern of expertise development at the economy level, as discussed in the next section. We must note here that in the model changing jobs is in no way disruptive, either to the individual or to the departments involved. This is obviously unrealistic, so the results on the job market should be interpreted with caution.

4.6 Expertise at the economy level

The last aspect of specialization we examine is the extent to which individuals (and as a consequence departments) tend to develop the same expertise all over the economy. The alternative is that aggregation preserves diversity even though we observe specialization both at the individual and at the department level.

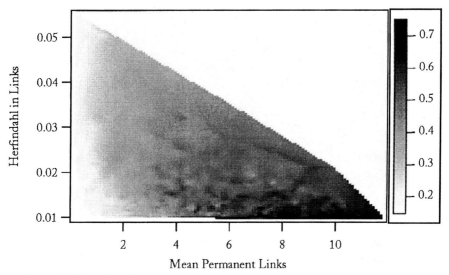

Figure 10.9. Herfindahl index over aggregate knowledge stocks: specialization at the economy level

Figure 10.9 depicts the Herfindahl index H of economy-wide specialization. As H is obtained by pooling all the existing knowledge in each category, if one category grows more than the others it indicates that specialization on this discipline is taking place in the economy as a whole. What is clear from Figure 10.9 is that the extent to which one field dominates is highest when the permanent network is dense, and more so when the network is concentrated on the fewest possible number of people— networking stars. This is similar to what we observed in Figure 10.5 at the individual level. People tend to become experts, and the economy itself tends to focus on a specific type of knowledge when the number of permanent connections and the concentration of them is increased. While this might sound counter-intuitive because more links could *a priori* imply a more even distribution of all there is to distribute, it must be kept in mind that links are conveying knowledge in the domain of expertise, and people's expertise is more likely to converge when they repeatedly broadcast to each other, rather than when balancing trades take place (as is the case within departments). More concentration in links also favours the emergence of a dominant field: more stardom means a small number of people influencing a large number of individuals, and quickly diffusing their fields of expertise. It is worth noting that while we would probably like people and/or departments to specialize, it might be questionable to have a specialized economy oriented towards the production of a single type of knowledge. It is also interesting to see that the point in the (p, λ)-space that maximizes knowledge creation is characterized by low specialization, be it at the individual, department or economy level.

5. CONCLUSION

In terms of knowledge growth, inducing knowledge mobility is a good thing. This can be achieved by establishing an on-going job-market or by promoting networking, i.e. the establishment of inter-department connections among scientists. Both are effective in increasing knowledge production. The intensity of networking has a non-monotonic effect on knowledge levels. It is possible to have too much networking. This stems from the fact that increasing networking activities imposes a cost on other valuable activities that take place within a department. There is an interior optimum for the amount of networking in the economy—a few links on average is optimal. The second thing we have explored in this paper has to do with the distribution of networking. As with so many distributions in science, the distribution of networking activity is likely to be relatively highly skewed. Our results indicate that for any level of networking, making the distribution of links more homogeneous improves knowledge production. On the other hand, networking reduces the dispersion in knowledge levels. Both at the level of the agent and at the level of the department, knowledge levels become more homogeneous as the number of permanent links increases. Global distribution of knowledge clearly permits distant agents (and departments) to acquire each other's knowledge. While homogenization may be good from the point of view of European social cohesion, if it implies the elimination of excellence, either of individual "genius" or elite departments, it is not obvious that it is good for science. A third effect of long distance networking is to change the economy from a collection of relative generalists to a collection of specialists. The specialization stems from the networking aspect of the structure, and suggests that networking does create the synergies that it is often presumed to do. When two agents are directly connected, and specialize in adjacent knowledge categories, they can create a strong positive feedback between them in which they improve side-by-side so to speak, each one's improvement directly helping the other. As this happens, the two agents become more and more specialized in their two sub-disciplines, as their knowledge there increases fastest. Surprisingly, this is true at all levels of aggregation: Agents specialize; departments specialize; and the economy as a whole specializes. While the first two seem unproblematic, and even valuable, the third, specialization at the economy level, seems possibly dangerous. Specialization at the economy level creates serious risks of begin caught unprepared for new developments, and can provide a serious obstacle in catching up with the world leaders in new fields. Even at the optimal number of links ($p \approx 0.2$; roughly 3 permanent links on average) we see that specialization at the economy level is significant. This suggests that it may be optimal from the policy point of view to sacrifice some knowledge production in the name of preserving variety in the knowledge stock. It may be that policy could focus more heavily on the distribution of networking activity rather than on its quantity. But how does the job market interact with all of this? It may provide another venue for increasing knowledge production. Provided the mobility is not too disruptive either to the agents or departments involved, reducing job market frictions increases knowledge production, apparently thereby reducing the need for long distance networking. It seems to do this, furthermore, without large effects on the specialization of the economy. This paper has examined three aspects of knowledge distribution within a scientific community. It turns out that the interplay among the different aspects is not trivial, and there is a rich set of outcomes depending on details of the mechanisms involved. Even though the model is highly stylized, it suggests that there may be tradeoffs that need to be understood both before we understand how knowledge is diffused, and before we design policies to improve it.

NOTES

[1] See Dasgupta and David (1994) for a detailed discussion of open versus closed science and policy implications drawn therefrom. For a general overview of the economics of science, see Stephan (1996).

[2] See Kogut and Zander (1992) for a discussion of this idea.

[3] See for example, von Hippel(1994); David and Foray (1995); Cowan and Foray (1997); Cowan et al. (2000); or the TIPIK project papers in the special issue of *Industrial and Corporate Change*, 9, 2000.

[4] See Dasgupta and David (1994).

[5] Permanence is a relative notion of course, and people may change jobs frequently or infrequently, and they may create and destroy long distance, "permanent" connections rapidly. But in aggregate, it is reasonable to assume that changes in networks due to job mobility operate on a shorter time-scale than changes in our ongoing network connections.

[6] Clearly, in reality every action is not a barter, but it does seem to be the case that over a reasonable length of time, within a department people talk routinely to those people with whom knowledge flows in both directions.

[7] This can be interpreted as an agent working on a problem over a period of time, and asking his colleagues about aspects of it throughout this period. For simulation purposes we compress this into one period.

[8] Note that this implies that there is an implicit relative price of department links to permanent links. We assume below that this price is 1, so the two types of links have the same costs to maintain. This could be generalized without qualitatively changing the results.

[9] Those who have many permanent links could do so either because they are seen as desirable colleagues by agents everywhere (they are in demand), or because they have a taste, or skill, for the activities needed to maintain permanent, long distance links.

[10] The algorithm described here is similar to the well-known algorithm of Watts and Strogatz (1998) and Watts (1999) for studying small worlds. The structure described here could as well be used to study small world effects, but that is not our concern in this paper.

[11] We remove department links equal in number to half the agent's permanent links in order to keep the density of the global graph constant. Consider: each time a permanent link is created, 2 agents receive one more permanent link. If each of them removed one department link, the total number of links in the economy would decrease by 1. This reduction in total density of the graph is a complication we wish to avoid, so we use the algorithm described

to keep density constant. This implies that some agents will have more, and some fewer than d-1 links, but the average will be constant and equal to d-1.

[12] The strictly partial assimilation arises from the fact that tacit knowledge is needed to assimilate and use fully any piece of information (cf. Cowan and Foray, 1997). Further, the value of a piece of information lies in great part in its integration with other information, so typically it is not possible simply to 'add' a piece of information to an existing information structure. Put another way, absorptive capacity is never perfect (Cohen and Levinthal, 1989 and 1990). Note also that with $\alpha<1$ the model has the property that knowledge degrades as it is transmitted. Thus, the longer the path a piece of information travels, the less value it is to the recipient.

[13] A slightly more detailed method for ranking departments or individuals would be based on the question, "If I were to join that department, how many potential beneficial trades are there? ", or the converse, "If we hire this individual, will existing members of the department be able to make many trades with him? ". Using this method for ranking individuals and departments makes no qualitative differences to the results.

[14] We use as the basis of the frequency distribution the function $g(x)=\lambda^{x+1}$ where $x\in[0..50]$. In order to use it to assign links, this function must be twice re-scaled: first to ensure that it has the right number of agents; then to ensure that it has the right mean.

[15] Each point shown in the plane represents one run of the simulation, with linear interpolation between the points.

[16] Given the structure of our stylized job market, it is possible that agents on the market would be selected by their current departments. Thus there can be a discrepancy between the number of participants in the job market and the number of agents who change jobs. In this section we are discussing the latter.

REFERENCES

Cohen, W. and Levinthal, D. (1989). Innovation and learning: The two faces of research and development. *The Economic Journal, 99*, 569–596.

Cowan, R., David, P. and Foray, D. (2000) The explicit economics of knowledge codification and tacitness. *Industrial and Corporate Change, 9*, 211–253.

Cowan, R. and Foray, D. (1997). The economics of codification and the diffusion of knowledge. *Industrial and Corporate Change, 6*, 595–622.

David, P. and Foray, D. (1995). Accessing and expanding the science and technology knowledge base. *STI Review, 16*, 13–68.

Dasgupta, P. and David, P. (1994). Toward a new economics of science. *Research Policy, 23*, 487–521.

Erdös, P. and Renyi, A. (1960) On the evolution of random graphs. *Publications of the Mathematical Institute of the Hungarian Academy of Sciences, 5*, 17–61.

Gale, D. and Shapley, L. (1962). College admissions and the stability of marriage. *American Mathematical Monthly, 69*, 9–15.

Kogut, B. and Zander, U. (1992). Knowledge of the firm, combinative capabilities and the replication of technology. *Organization Science, 3*, 383–397.

Stephan, P.E. (1996). The Economics of Science. *Journal of Economic Literature, 34*, 1199–1235.

von Hippel, E. (1994). "Sticky Information" and the Locus of Problem Solving: Implications for Innovation. *Management Science 40, 4*, 429-439.

Watts, D. (1999). Networks, Dynamics and the Small World Phenomenon. *American Journal of Sociology, 105*, 493–527.

Watts, D. and Strogatz, S. (1998). Collective dynamics of small-world networks. *Letters to Nature, 393*.

Index